Headteachers at Work

Valerie Hall, Hugh Mackay and Colin Morgan

Open University Press
Milton Keynes . Philadelphia

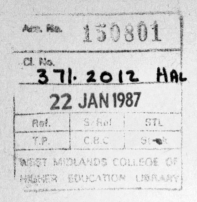
Open University Press
Open University Educational Enterprises Limited
12 Cofferidge Close
Stony Stratford
Milton Keynes MK11 1BY, England
and
242 Cherry Street
Philadelphia, PA 19106. USA

First Published 1986

Copyright © 1986 Valerie Hall, Hugh Mackay and Colin Morgan

British Library Cataloguing in Publication Data
Hall, Valerie. 1943–
  Headteachers at work.
  1. School superintendents and principals
  —Great Britain
  I. Title   II. Mackay, Hugh   III. Morgan,
Colin
371.2'012'0941   LB2831.976.G7

  ISBN 0-335-15244-9
  ISBN 0-335-15243-0 Pbk

Library of Congress Cataloging in Publication Data
Hall, Valerie.
  Headteachers at work.

  Bibliography: p.
  1. High school principals—Great Britain.
2. School management and organization—Great Britain.
I. Mackay, Hugh.   II. Morgan, Colin.   III. Title.
LB2832.4.G7H35 1986   373.12'012'0941   86–8566
ISBN 0-335-15244-9
ISBN 0-335-15243-0 (pbk.)

Text design by Carlton Hill
Typeset by Mathematical Composition Setters Ltd
Printed in Great Britain at the Alden Press

Contents

V What Others Say about Heads 183

VI Conclusion 203

List of Figures

List of Tables

Preface

We are grateful to the Leverhulme Trust, which provided the funding for the research on which this book is based. We could not have carried out our work without the co-operation and support of a large number of individuals in teacher organisations, other trades unions, LEAs, and schools; especially the fifteen heads who allowed us to observe them at work. In particular, we are most grateful to the four headteachers whom we observed for something over a year. Finally, we should like to thank our secretary, Julia Bullough; our colleagues at the Open University, especially Professor Ron Glatter; and, particularly, Colin Fletcher for his editing of our manuscript.

For confidentiality, all of the names which we use (of headteachers, schools, towns, Authorities, etc.) are fictional.

• | •

Introduction

The study of headship we discuss here represents one of the growing number to have taken place in Britain in the last decade. Indeed, only during this period has headship become a focus of significant interest within educational studies. Certainly within the same period government has discovered headship as a policy priority in creating 'effective' schools, however these are defined. Our own focus has been on secondary headship in action. In this Introduction we set our study first in the wider policy context, and second, in the context of other headship research both at home and abroad. We also describe the bases we used for evaluating our findings.

In the 1970s a profound change took place in the role of central government in educational policy-making which was to have far-reaching repercussions for school headship. It began in late 1976 with a Labour government but was continued uninterrupted by the Conservative administration since 1979. For decades previously, central government's prime concern had been with the *context* of publicly provided schooling rather than the *content*; that is, with matters of 'provision' and 'access' rather than with issues of curriculum or quality of performance. The historic posture of government towards content was conveyed well in the celebrated statement, 'Minister knows nowt about the curriculum'. This was reputedly the dictum of George Tomlinson, Minister of Education in the Attlee Government, but Butler before then, and Crosland since expressed much the same view (Glatter, 1976). Hence, the successive Ministers or Secretaries of State who implemented the major system changes of raising the school leaving age and comprehensive reform were largely unconcerned with headship or 'within school' matters. This long tradition of leaving to others what went on inside schools came to a sudden halt with central government's unprecedented intervention at Prime Ministerial level.

James Callaghan's speech at Ruskin College, Oxford in October, 1976, changed the boundaries of control of education in England and Wales. His speech, 'Towards A National Debate' (later christened 'the Great Debate') set in motion a range of concerns about what schools were doing:

> unease by parents and others about the new informal methods of teaching ...
> you (the teachers) must satisfy the parents and industry that what you are
> doing meets their requirements and the needs of the children ...
> the strong case for the so called 'core curriculum' of basic knowledge ...
> In today's world higher standards are demanded than were required yesterday.
> Therefore we demand from our schools more than did our grandparents.
> (Callaghan, 1976)

Callaghan had brought school curriculum and performance on to the
political stage of central government. He did not directly refer to the place
of headship but the assertion of a link between the quality of headship and
school 'success' emerged as one of the early main discussion topics in the
wake of this new policy paradigm. However, at the time that he spoke, the
received view was that the running of schools was safely entrusted to what
was called 'the headmaster tradition'.

The term, 'the headmaster tradition' developed to describe a role model
of headship which had stabilised in the nineteenth century. The context was
of rapidly growing public schools which needed to appoint a range of
assistant masters and were led and influenced by dominant personalities,
chief of whom was Arnold of Rugby.

> The originality of Arnold lay in his regarding his school first and foremost as
> a community which shaped the character of his boys as well as their minds.
> Moreover because of his sense of pastoral mission ... he was convinced that
> he must be the centre of that community and exercise his influence on every
> individual member of it ... Throughout, to parents, old boys, and his many
> friends and correspondents he never tired of showing how his work at Rugby
> was a vocation. (Baron, 1975, p. 289).

The supremacy of the nineteenth century head was based on his possessing
all of the powers of a nineteenth-century employer, especially as staffing was
almost wholly in his hands. Through the various headmaster associations of
that time the role and tradition was dispersed far and wide, so that:

> ... the man working in some obscure county grammar school, or some newly
> founded municipal secondary school, was brought into touch with the great
> figures of the day, heard them declare with passion their determination to
> defend their independence against central authority and (proposed) local
> authorities ... and was strengthened in his own resolve to assert his authority
> over his school and its destiny. (Baron, 1975, p. 291)

Thus arose a role model of headship as paternal, autocratic in decision-
making, possessing authority by virtue of personal qualities — notably
scholarship and moral values — and imbued with a sense of pastoral mission

to secure influence on each pupil and every aspect of the running of the school. Though first established in the public schools, it was adopted in the state provision with the minor adaptation necessary to cope with local authority control (see Bernbaum, 1976), and was to be the model for decades to come. In the two decades following the 1944 Education Act, headship and its traditions were largely taken for granted; even the appearance of the large co-educational comprehensives in the 1960s evoked little discussion of headship by the profession and none was initiated by central government. There was however a growing academic interest which had noted the need for traditional views of headship to be revised from the basis of research evidence.

In particular, the empirical work of Hughes (1972) demonstrated the relevance of new interpretations of the headship role, which challenged the traditional model of 'the autocratic pastoral missioner'. Hughes showed that there was a 'leading professional' interpretation or model of headship which saw its source of influence to be based upon teaching, openness to consultation with colleagues, external professional influences for innovation in curriculum and teaching methods, as well as involvement in educational activities outside the school. Hughes also found empirically that there was an additional interpretation of the headship role which he described as a 'chief executive' model. This had an internal aspect: the division and allocation of work, including the classification of staff responsibilities and delegation of responsibilities; and the coordination and control of organisational activity (including staff supervision, an insistence on deadlines and a general emphasis on efficient procedures). Externally in this role interpretation there was concern with the relationship of the school to the wider system, particularly the school's governing body and the local education authority.

The work of Lyons (1974) and Richardson (1973) were also milestones in British studies of headship. Lyons' survey provided descriptions of what heads and other senior staff said they did in their jobs, in administrative terms. He identified what he called 'MATS', the major administrative tasks in the running of the relatively recently established large comprehensive schools. Richardson, on the other hand, studied a single comprehensive school, and her work stands until now as a lone example in Britain of an account of secondary school headship based on observation.

In addition to research studies, the 1970s saw the emergence of more prescriptive writings (e.g. Allen, 1968; Barry and Tye, 1972; Poster, 1976) on how traditional conceptions of headship needed to change, and allow for the acquisition of management skills. These advocated that headship should be based, at least in part, on managerial technique and training, rather than depend on personal mystique or professional teaching expertise. Such a view had its opponents. R.S. Peters (1976), for example, rejected a view of the head as a manager who 'should run a school as if it was a modern industry'.

Other writers, whilst eschewing any simple industrial analogy for schools, saw relevance in viewing secondary school headship from a basis of managerial or organisational theory. For example, Bush (1981, p. 58) used role theory to create an hourglass model of headship, with the head at the neck of the hourglass receiving pressure upwards from the staff within the school, and downwards from the external role set. We ourselves published a view of secondary heads' tasks (Morgan, Hall and Mackay, 1983) based on a model propounded by Katz (1974). We did not, of course, know at the time whether such a theoretical view of headship corresponded with headship as it was practised. The absence of an empirical foundation for descriptions of secondary headship in Britain in the 1980s prompted our present study.

In some countries research on headship is more firmly and longer established, wider in scope, and based on close links between the teachers (and researchers) of educational administration, management, and heads. The studies made abroad since 1960 are numerous. Those from the United States, Canada, and Australia have had particular significance for us. In the United States studies have concentrated on two aspects of the principal's job: what they do and what constitutes effective performance. A variety of approaches have been adopted. Both Martin and Willower (1981) in the United States and Willis in Australia (1980) used Mintzberg's structured observation techniques to record the range of the principal's activities over specified periods of time. These aimed to overcome what they saw to be a continuing problem of lack of observational data about what principals actually *do*:

> In short, there has been considerable concentration on normative approaches with virtually no basis in what principals actually do in their work (Willis, 1980, p. 27);
> An obvious strategy for examining role behaviour is to observe the task-performance patterns of persons in the position in question. Surprisingly, this strategy of observation seems to have been ignored by most educational researchers, (in the U.S.A.) (Martin and Willower, 1981, p. 69)

The contrasting approaches, which concentrate on the collection of qualitative data to explain leadership behaviour, have been summarised by Greenfield (1982). Amongst them is the ethnographic account of Wolcott (1973), who shadowed one elementary school principal for a year. For Wolcott the purpose was unambiguous:

> This study is not designed to provide an evaluation of the role of principal but to provide a description of what the principal does. (Wolcott, 1973, p. 319)

From the United States, important recent studies which have endeavoured to explore what constitutes effectiveness are Blumberg and Greenfield's *The*

Effective Principal (1980) and McCleary and Thomson's *The Senior High School Principalship* (1979). Both use perceived reputation by different constituencies as their criterion for identifying 'effective' principals, and structured interviewing as the methodology. The guiding principle of McCleary and Thompson's study, undertaken for the National Association of Secondary School Principals, was that 'the principal is the key to a good school' and their intention was to profile the characteristics of the effective principal, so that future training needs could be identified. Blumberg and Greenfield developed from their interviews with eight 'effective' principals, eight different models of principalship, each of which was associated with effective performance: organiser, value-based juggler, authentic helper, broker, humanist, catalyst, rationalist and politician.

In the United States there has been important discussion of the methodological issues involved in studying headship. For example Murphy, Hallinger and Mitman (1983) outline the limited generalisability of findings, the lack of explanatory models, the lack of behavioural indicators for leadership and the premature application of research findings. They suggest that there continues to be uncertainty as to whether it is effective principals that create effective schools or effective schools that create effective principals. In the policy context of the late 1970s which we discussed earlier, there was in Britain a more certain view: that it is effective heads that account for good schools.

Callaghan's 'Great Debate Speech' had invited the question of what constitutes school success or effectiveness, given the issues or alleged shortfalls he had identified. In the flow of discussion documents, Green and White Papers, and Education Bills which followed, the government itself was to suggest an early answer. *Ten Good Schools : A Secondary School Enquiry* (DES HMI, 1977) argued the centrality of the headteacher. In the view of Her Majesty's Inspectorate which carried out the study, a successful school was one with a good headteacher:

> The schools visited differ in many respects as institutions, although each can demonstrate its quality in its aims, in oversight of pupils, in curriculum design, in standards of teaching and academic achievements and in its links with the local community. What they all have in common is effective leadership and a 'climate' that is conducive to growth ... Emphasis is laid on consultation, team work and participation, but, without exception, *the most important single factor in the success of these schools is the quality of leadership of the head*. (DES HMI, 1977, p. 36. Our emphasis.)

The discussion document ends by describing the effective leadership displayed by the headteachers in the ten good schools:

> They appreciate the need for specific educational aims, both social and intellectual, and have the capacity to communicate these to staff, pupils and

parents, to win their assent and to put their own policies into practice. Their sympathetic understanding of staff and pupils, their accessibility, good humour and sense of proportion and their dedication to their task has won them the respect of parents, teachers and taught. They are conscious of the corruption of power and though ready to take final responsibility they have made power sharing the keynote of their organisation and administration. Such leadership is crucial for success.

Ten Good Schools marked the beginning of a major interest in headship on the part of central government. Soon afterwards the DES commissioned the POST project on the Selection of Secondary School Headteachers at the Open University. The NFER project on the early years of headship was started, and the DES funded on a pilot basis the National Development Centre for Schools' Senior Management Training, in Bristol. In 1983 a policy of specific grants for twenty-day and one-term headteacher training opportunities was introduced, leading to an unprecedented level of course provision and examination of what headship in the school should mean.

It was within this context of central government's interest in headship and concern with school's success that our project was funded by the Leverhulme Trust. Our research was undertaken between mid-1983 and mid-1985, and during this period central government's growing concern with the leadership and the running of schools was further evidenced by the publication of statements of major policy intent in two White Papers, 'Teaching Quality' (1983) and 'Better Schools' (1985). We take up in Chapter 13 some of the issues these documents raised in the light of our findings.

Our research approach was based on conclusions drawn from a study of the literature. We chose an ethnographic approach resembling Wolcott's, although we have also included data about the distribution of tasks which can be compared with studies that have used Mintzberg's work as their basis. The literature demonstrated the possibility of understanding headship, first, from what principals and others say about the job, in interviews or questionnaires; second, from the application of structured observation techniques recording times, participants, locations and purposes; and third, from an ethnographic description which, as Wolcott describes it, is committed to understanding and conveying how it is to 'walk in someone else's shoes' and 'to tell it like it is' (Wolcott, 1973, p. 113). We hope to have achieved what Greenfield advocates, 'a close match between the world as researchers construe it and the world as people perceive and act in it' (Greenfield, 1982).

This research can claim distinctiveness among studies of headship in Britain as it was based on extensive observation of headteachers at work, both within and outside of schools. Altogether fifteen heads were observed at their daily work, four of them in depth on a regular basis for a year. Our study of secondary headship is to be distinguished from others on grounds of both methodology and policy-relatedness. Our methodology was chosen to ensure an accurate account of what heads do rather than what they, or theoretical analyses, say they do. Our evaluation of the research findings in Chapter 13 has as its framework the policy context described. We shall discuss the findings under five headings which are pertinent to the curricular and managerial issues in schools and being raised by the continuing policy debate:

a *Commonalities in headship performance:* the extent to which the headteachers of maintained secondary schools interpret and perform their jobs in similar ways;

b *Contrasting interpretations of secondary headship:* the significant differences between secondary school headteachers in their performance of the job;

c *The LEA and headship practice:* the correspondence between LEA expectations of headship and the views and practice of the heads themselves;

d *Secondary headship and public policy expectations:* i.e. the extent to which secondary school headship as currently interpreted matches certain expectations expressed by central government in White Papers etc.;

e *Headship theory and practice:* the correspondence between views of secondary school headship grounded in managerial and organisational theory and the way headship in practice was observed to be.

From a broader perspective the question also arises as to whether our findings have implications for the future determination of policy in headship selection, headship development and training, LEA and heads' spheres of responsibility and ignored or underdeveloped aspects of headship. Our findings can be seen both as raising issues about current policy directions, and also about the possible need to identify new policy directions.

•|•

Headship in Action: Contrasting Interpretations

This section describes the main features of the job performed by all second-ary heads, and delineates the ways some heads differently interpret the demands of headship. We draw on two sets of data: first, that which came from observing fifteen heads for a single day; and second, that which came from observing four heads over a period of about a year. The overall picture of headship in action forms the basis for the detailed description and analysis in the next section, in which we consider specific elements of headship as performed by the four heads.

•2•

Fifteen headteachers observed for a day

The single day studies of fifteen heads were drawn from a representative sample of schools in nine LEAs in England and Wales. They included some of those with the most difficult social and racial problems, as well as those serving the most socially favoured catchment areas (see Appendix for details).

The fifteen heads were observed throughout the day and fieldnotes kept of all that they did. This ethnographic method captures the essential elements of the job and the minutiae which the incumbents themselves would recognise. The fieldnotes were analysed to reveal the predominant features which headteachers share in common as well as the ways they interpret their jobs differently.

The main features in the working day are: *fragmentation of activity*. i.e. heads carry out a large number of different acts; *people intensive* i.e. heads interact with a variety of people; and *range of tasks*, i.e. educational, administrative, and managerial activities both internal and external to the school.

Fragmentation of activity

The number of 'acts' engaged in on a daily basis is shown in column 2 of Table 2.1; the picture is one of a job with a high degree of fragmentation. An 'act' was defined as a discrete *activity* undertaken by the head with unity of purpose, or a discrete *interaction* between the head and another person or persons with an essential unity of purpose. This definition of 'act' avoids double counting where interruptions take place.

This fragmentation of the job has been commented on by others, initially by Lyons' study (1974) of the administrative tasks of heads and senior teachers in large secondary schools. Clearly in this respect there has not been

Table 2.1 Fifteen headteachers observed for a day—
fragmentation of activities

Headteacher	Total no. of separate 'headship acts'	No. of scheduled meeting with individuals or groups	Nature of longest sustained activity	Length of longest sustained activity (minutes)
A	30	0	Teaching	35
B	47	1	Teaching	20
C	35	0	Teaching	67
D	51	1	Working party (curriculum)	28
E	32	1	Teaching	123
F	29	0	Teaching	60
G	35	0	Teaching	90
H	29	0	Discussion with deputy head	26
I	47	1	Discipline meeting with head of dept.	45
J	66	0	Teaching	69
K	29	4	Curriculum committee	74
L	32	3	Meeting with head of dept.	77
M	22	1	Teaching	22
N	27	3	Senior staff meeting	131
O	26	3	Meeting with head of dept.	41

any substantial revision in the way comprehensive school headship is performed. Table 2.1 also shows (column 3) where the head was engaged in pre-planned formal meetings with groups or individuals on the staff. Table 2.2 which is taken from the log of school K, illustrates these different types of headship activities, i.e., where the head works on his own, where the head is in interaction with others, and where the head is in a scheduled meeting.

The overall picture in Tables 2.1 and 2.2 is not different in kind from those found from studies of managers in other occupational settings (e.g. Mintzberg *et al.*); it is characterised by variety, fragmentation, and the brevity of many transactions. There are, however, two interesting dif-

Table 2.2   Headship activities—the pattern of fragmentation

12.55	Leaves for lunch. Goes over to house blocks.
1.02–1.05	Returns; discusses 'temporary woman' with secretary.
1.05–1.11	Sees two girls who have had bad reports from staff.
1.11–1.18	Goes to see welfare assistant about a meeting later that day.
1.19–1.39	Works on updating school handbook—especially the definition of senior staff roles.
1.40–2.00	Discusses with welfare assistant in his study the professional scope of her work; also the timetable pattern of her working.
2.00–2.20	Walks about school outdoors. Coffee and chat.
2.35–3.25	Scheduled meeting with two deputies and head of department (remedial) about work of the department.
3.27–3.35	On the telephone regarding NAHT matters.
3.35–3.40	Reads and signs mail.

ferences: the incidence of teaching as the longest sustained activity for many headteachers: and the proportion of scheduled meetings in the totality of the job. Regarding this latter aspect, research on how top managers spend their time has suggested that notwithstanding the reactive nature of all managers' jobs to issues and events initiated by other people, they can expect to spend over 40 per cent of their time in formal meetings (for example, see Dill, 1984). The evidence of Table 2.1 is that this is not the case for headteachers.

The extent to which heads are engaged in teaching (Table 2.1 column 4) can be taken as important evidence of how some heads view their role. In the conventional analysis of a top management position, the expectation is that the leader-manager eschews direct involvement in the generic professional activity which occupied him or her on the career path; and uses previous professional knowledge as the base of a new role concerned with overall policy development, quality control, and supervising the development and productivity of others. It would appear that secondary school headship may not mean for many a 'top management' perspective as understood in industry, or, indeed, as professed by some headteachers.

People intensive

The overwhelming percentage of all headship activity is interpersonal. We found that heads had contact with eleven groups, with a contrasting weight of contact between them. A contact is defined as an interaction between the head and one or more people in the catergory specified. Whether the head is with one, two, or even thirty plus people at the time, only one contact is counted. In assembling the data heads' contacts with their secretaries have been omitted; contacts with the LEA included those with educational welfare officers, educational psychologists, community liaison workers, and builders and electricians; and youth tutors have been counted as teachers. The community included contacts with employers, suppliers of services or persons (other than parents) outside of the school.

The total number of contacts varies from 20 to 70 with an average of 37. Not surprisingly contacts with the main groups within the school, teaching staff (49 per cent) pupils (20 per cent) and non-teaching (ancillary) staff (11 per cent) are the predominant contacts and the relative weighting of contact with these three groups was fairly consistent, across all schools. Of note is the level of contact with pupils which occurs in comparison with five other groups—LEA staff (7%), community (3%), other headteachers (3%), governors, professional associations (all 1%)—with which the heads have regular contact. This level reflects the emphasis placed by some heads on both teaching and pastoral work with pupils.

Range of tasks performed daily

The complexity of running the comprehensive school has, in recent years, received substantial comment. What have not received significant comment are the implications of the complexity of the range of tasks to be carried out and the amount of activity that heads themselves give to the different task areas. Hence, whilst there are 'official' and analytical statements about what it is assumed comprehensive school headship encompasses, the correspondence between headship in action and the policy statement or theoretical view has remained problematic. Also, the extent to which headteachers interpret the task differently has only been known, if at all, on anecdotal rather than systematic bases. Table 2.3 shows the distribution in percentages of the time of the fifteen heads across six broad task categories.

The broad categories of task used in Table 2.3 were in part suggested by a reading of the data, and in part derive from our own previous work (Morgan, Hall and Mackay, 1983). The definitions of each task category are as follows:

1 Teaching

Formal class teaching, and 'teaching activities' such as marking pupils' work or formally discussing with pupils their progress in particular subjects, their choices of new courses, or the relationship of subject choice to future career.

Table 2.3 Fifteen heads observed - percentage of time spent across main categories of task

Head	Teaching	Figurehead/ ceremonial/ ethos	Educational policy and curricula matters	Operations management and routine admin.	Human management staff, pupil problems etc.	External management parents, governors, etc.
A	14	12	0	25	36	1
*B	41	4	3	32	8	12
C	31	12	0	18	27	12
D	0	20	26	19	28	7
E	34	19	1	18	17	1
F	16	9	17	37	16	4
G	26	0	7	45	9	13
H	0	8	3	39	36	14
I	0	9	0	39	35	17
*J	14	12	0	35	33	6
K	0	13	37	33	14	3
*L	13	7	14	20	27	19
M	17	16	18	24	20	5
N	0	0	23	57	20	0
*O	0	14	2	56	14	14
Average	13.7	10.3	10.0	33.1	22.6	10

* In depth study school

2 Figurehead/ethos/ceremonial

As a consequence of formal authority, the headteacher symbolises the school both to people inside it and to members of the community. As the highest status person in the school, the head's position has a figurehead function and symbolises the values to be upheld. The ethos set gives important meanings about what the school stands for. Hence, this category includes all those activities which are either *ceremonial* (such as assembly, or speech day), day to day *figurehead* (such as being the person whom important visitors to the school see, or presenting merit awards to pupils in his or her room), or in a variety of ways, setting the *ethos* of the school (for example, by stopping pupils in the playground to remonstrate about crisp packets and getting them to pick them up; or seeing pupils 'sent to the head' for infringing school rules).

3 Educational policy and curricula matters

These include all activities connected with the setting of the main aims and objectives of the school; the provision of an academic and pastoral curriculum to meet the needs of the whole range of pupils; and the arrangements and methods of teaching. As we indicated earlier, it was the special emphasis which some heads said they gave to innovation in curriculum, and teaching methods that Hughes (1972) took to define the 'leading professional' interpretation of headship.

4 Operations management and routine administration

This includes first, the routine administration of form filling and statistical returns, general record-keeping on pupil progress, keeping and monitoring registers, dealing with the mail, and matters to do with the physical buildings and plant; and second, the major logistical or control arrangements that have to be planned, such as timetable arrangements for teaching, examinations, meetings coordination arrangements with feeder schools and FE and HE colleges, the definition of staff tasks, job descriptions and delegation of responsibilities of senior management, and the evaluation of progress on all aspects of school policy - including effective standards of teaching in the classroom. Although not exclusively so, the former category of routine administration activities can generally be seen to be reactive matters as far as the headteacher is concerned, whereas the latter category of *operations management* requires considerable pro-activity.

5 Human management

Human management is the effective communication with, and the motivation, supervision, and development of staff; dealing with pupils; and the solving of problems and resolving of conflicts among staff and pupils.

6 External management

External management covers dealing with parents, LEA officers, headteachers of other schools, and with the chairman and other members of the governing body.

Of the six broad categories defined above, 40 per cent of heads dealt with matters in each of these task areas on the days they were observed, and over 80 per cent of heads dealt with matters in five of the task categories (see

Table 2.3). Fragmentation of the job in terms of the sheer volume of separate acts carried out needs therefore to be supplemented with the additional finding of a wide range of *different* tasks every day.

The time spent on the six task categories differs. These heads as a whole spent more time on teaching than on the 'leading professional' matters of curriculum or other educational policy; considerably more time on operations and human management than on educational policy; and some 10 per cent of their daily time in school on external management matters.

The broad task categories used in Table 2.3, however, conceal some important differences within them. For example, category 4 covers both routine administration and more strategic management. Analysis shows that routine administration overwhelmingly takes up headteachers' time in this category. Further, our human management evidence shows that heads spend almost equal time on staff and pupil issues; there was no day on which some pupil management problems did not arise. Whilst heads therefore have most 'people' contact with teaching staff—49 per cent of contacts—in their working day, it is the much smaller level of issues relating to pupils—20 per cent of contacts—which claims just over half (54 per cent on average) of their human management time.

Tables 2.1 and 2.3 also suggest three main differences in secondary heads' interpretation of role: (i) the position of teaching as a substantial part of the

Table 2.4 Fifteen heads observed for a day—number of scheduled meetings and time spent on educational policy and curricula matters

Schools with no scheduled meetings	% time spent on educational policy and curricula matters	
A	0	
C	0	
F	17	
G	7	Average = 4.5
H	3	
J*	0	
Schools with 3 or more scheduled meetings		
K	37	
L*	14	
N	23	Average = 19
O*	2	

* In depth study school

job; (ii) the use of scheduled meetings with staff and (iii) the volume of daily headship acts, or as it could otherwise be described, the incidence of fragmentation.

The overall incidence of teaching was high, 13 per cent of the total time. This figure conceals striking differences, though. Whilst over a third of heads did no teaching on the days they were observed, a quarter spent over 30 per cent of their time teaching, and one head ('B' in Table 2.3) spent over 40 per cent of his time that day in teaching.

The number of scheduled meetings with individuals or groups of the staff showed interesting differences. Two-thirds had none or one, whilst a quarter of the heads had three or four. One of these heads ('L' in Table 2.3) also demonstrated the close relationship which we found between the number of scheduled meetings and the amount of time given to educational policy or more purely professional, rather than administrative, matters (Table 2.4).

Some heads have a very high level of interaction. A quarter of the heads observed carried out over 45 discrete acts as defined earlier and for 'J' (Table 2.1) the total was 66. His high level of interaction or fragmentation of tasks was a consistent characteristic. He presented himself in person, 'on the hoof' to all around (and outside) the school consistently.

These contrasts in interpretation of the job are illustrated in the description we now give of the working life of the four heads we studied in depth.

•3•

A week in the work of four headteachers

Here we aim to convey graphically as well as analytically what headteachers do and the idiosyncracies of their individual interpretations. By providing narrative accounts as well as logs and summaries, we are following in the path set by Wolcott (1973), 'to tell it as it is'. The multiplicity of tasks make it difficult to convey a 'typical' day or week. At different times of the school year, different sets of activities are dominant. In the course of our observations, for example, situations such as the teachers' industrial action occurred, which interrupted the normal flow of events.

We have chosen to represent a 'week in the work' of each of the four heads, in the following ways:

Monday ● A narrative of a composite rather than actual day, to convey the typicalities. In this is each head's usual response to the different situations which occur. In other words, they are not 'typical' days but days which typify the nature of the job as they perform it.

Tuesday ● A log of all the events recorded during one day's observation (of each of the four heads). This gives an indication of the pace, scope and direction of each head's working day.

Wednesday, Thursday, Friday ● Logs of three other working days for each head, noting all events occurring in those days lasting more than five minutes. We have noted the fragmentary nature of the job and the pre-eminence of tasks and actions lasting less than five minutes. We aim to show here the frequency and type of events of a longer duration.

In this way the working week constructed stands as an illustration (on a composite basis) of the features of each headteacher's work.

A week in the work of Mr Shaw

MONDAY ●

Mr Shaw left home at 8.10 after breakfasting with his wife, who worked part-time as a doctor. One daughter was at university, the other working as a teacher in London. His fifties, semi-detached house was in a quiet cul-de-sac some ten minutes drive from the school, in a suburb adjacent to his school's catchment. His involvement in a number of activities associated with the twinning arrangements and parish church of Litton School's community allowed him to feel part of the area. He had been head of Litton since 1968, having completed all his previous teaching career in the same LEA.

Litton school is a mixed 11-18 Comprehensive. It has a sixth form of about 130 students with about 1400 pupils and 77 staff. It lies on the outskirts of a large city, in a suburb with a number of factories and workshops, but also drawing from the outlying villages. Building began in 1968 and the school consists of a bright, modern administrative and teaching block, a purpose-built sixth form centre and a number of smaller blocks, more shabby with age. It stands on a busy arterial road, away from housing and amidst a wide expanse of playing fields and open space.

8.20
Mr Shaw arrived at school and parked his car in the reserved space in front of the main entrance doors, used only by staff, sixth formers and visitors. The foyer was still quiet and he went straight through to his room, calling greetings to the office staff already in the adjacent office. Pausing only to deposit a bulging battered briefcase on his desk, take out and check his diary which he claimed to use as his in-tray and carried everywhere with him, he returned straightaway to the entrance hall, to greet staff as they arrived. As they came into the foyer, each teacher turned over his or her ring on a large board, from which the deputy responsible for arranging cover, was checking who was in or out. They glanced at the notices on the board beside the rings and checked to see if anything was in their adjacent pigeon hole.

8.40
Soon the foyer started filling up. Mr Shaw greeted individual teachers as they arrived, enquiring after their weekend, discussing various matters. Mike Reid and Sue Wilson, his deputies joined him and they stood as a trio, watching arrivals. At 10 minutes to 9 the foyer had nearly cleared and the two deputies, Ron Brown (senior teacher) and Mr Shaw stood chatting for a few minutes, about different members of staff. At 9.00 a.m. when the foyer was completely empty, Mr Shaw went back to his room calling in the office on his way to pick up his post. He placed it on his desk, together with the notices the head-boy had given him to read out over the tannoy.

Mr Shaw's study was in the administrative block, which constituted the main entrance to the school, adjacent to the general office. The large bright room was the result of his own design when he had three rooms knocked into one. It was his choice too, to have it in the middle of the school. One wall consisted entirely of windows with undrawn curtains, looking on to the corridor. The design of this was also deliberate, so that people could see when he was talking to someone and when to come in. Since he held a large number of meetings in the room, he considered it important to create a good environment. A large table filled one end of the room, with up to fifteen chairs around it, during meetings. On a small trolley was a kettle for coffee after working-lunches. His own desk was at the other end with easy chairs grouped round a coffee table to one side. On the walls were a variety of prints and on the window sills and cupboard were shields and other trophies won by the school. By the side of the coffee table was a table-top peg board model of the school's year system. A row of drawers stood behind his desk, each one labelled and a large cupboard at the opposite end held more files and books. As well as papers, his desk held a conference telephone system ('useful so the whole senior management team can listen in on conversations'); there was also a public address system. His secretary worked with other clerical staff in the adjacent general office, with an adjoining door.

9.00
The phone went, a mother wanting to know if he could take her eleven-year-old daughter into the school, as they had just moved into the district. He advised her that they were full in the first year and she would have to make a separate appeal to the county.

> You have an eleven year old child and you want to change? You have to write to the chief education officer. The decisions on first year entries are made at county hall not at individual schools. Do you live in my area? (No). I should say that the chances aren't strong. The number you need to ring is ... schools department, then ask for a personal call to Mr Pearson and he'll tell you exactly what to do. Why have you left it so late? ... Because all these things are sorted out much earlier. If the Authority says yes that's fine by me. If they say no I have to abide by that. ... Goodbye.

He jotted down different requests staff made earlier in the entrance hall; to go on a course in school time; to look at a new homework book for history. He went out into the corridor to chivvy some girls who were dawdling their way to the assembly hall.

> Come on girls, hurry up (louder). Come on, you're holding everyone up. Take your coat off. (Pulling a boy's tie out of his shirt). That's better.

9.05
When there were no more pupils in the corridor, he returned to his room to give the daily messages out over the tannoy. These were relayed to all

assembly points in the upper and lower school buildings. He praised the tidiness of the school, 'please keep it like that'; gave details of CSE oral exams, room changes, rehearsals for Showboat, netball practices; read out the results of matches and details of the Drama Club and Seekers' Club meetings; 'finally, don't forget point number one I started with. The place is looking much nicer. Keep it that way.'

9.10
Notices finished, he crossed between the buildings, telling off some latecomers on the way, and waited at the back of the lower school hall, where the head of lower school was addressing the pupils. Taking his place at the front, Mr Shaw congratulated the twenty five pupils in turn who came up to receive their commendations for work and behaviour during the year. When he had finished, he asked the children,

> Now, I don't think I'll have to ask this question more than once again. How many here have now got at least one commendation?' (Nearly every hand in the hall went up, the whole of the first year). 'That's marvellous. Let's hope it's everyone.

9.35
On his way back to his office, Maureen Osmond (head of geography) caught up with him to tell him about her unsuccessful job interview the previous Friday. He commiserated, and told her that, although she had not got the job, he had heard that her interview went very well.

9.40
Outside his room a dozen or so children were queuing to collect distinction certificates. He took a pile from his desk and asked each pupil in, shaking hands and congratulating them.

9.50
Vivien Collins (commerce) came in, worried about the insurance forms that all employers were now expected to fill in for work experience pupils. Mr Shaw sat down with her at the coffee table and they discussed the difficulties. He suggested local businesses who might be interested in taking on some of the pupils, which she noted down.

10.05
The girl on reception (a different third-year pupil each day) rang through to say that Mr and Mrs Simmonds had arrived and were waiting in the entrance hall. While they were being brought to his room, the bursar rang to remind him that the estates officer was coming that afternoon. Mr and Mrs Simmonds came in, with their grandson David, his mother and a voluntary social worker. David had been suspended from another local school and was being transferred to Mr Shaw's. Around the coffee table, Mr Shaw explained to them the implications of the move and what the school would expect

from David. His mother remained silent. David's grandparents and the social worker did most of the talking. At one point Mr Shaw broke off to ask the head of the special education unit to join them, as this was where David would spend most of his time on first entering. Mr Shaw then discussed with David his interests, what he was good at and how he thought he might fit in. He pulled out the pegboard model of the school's pastoral organisation, that he always used to show to visitors and explained to David where he would fit in. When they had gone, he made the necessary adjustment to the figures in the admissions book, and wrote memos to the different members of staff who would be working with David. He also wrote a note to the head of music about David's interest in playing drums and asked him to follow it up.

10.40
Jenny, from the office, looked round the door and asked if he was ready for his coffee. She brought it on a tray with biscuits and Mr Shaw sat at his desk drinking and sorting through the post. He took some papers through to the office and asked Mary, his secretary, to run off 60 copies of a paper he had prepared for a conference of his professional association. The phone rang while he was out and he hurried back in to take the call. It was the county's special education officer to whom he had written, requesting additional help in the school's special education unit. While he was talking, Mike Reid (senior deputy) came in and Mr Shaw indicated he should wait and listen to the conversation on his loudspeaker phone. 'You'd better listen in on this Mike, in case I get it wrong.'

(to the special education officer) . . . The first is an important issue, all the extra special unit people we've got coming in. What about all the extra staff we were promised . . . We'd better find somebody quick. Could you blow the cobwebs off the section's files and look at that . . . We're still left with this residual problem of Robert Wainright. This isn't the right school for him . . . But meanwhile we are stuck with looking after him. (The officer reassured him that it might only be days). Yes, I realise it's a logistic problem. I appreciate you're stuck with resources. You've given us extra people and we've used up your resources. We're not just trying to grab more resources. I've never met such a remedial child. (The officer said again that they would try and move him as speedily as possible). O.K. Bob, I'll wait until I hear from you. Bye.

Putting the phone down, he looked at his deputy and raised his eyebrows, 'It's like dealing with a soggy sausage,' he said.

11.00
Meanwhile the other deputy, senior teacher and director of studies had arrived for the regular Monday senior management team meeting. Mr Shaw got out from drawers he used as a filing system one labelled 'senior management team' and sat down at the coffee table with the others, to go through

its contents. Before they could begin, the phone went again. The head of another school in the Authority wanted advice from Mr Shaw in his professional association convenor role, about an industrial tribunal case, Mr Shaw said he would ring him back soon after lunch. The senior management team meeting began with a discussion on the quality of tutor teams across each year. Mr Shaw wondered whether one particular tutor needed replacing. The others were emphatic that it should not even be considered. 'O.K,' he said, 'I'll take my little idea away and run away with it!'

They were equally adamant that another tutor should retain his scale point, although Mike Reid agreed with Mr Shaw that they could probably carry themselves a lot of the jobs done by the tutor. Mr Shaw added, 'either we've got to give him more to do to justify his scale point or it ought to go'. Sue Wilson suggested that the tutor's time could be used better than it was. Mr Shaw acknowledged that there were tremendous possibilities for a mess if the tutor was not left in charge. They moved on to other possible staff changes as a result of redistributing points, on the imminent departure of one of the deputy heads of lower school. 'It gets like this every year,' Mr Shaw said, 'pieces on a chess board.' The meeting finished at 5 minutes to 12 and Mr Shaw returned to the day's post at his desk.

12.00

At twelve, there was a knock and Jim Murray, head of Raleigh House, looked round the door. He reminded the head that he intended seeing Peter Smedley, a fourth former, to get him to sign a contract about future behaviour. Mr Shaw took out a piece of paper from his briefcase. 'I haven't got the contract typed yet. I've written it. Have a look at it and see what you think.' Murray read it through quickly and suggested a further point, which Mr Shaw added in.

(Mr Murray) 'Peter's out there now, with red trousers on.'

(Mr Shaw)   'Oh, he's not, he's never.'

(Mr Murray) 'Are you going to see him with red trousers?'

(Mr Shaw)   'Can we contact home? Let's try.'

He phoned through to Peter's mother and Mr Murray listened in on the loudspeaker phone.

> Hello, Mrs Smedley? Mr Shaw, Litton School. I've got Peter outside. Did you check him before he left home? (Mrs Smedley said not and wanted to know why). He's in red trousers. (She apologised, saying that it was her fault as Peter had ripped his grey ones and not told her). I wanted to talk to you first in case you had a battle with him and he said no. (She apologised again). That's O.K. then. It's just he's on pain of death to behave properly or else and he turns up at school without uniform. O.K. then. Thanks very much. Bye.

12.05

He took the contract through to the office to be typed and was stopped by a teacher asking if he had looked at some lesson plans yet. 'I'm sorry, I just haven't had a moment.' While they were waiting for the contract to be typed Mr Shaw and Mr Murray chatted about the new history syllabus, that they were both involved in teaching. His secretary brought in the typewritten contract and Mr Murray called Peter in.

Mr Shaw:	Right, come in Peter. (They all remained standing). I've just had a word with your mother about your trousers. (Peter muttered they were ripped). Take your hands out of your pockets my lad. (Giving him the contract.) Will you read that out loud. (As the boy read it Mr Shaw kept stopping him, saying, 'do you agree' after each command). Will you sign three copies? (Peter agreed and signed three copies, which Mr Shaw countersigned). This is a contract which means it's a document we all agree on. Peter. Right? And remember what I said to you yesterday about pressures from other people. We don't want to make life a misery for you, old son.

12.15
Peter and Mr Murray left. Mike Reid (deputy head) came in with the reference Mr Shaw had asked him to put together about the head of geography, who was applying for jobs elsewhere. Mr Shaw read it through carefully, making a couple of word changes so that it was more personal, 'as it was addressed to me'. He also added to it a comment that the head of geography was 'totally unstuffy'. He asked Mike Reid to check that the rest of the senior management team had seen it, so that he could ring it through to the other head after lunch.

12.20
Mr Shaw went back to his desk and drafted a letter to a parent who had complained about her daughter being given a detention. In her view, if teachers were giving up all out-of-school activities during the teacher's dispute, then she refused to let her daughter be detained in her own time. Mr Shaw wrote:

> This raises serious implications for school discipline. I would appreciate it if you would make an appointment to come and see me.

He buzzed the intercom and asked for the manager of the local bank who acted as a trustee to the school's special fund. He wanted to check whether Mr Lawson was willing to continue in that capacity. Just as he'd finished, the head of chemistry came in to ask for more money to meet the increased price of text books. Mr Shaw asked him to do a costing, then they would consider it.

12.25

Two sixth formers came in with their leaving forms to be signed and Mr Shaw chatted with them for a few minutes about their final plans. He asked them their reasons for choosing the technical college rather than staying on into the sixth and then wished them well. Mike Reid brought the reference back in; it had been typed and the other senior management team members had all read it. Mr Shaw sat down at his desk, to read the final version through carefully:

> It's very important reading carefully references that are typed because you just need a 'not' left out and you change the whole thing.

12.35

While he took some papers through to the office for typing, his senior colleagues arrived for the regular weekly lunch with pastoral staff. They had already collected their dinners on trays from the canteen and sat down at the large table at the end of Mr Shaw's room, and started eating. Other house heads, house deputies and year tutors arrived, having collected their dinners. They were joined by the youth tutor and education welfare officer. Together with Mr Shaw, there were seventeen gathered around the table. While they were chatting and eating, Mr Shaw went to the canteen, to the top of the queue, to get his own dinner. It was the custom during working lunches for business to begin only after the pudding. He sat at the top of the table with his deputies, senior teacher and director of studies on each side. Everyone was chatting across and down the table and busy eating. At five to one, they started clearing the plates to one side and, while Sue Wilson and Sid Thomas got the coffee (using the kettle and cups which Mr Shaw kept in his room for the purpose), the formal meeting began.

1.10

The meeting was used primarily for information exchange and dialogue tossed around the group, with Mr Shaw listening, joining in and introducing the next topic each time. He began by going through the special drawer he had beside him, into which he filed anything relevant to the group, and handed out letters, court reports, reading matter, etc. to the relevant individuals.

> Let's make a start folks. Jim (senior teacher), the people who actually helped with this charity, do you want them certified? . . . (handing out court reports). Edward Gee, criminal damage as taught by his ex-house! (The head of careers asked if they could get magistrates to indicate when an offence took place) . . . Well, I had Jeff Jones turn up in my kitchen last Saturday. He now works for Dynorod so watch it! Right, quickly ins and outs. Any imminent outs or in in year one (They discussed each year in turn). How's Peter Bright settling down? . . . What do you mean 'too well' he looked angelic . . . we were all set to take Tim Dower . . . He never came . . . are you sure about this? We're on

a knife-edge. If that takes us up to 241 again that's tricky ... We must check on that because I had a letter from a father this morning. (Finishes handing out papers). Right, that's all my youngsters. Now from you ... (Each house head gives a report on individual pupils). We could Litton School him, put it on for a piece of gradualism. (The house head pointed out the boy had already been put on the school's own suspension system) ... In a similar vein, Mary Carter, it's such a dodgy home background ... who actually does she live with? I wonder if it would be better to ask her mother up and say this is what we'll have to do. (To the education welfare officer). Can you get hold of Mrs Carter and get her to come up and see us. (They discuss a number of pupils, Mr Shaw recognises all their names). They move on to finding the culprits for a recent outbreak of thefts, complaints about the dangerous road outside the school and report deadlines. How are you going to get them to us by Friday? What we've always said is once it's left at department level it's flexible. I don't mind receiving them Saturday morning. All I can suggest is look at it flexibly and let us know. (He explained the new phone system, an outbreak of hepatitus and the problems of leaving children unsupervised in the laboratories.)

1.50
At 10 minutes to 2 the meeting ended, with Mr Shaw arranging to speak to all the boys the next day about the damaged toilets. The pastoral staff left and Mr Shaw went into the corridor to commandeer a couple of boys to take the trays of dinner plates back to the canteen. He pushed the tables back against the wall and re-arranged the chairs, before going back to his desk.

2.00
First he rang Mr Wilson, the head who had contacted him that morning. Mr Wilson told him that he was being threatened with an industrial tribunal, by a teacher who felt he had treated unfairly her application for a job. Mr Shaw commiserated and offered his support as their professional association's local convenor, if Wilson should have to go to court. They agreed that the Authority, as the employers, should be Wilson's representative in that event. As soon as he had finished talking to Wilson, he asked for a call to be put through to another headteacher who had requested the reference on the head of geography. While he was waiting, the bursar rang through to say the estates officer had arrived.

2.10
Mr Shaw asked them to come along, to his room. First, he read out the references on the phone, concerned that the request for it had come after the deadline given. Reassured that it was not too late, he joined the bursar and Dick Montgomery from the Authority's estates department, round the coffee table. They discussed proposals for alterations to different parts of the site, Mr Shaw taking Montgomery into his confidence about future plans. Then they walked round the school, checking which parts needed repairs. Mr Shaw was concerned that, although the school had been externally decorated

recently, the interior was noticeably shabby. Two boys in the corridor, wearing coats, took them off when they saw him. He shouted at another two boys hanging around in the corridor and they disappeared.

2.40

When Montgomery had gone, Mr Shaw returned to his office. The head of the fifth year followed him in and asked for permission to go on a course at the polytechnic one afternoon the following week. Mr Shaw standing at his desk, sorting through papers, agreed. He sat down and started looking through the pile of financial bids from departments for money from the school's special fund, for next year. He was pleased that everyone had submitted their bid on time. He took them through to his secretary and asked her to open a file for them. He opened a letter from his professional association, asking him to contribute a chapter for a book on curriculum. He put it aside, to look at more carefully at home.

2.50

Looking at his watch, he jumped up suddenly and went out into the corridor to watch the children changing classes. Within a minute he was back in his room with a form tutor concerned about a third year boy recently arrived from Africa. In the tutor's view the boy was very depressed, and felt he was not being allowed to practise his religion at home or in school. Mr Shaw looked at his diary, to see when he could speak to Amin.

> Tomorrow's hopeless, absolutely gruelling. I could see him Period 1 on Friday. Do you want to be in on it? (The tutor said he would like to be but it was not essential) Will he unburden to me? I'll have a go at Sam (the RE teacher) from my Methodist standpoint. Then I'll ask Amin's foster parents down and explore and see if there is an alternative way whereby he goes to the mosque.

2.55

As soon as the form tutor had gone, Mr Shaw hurried around his room, setting up the slide projector and rearranging chairs ready for the fourth-year history class he taught each week. He could hear them outside the room waiting to enter. He hurried into the office to gulp down a cup of tea that had just been made, then called the class in to start the lesson. He gave them details of the history trip he had arranged for the following week and showed them slides of the area they were to visit, encouraging them to ask questions, which they did in great number.

3.45

About an hour later, when the lesson had finished, Mr Shaw left the equipment as it was and went out to watch the children boarding the buses which drew up outside the school drive. He shouted at some boys who were pushing to get on and had a quick word with one of the drivers about a complaint from other passengers. As the school grounds emptied, Mr Shaw returned to his room and cleared away the projector and chairs, getting ready for the monthly heads of departments meeting at four o'clock.

4.00

Sid Thomas (director of studies) brought in the agenda and Mr Shaw added a couple of items to it. The heads of department started ariving, some flicking quickly through the departmental minutes books which Thomas had laid out on the table at the back. The room was crowded, with seventeen department heads, the deputy, senior teacher, director of studies and Mr Shaw. Mr Shaw sat at the front of the room, with his senior staff colleagues, facing the group. He began with apologies from those who were unable to attend and asked staff to add two items to their agenda.

He began:

> Can I take item one, a second in-service day. We need a second one, Can I throw out to you an idea and see what you think about it. We have to take very urgently the 16+ developments. I thought we could invite someone in who is close to the throne in 16+ development and in the second session invite in a whole lorry load of umbrella men, for example, the chairman of the working party on 16+ syllabuses. What do you think? (Murmurs of agreement). Alright, I think we really ought to do more about it. (There was discussion across the room about what 16+ exams might look like.) Did you hear anyone speak at the conference who was outstanding who it would be worth having? Did you get on to the child who is borderline, the sorts of arrangements? We are in for a very interesting decade. (The head of maths commented that schools would probably be squeezed out of consultations.) This is why I said any opportunities you can seize to get in on working parties, you should. A whole heap of stuff has come through that we've circulated. It does look as though we ought to keep this very firmly at the front of our agenda.

He went on to the next item, his proposals for keeping in closer touch with what was going on in the departments.

> Are there ways we could a little more systematically, we being the entire senior management team, get along to departments to see how things are going, whether the shoe pinches etc ... It sounds wet and ridiculous, but how about adopt-a-department month, where the department can get us to do whatever it wants. If it wants an in-depth chat or for us to come and have a look or looking at kids ... But this way, first you know your department aren't going to be overloaded and second, with the emphasis back with you, what do you want us to look at? ...

The heads of department showed interest and he asked them to debate it and feed back the results to the senior management team. He handed over the third item, about the first years' residential weeks, to the head of lower school. Mr Shaw supported his request for feedback and agreed to consider the possibility of releasing more staff to go down to the residential centre to see what curriculum work would be feasible. The head of commerce led the next item, arrangements for the fifth year mock exams. Having urged staff to make sure fifth year projects were handed in on time, Mr Shaw turned to item six, the school's open day:

> I'd just like to thank you all for what you did on Open Day. We've had some very nice comments, how much people appreciate the staff who spoke to them and who thought it looked marvellous.

Moving on to rough books, he said:

> At least one parent has moaned at me why don't we issue rough books. Can you please debate it in departments and let's have a feedback in the minutes.

A short discussion of the pros and cons of rough books followed between different heads of department, then Mr Shaw moved them on to the fourth-and fifth-year course choices. He acknowledged their concern about the uncertainty of future staffing levels, with a smaller intake and urged them to share any problems they saw emerging. The head of science was concerned about the behaviour of those in the lower sixth whose motivation in his view was not good and who were difficult to control, since they were voluntary pupils. Mr Shaw responded:

> You've got to be sympathetic to the national situation, that some are there because of problems not of their making, like unemployment. But there is a cut-off point. Be humane, but then you have to say to them, you're wrecking the environment.

He gave them details of a free offer of computers from the Authority, 'and anything one is offered, we don't turn down!' He went on to praise the head of history for a new homework book that he had produced for the school:

> This is passing on good practice. It will stop any good ideas coming up I know! But seriously I do commend the history department on this. It was science's turn to be embarrassed last time. (Holding the book up.) It's a sort of programmed response to learning. (To the head of history) Would you like to say something, Melvin? ... How expandable is it for able youngsters? I did give a small central grant ... Again, thanks very much to the history department. Don't be shy about bringing up your ideas and we can put into the common pot good ideas we can all learn from.

He asked them to make sure that each pupil's career form was completed properly, to ensure that potential sixth formers did not slip through their fingers. There was laughter when he described the new telephone system as tying everyone down equally. Someone muttered that at last it would be revealed who really made all the phone calls. The head of science suggested that the technician should be thanked for all his help recently. Mr Shaw agreed and underlined that they should not take the technician's additional help for granted. There was a brief discussion on exam dates, speakers for the general studies sessions and how qualifications should be set out in the prospectus. When Mr Shaw confessed he could not remember how they had arrived at the present system, someone pointed out, 'we couldn't agree, so you decided!' He ended the meeting at 5.20, urging everyone to have their departmental minutes with him before half term.

5.25
He left, carrying a bulging briefcase. Having finished tea, read the paper, taken the dog for its usual evening walk, he phoned his professional association's treasurer about plans and projects. Then he wrote a letter 'in response to a silly parent letter', an editorial for the school's newsletter for parents, and looked again at the request to write a chapter on curriculum for a forthcoming pubication. Before going to bed at 10.30, he glanced through the history syllabus material he had been working on that weekend.

TUESDAY

8.25	Head arrives. Puts briefcase in his room
8.30	Stands in foyer talking to staff.
9.00	Stands in corridor watching children go in to assembly
9.10	In his room, reads out notices over tannoy.
9.15	Hurries over to lower school building. Scolds three latecomers on the way.
	Takes over assembly from head of lower school. Praises children for smartness, sport, admonishes for litter, unpunctuality, not being properly equipped.
9.35	On way back to room, counsels teacher on failed interview.
	In room, congratulates children lining up for distinctions.
9.50	Commerce teacher in to discuss work experience.
10.25	In office, speaks to bursar about groundsman.
	Clerk brings in coffee.
10.35	Head of lower school in to discuss feeder primaries.
10.40	Phone to special education officer (LEA). Not there.
	Reads through post, drinks coffee.
10.42	Four girls in for reprimand for playing near stream.
10.43	Signs post.
10.44	Head of sixth in to confirm 'options' meeting
10.48	Phone from bursar about netting.
10.50	Senior staff arrive for 'options' meeting.
11.34	Meeting over. Teaches fourth year history class.
12.35	Clears room. Fetches lunch.
	Pupils on school council in with lunches for monthly working lunch.

1.40   Working lunch over. Clears plates and chairs.
         Phones YHA. Not there.
         Chats to deputy about residential course.
1.55   Teacher brings boy in for final warning.
2.14   Bursar in to complain about boys' behaviour
         Head goes out and shouts at boys.
2.17   Secretary in with 'distinction' lists for checking.
2.30   Takes signed fifth-year reports into office.
2.31   Collects papers from bursar.
2.38   Phone from parent about possible new entrant.
2.42   Phone to other head on professional association business.
2.50   Phone from local firm's training officer.
3.14   Phone to education welfare officer (LEA), Not in.
3.15   Phone to special education officer (LEA). Discusses pupil.
3.30   Empties in-tray.
3.35   Secretary in with some papers.
         Head takes booklet to cook
3.40   In office, putting teaching equipment away.
3.45   Out to school drive to supervise pupils boarding buses.
4.00   In foyer, checking display.
4.05   To canteen for tea with staff staying on for parents' evening.
4.30   To large hall for parents' evening.
         Greeting parents, discussing pupils, talking to staff.
10.00   Leaves

A log of more extended events (more than five minutes) in Mr Shaw's working week

WEDNESDAY

8.20   Arrives.
8.30—9.00   In entrance hall to greet staff.
9.30—9.50   Paperwork.
9.53—10.07   Counselling unhappy first year pupil from abroad.
10.07—10.45   Discussion with head of house and deputy about boy stealing
                 pornographic magazines.
10.45—10.52   To staffroom, chatting to staff.
10.52—11.52   Meeting with senior management team.
11.55—12.23   Counselling parent and son.
12.23—12.40   Discussing career with teacher.
12.40—2.00   Working lunch with commerce department.
2.00—5.20   Attending and addressing conference on parental involve-
                 ment in schools at local university.

6.40—9.45	Governors' meeting at school.
9.45	Leaves

THURSDAY

8.30	Arrives
8.30—9.00	In entrance hall to greet staff.
9.40—10.35	Teaching
10.45—11.45	Meeting with other LEA heads in another school.
12.40—1.45	Working lunch with senior management team.
3.30—4.30	To county hall for union meeting with finance committee.
5.15—7.15	To nearby town for professional association meeting.
7.15	Home.

FRIDAY

8.20	Arrives
8.30—8.50	In entrance hall to greet staff.
8.50—8.57	Greets career inspectors visiting school.
9.07—9.26	In room, disciplines boy.
9.35—10.35	Teaching
10.45—12.00	To county hall for curriculum review group meeting.
12.30—2.00	Working lunch with pastoral staff.
2.15—2.25	In room chatting with HMIs.
2.25—2.36	Parent in enquiring about admitting son.
3.05—3.45	In room, with head of careers and careers inspectors to discuss their impressions.
3.45—3.55	Supervising buses in school drive.
4.04—4.11	Paperwork.
4.16—4.45	Paperwork.
4.45—5.00	Head of careers in to discuss inspectors' report.
5.10	Leaves.

A week in the work of Mr Dowe

MONDAY

Mr Dowe left his link house in a pleasant suburb just over the boundary of his school's catchment area at 8.10 each morning, to make the five minute drive to the school. His children had both left home to go on to further study and his wife had recently given up her own teaching post. He had never felt entirely comfortable in his catchment, having come from a totally different part of the country; he was aware of not having been brought up in this part of the world. He had been head of St Mary's for six years, having previously been a head for seven years in a large industrial city in the north.

St Mary's was an 11—18 mixed comprehensive school with over 1700 pupils and nearly 100 staff. There were over 200 pupils in the sixth form. The school had developed from the original secondary modern building, to which more buildings had been added in the 1960s and 1970s. It was on two sites, the larger one surrounded by playing fields, and the smaller built in the late 1970s, plush and pleasant. St Mary's was in a small residential town, very close to a large administrative city, for which it acted as a commuter base. At one end of the school's catchment housing was predominantly owner-occupied, comprising what was virtually a stockbroker belt. At the other end was a large, mainly white, local authority housing estate.

8.20

Mr Dowe parked his car in the corner of the car park nearest his room; he could choose his parking space because only two teachers with cars had arrived earlier than him. He walked with his square, maroon attaché case to his room where he hung up his coat and unpacked his case, sorting through some of the papers he took out.

Mr Dowe's room was adjacent to the administrative office at the upper end of the school buildings. It was large, but had no armchairs or coffee table. As well as a couple of filing cabinets and a table on which prospectuses and handbooks were laid out, he had a glass fronted bookcase and a row of teaching books on a table; a shield and a few framed photos also stood on this. One wall was a window—the one behind the head, who sat with his back to the window, facing the door. As well as a pile of collapsible chairs, which pupils took to sit on when they came for lessons, he had about eight desk chairs with arms, around two walls. One or two of these would be put to face his desk, and it was here that visitors would sit; some would not get as far as sitting, but hover on the room side of his desk. The three walls of the room without windows were covered with large posters for mainly Shakespearean plays; and on the wall beside his high-backed, black swivel chair, Mr Dowe had a Sasco year planner and several timetables.

He went across the corridor to photocopy from a book for his class today. On the way he chatted with Mike, the head of art, who was just going into the staffroom, next to Mr Dowe's room. Judith, his secretary, had also just arrived, and he chatted briefly with her. Then he made his photocopies.

He returned to his room with a coffee, and a pupil knocked on the door and came in to ask Mr Dowe the date of his intensive course in Latin at the end of the term. The NUT representative came in to ask the head to clarify with staff about the invigilation of internal exams after school hours. There was some confusion about a letter Bill, the deputy, sent out yesterday. Mr Dowe agreed to put up a notice clarifying the matter, though he did not think there should be any confusion. John Dunn, the senior deputy, brought him some literature which he had received from an anti-peace movement group. 'I thought you should have this.' (Mr Dowe had had some trouble recently over an allegation in a letter to the local paper of political bias in the school.) They chatted briefly about the Secretary of State for Education's latest statement on 16+ examinations. John left and Mr Dowe went to dictate a note to Judith for the staff, asking her to display it prominently in the staff room. On the way back across the corridor he greeted Len, the caretaker.

9.17
His class of eleven 'A' level classical studies pupils entered Mr Dowe's room, helped themselves to the collapsible chairs in the corner and settled down. Mr Dowe taught from behind his desk, in a seminar style: he taked about Horace's Odes, and asked the pupils questions as he went through the material.

10.26
At the end of the lesson, his secretary brought coffee in, and a pupil came in. Mr Dowe did not know her, and the pupil reminded him that he had seen her mother the previous day. He remembered this, but had forgotten why she had to come to see him, and had to ask her. It was about the set she was in for physics, and he asked a few questions and said he would have a word with Mr Lewis. The pupil departed and Mr Dowe expressed annoyance with himself: 'That's a sign of old age, you forget.' It reminded him to look at the wall chart he had put up recently to record appointments, something he thought he would never need. A sixth-form pupil who had recently entered the school asked to borrow a video cassette of *Twelfth Night*; *Twelfth Night* was on the syllabus here, but was not at her previous school. Mr Dowe rang the caretaker and asked him to turn the heating off. He was strongly against nuclear power and the wasteful use of finite fossil fuels, and was critical of public buildings with high heating and open windows. He rang Dave Jones in the LEA staffing section, but there was no further news regarding the posts he wanted clearance for. He expressed frustration that Dave said exactly the same yesterday. A pupil came in to ask if she could change her 'A' level subject options, which Mr Dowe started to deal with. Mr Kite, head of German, came in to discuss something a parent phoned Mr Dowe about yesterday; so the pupil was asked to wait outside. For the next ten minutes they discussed the staffing implications of a particular curriculum option; then Mr Kite left; the pupil returned, and Mr Dowe made a note of the details on a piece of paper, after he failed to find the appropriate form in the adjacent deputy's room.

11.05
Mr Dowe rang his senior mistress to discuss curriculum initiatives:

I hear you were at the examining board meeting yesterday ... Did you discuss the 16+ ... The TVEI thing suddenly drops on my table, it says schools will be expected to do this from next year ... There's been *no* consultation with teachers ... I'd like to get some lowdown on what HMI think ...

He told her his colleague heads' reactions to particular initiatives, including equal opportunities, at a regional conference he had attended last week. They discussed some details of the management of the teachers' dispute within the school, the progress of a pupil who had recently joined the sixth form, and of one of the school's most troublesome pupils. Mr Dowe concluded the call, 'Thanks very much for all the reporting, keeping me up to date.'

11.28
The senior deputy came in to clarify what to do about cover for an impending school trip. It was a complex matter involving half classes, departmental co-operation, and the various teacher union affiliations of particular teachers. A letter had to be written, and Mr Dowe concluded, 'Can I see it before it goes out, John?'

11.34
Mr Dowe expressed concern about interviewing for a post on Wednesday during the industrial action, and whether internal candidates would come; again, it involved the matter of cover, 'but I don't want to raise it with them just in case they say 'No'.' He popped over to his secretary's office, 'I'd better get a letter through to Jimmy Hall's father and mother, 'cos he's not in school again today.' This was the boy referred to during his discussion with his Senior Mistress. The Senior Deputy's room was across the corridor, next to the secretary's and while over there he clarified with John that the school's letter to parents (about children being sent home) had to be completely rewritten—the circumstances were different with this spate of industrial action.

11.58
Mr Dowe put on his coat and went home to have lunch. He liked to have a break; have a quick read of the *Guardian*, listen to the news, and lunch with his wife.

12.30
He returned to school, and joked and chatted with a small group of sixth-form girls who were sitting on a wall between the car park and the school building. On entering his room he found two notes on his desk which had been put there in his absence: one was from the senior mistress, about an increasing trend amongst girls at the school to wear pencil skirts and suggesting specific action. The other was from the school's NUT representative, letting the head know that the school had *not* been selected for next week's action. The phone rang and the office explained the incoming call as they always did. The caller had rung earlier when Mr Dowe was teaching. He was never interrupted then. It was the elder brother of one of five pupils, an Asian, whom Mr Dowe had disciplined the previous day. He had written

to the boy's parents, and this boy was ringing up offering the head support and urging him to take a firm stance with his brother. Mr Dowe had an enthusiastic conversation with him: 'having seen the boys yesterday, as far as I'm concerned the matter is closed . . . I think you did the right thing . . . Thank you for ringing.' Just before the conclusion of this phone call, there was a knock on the door, and a pupil entered tentatively. Mr Dowe indicated to her, one of his sixth formers, to come in and sit down. When he had finished, he turned to her, 'Right Sarah, sorry . . .', and went through her essay with her. A few minutes later she departed, and on her way out met Mr Dowe's secretary coming in, to tell him that James Barber, his colleague on the examining board, had phoned while Mr Dowe was on the line; he tried to ring him back, but James' line was engaged.

1.02
Mr Dowe went to teach his regular lower sixth general studies class. Walking along the corridors he greeted several pupils, mainly sixth formers whom he taught—and staff. One teacher asked him about having time out of school for him to be involved in a competition his 'A' level set has entered; another reported briefly on a meeting he went to last week at the teachers' centre. He passed the senior mistress telling off a pupil for her uniform, and entered the rather bare classroom where he was teaching this lesson. Although he taught his classics and English classes in his own room, the general studies classes were too large for this. All pupils in the sixth form took general studies, and so this class was a mixture of pupils re-sitting 'O' levels, and those taking full 'A' level and vocational courses. It was one of Mr Dowe's innovations, and a policy to which he was firmly committed, to make general studies compulsory for all sixth formers. The lesson was about applications for education courses, and especially about the selection of courses and completion of forms, with a strong emphasis on the UCCA system.

2.20
The lesson finished, and Mr Dowe returned to his room, having acknowledged several teachers and pupils en route. Coffee was waiting for him there, as was usual at break time. He called Judith in to take a dictated letter—to the director of education, with copies to the chairman of the education committee and the chairman of governors—on the effects of industrial action. At their meeting yesterday all the heads in the county had agreed to send such a letter. He referred to lunch arrangements, children returning late, pupils being told to stay at home, the effects of 'no cover', the supervision of practicals and the cancellation of specific meetings. He wrote:

Neither my colleagues nor I can spend much time planning or thinking (and he concluded) I would urge Docklands (LEA) to exert its influence to end the deadlock in the present salary negotiations.

2.32

Judith departed, and the parent of a child who might come to the school arrived, by appointment. He was the director of a regional quango but had started his working life as a teacher, and had just moved from Edinburgh. Mr Dowe chatted about his move, gave him the relevant booklets, asked him if he had written to the director of education and gave him his own home phone number, 'one of the really important things'. He took details of the parent's daughter, and chatted about the Scottish educational system. Mr Dowe rang his deputy to check that particular 'A' level options could be taken. They discussed his daughter's educational level—which was complicated because of the different exams in Scotland. Mr Graham, the parent, said 'I'd welcome you and your colleagues' advice on whether she is behind, and whether to catch up or do two 'A' levels.' He enquired about uniform, making notes, and moved on to results. Mr Dowe was confident that his school's exam results were favourable and gave him details in relation to county averages and particular subjects, as well as entry policy, number of passes and 'A' grades, and Oxbridge entries. Mr Graham asked about the size of 'A' level groups, how they were made up, and enquired about whether other children from the hamlet where he was moving came to the school and how they travelled there.

3.24

Having spent longer with this parent than he would normally do on possible new entrants, Mr Dowe signed the letter his secretary had just brought in and went to find his head of English to see if he approved of his contribution to the lower sixth's exam paper. Francis (head of English), was in the lower staff room, and they discussed the paper. On the way back Mr Dowe stopped to sort out a riotous class and to make a girl apologise to the teacher. After, he attributed the situation to the hot weather, since he knew that the teacher did not generally shout. He recalled previous difficult encounters with the father of the girl concerned, 'he's a ranter, he shouts down the phone at me.'

3.40

Mr Dowe stood in the corridor outside his room, chatting to pupils and encouraging orderly movement, without raising his voice to anyone. He joked with several pupils.

3.49

The corridor was clear, and Mr Dowe returned to his room, packed some papers in his attaché case, and left for home. He did much of his paperwork and telephoning at home in the evening, before and after dinner. Tonight, there was the additional task of marking the latest batch of exam scripts, so he was unlikely to get to bed much before midnight.

TUESDAY

8.20	Arrives. Orders coffee from secretary.
	Checks rooms are tidy after last night's adult education classes.
8.27	Walks round rooms turning heaters off.
8.31	In room. Checks through list of fifth-year option choices.
	Makes out interview schedule.
8.45	Takes list to staff room.
8.50	Back in room. Transfers incoming call to deputy.
8.55	Phone from chairman of the PTA.
9.00	Teacher in to discuss appointments with parents.
9.05	In corridor. Thanks teacher for forms. Tells child off for wrong uniform. Asks children if they are enjoying collecting litter. Speaks to teacher about syllabus.
9.18	Teaches sixth form classics class.
10.28	Teacher in for advice on dealing with parents of troublesome girl and to discuss changing her department.
10.38	Walks round corridors of other buildings. Tells children to walk straight. Speaks to teacher about text book, boy about 'A' levels.
10.48	In room. Asks secretary for coffee.
10.51	Discusses 'A' level options with fifth former.
11.02	Phone from local paper about head's participation in a sponsored slim. Continues 'A' level discussion. Pupil leaves.
11.13	Next pupil in to discuss 'A' level choice.
11.18	Next pupil in.
11.24	Education department phones to say meeting cancelled.
11.25	Next pupil in.
11.27	Local paper phones again to make appointment for photograph.
11.29	Asks secretary to get the school nurse on the line.
11.31	Next pupil in. Teacher in. Phone rings, nurse confirming time.
11.33	Next pupil in. Leaves
11.36	Makes a timetable on a sheet of paper for the next lot of pupils to see him in the afternoon. Takes to staffroom.
11.41	Next pupil in. Leaves.
11.48	Phones deputy head and asks him to come in.
	Discusses problem of handicapped child in school and staffing numbers.
12.00	Deputy leaves. Head goes home for lunch.
12.47	Returns to school. Goes to deputy's room to discuss scholarship level essays.
12.59	In room. Nurse and photographer arrive. Deputy in.
1.00	Rings for a pupil to come and check his weight. Has photo taken.
1.25	Opens post.
1.47	Pupil in to discuss sixth form choices.

1.53   Phone from supply teacher about to start.
1.55   Back to pupil. Leaves.
1.58   Next pupil in.
2.00   Teacher in with form about school trip.
2.02   Back to pupil. Leaves.
2.14   Next pupil in. Leaves.
2.19   Next pupil in. Leaves.
2.23   Phone secretary for coffee. Marks Latin book.
2.24   Parent rings about his son's swearing. Teacher looks in and goes. Rings careers teacher to make an appointment.
2.36   Pupil in to collect book. Explains errors to him. Leaves.
2.51   Deputy head in. Discuss redeployment notice from LEA, staff reference, pupil numbers and curriculum requirements.
3.13   Deputy leaves. Goes to other building to inform head of domestic science of supply teacher's visit. Speaks to boys watching games.
3.24   In room, goes through scheme of work for the maths department.
3.32   Rings teacher about pupil.
3.38   Finishes checking pupils' marks.
3.40   In corridor. Speaks to pupils and teachers.
3.48   Corridor clear. Back to room for meeting of working party on falling rolls.
4.30   Meeting over. Tells head of English about recent examining body meeting.
4.38   Leaves.

A log of more extended events (more than five minutes) in the rest of Mr Dowe's working week

WEDNESDAY

8.15   Arrives.
8.46—8.53   Rings LEA staffing about computer post.
9.00—9.11   Neighbouring head rings enquiring about one of Mr Dowe's staff who has applied for a job at his school.
9.12—10.07   To lower school annexe. Meets teacher about parental complaint.
10.07—10.13   Meets head of lower school to discuss staffing etc.
10.13—10.27   Meets caretaker to discuss problems with swimming pool.
10.45—11.50   Teaches classics class.
11.50—12.55   Back to main site lunch duty today. Drives around the area keeping an eye on pupils.
12.55—1.20   Home to lunch.

1.28—155	Teacher in to show head BEC work.
2.45—2.58	Walks around school looking for particular absent pupils.
3.10—3.39	Prepares for seminar.
3.46—4.55	Runs English 'A' level seminar.
5.00	Departs for home.

THURSDAY

8.18	Arrives.
8.42—8.50	Head of computer science delivers report on probationary teacher and discusses staffing.
8.52—9.11	Parent in to resolve perceived victimisation of her daughter by a teacher.
9.21—9.27	Teaches Milton to class of 20 pupils. Sets work.
10.32—10.40	Colleague rings about examination board meeting.
10.59—11.10	Goes to organise unsupervised class secretary has informed him of.
11.27—11.40	Rings a head in the LEA where he used to work to recommend a colleague's wife for a post.
11.52—12.08	Lunchtime supervision.
12.08—12.19	Allegedly victimised pupil comes to see head.
12.19—1.00	Home for lunch.
1.05—1.15	Teaches classics to class of 9 pupils—sets work.
1.15—4.00	Departs for the county heads' conference.
4.05	Travels home.

FRIDAY

8.10	Arrives
8.50—9.05	Meets three union representatives and deputy head to discuss position on industrial action.
9.07 9.15	Teacher in with pastoral information on pupil Mr Dowe teaches.
9.20—9.27	Pupils in for class. Mr Dowe sets them work and they leave.
9.30—12.00	With head of linked school for the handicapped to a meeting in LEA office with special adviser and assistant education officer (special), to discuss future policy and staffing for handicapped pupils.
12.15—12.34	Back in school for lunchtime supervision.
12.34—1.10	Home for lunch.
1.35—1.44	Head of geography in to discuss 6th form pupil complaining of victimisation.
1.50—2.10	Pastoral adviser in to discuss staffing and redeployment.
2.10—2.26	Dictates letter to LEA to secretary.

2.38—2.45	Goes to find 6th form pupils who should have come to see him.
3.30—3.42	Rings computer adviser re staffing.
4.17—4.25	Rings another head about grievance with the LEA.
4.25	Off to collect his son from the station.

A week in the work of Mr Mercer

MONDAY

Mr Mercer left home, dropping his two teenage daughters off first at their school, before arriving at Hillborough. His modern, detached house was about fifteen minutes drive from Hillborough, just outside the school's catchment area, where the city met the country. His wife, a former teacher, spent most mornings working with the local playgroup, of which she was the chairperson. Mr Mercer had been head of Hillborough for eight years, having previously been head of a nearby secondary modern school for boys.

Hillborough Comprehensive lies in a built-up area near the centre of a large city, the area being a mixture of residential, small industrial and commercial concerns and shops. The school has about 1,700 pupils, about 17 per cent of them from ethnic minority groupings. It has 97 staff and a sixth form of 80 pupils. As a result of steadily falling rolls, the organisational pattern of the school changed during our fieldwork from three to two lower schools (on different sites) and one upper school. The upper school buildings, where Mr Mercer is based, are a mixture of Victorian and modern, and have mainly hard courtyards and a few netball pitches. The school is surrounded by high-rise flats, small industries and main roads leading from the city.

8.30
Mr Mercer arrived as usual parking his car in the space reserved for him outside the window of his office. He called out a greeting to the office staff, as he unlocked the door of his room and hung his anorak on a stand in the corner.

Mr Mercer's room was large and comfortable, overlooking the long drive leading from the school's main entrance. It stood at the end of the corridor in the administrative block, separated from the general office, but with his secretary's room leading immediately off it. His desk and phones were in one corner, with two hard chairs in front, on which parents and staff were mainly invited to sit. In one corner there was a coffee table and four easy chairs, used for other visitors or longer discussions with colleagues. A large table filled the other half of the room, surrounded by hard chairs, the photocopier, the coffee machine and a glass fronted cupboard with cups and saucers. His academic gown hung on the back of the door and there was a rugby calendar and picture of the mining village from which he had come on the wall. A trolley for files stood by his desk, but he mainly used the large store-room, next to his, for files.

The room was cold and he checked the box outside his room to see if the heating had come on. It had and he returned to his room and wound the three school clocks on different walls, a weekly chore. Mrs Regan from the office knocked and brought in his mug of coffee, which he drank standing at his desk, sorting through the papers which had been left there. The bag with post from LEA had arrived late on Friday, and he had not had time to deliver its contents as usual. The door of his room remained open. He wandered out into the foyer and into the school office to collect post, greeting teachers as they came in. Back in his room he sorted through the post at his desk, sipping his coffee and pausing to gaze out of the window at pupils and staff now arriving in crowds. Suddenly, he dashed out to the front of the building and shouted at a girl wearing a flat, grey cap, to take it off.

He returned to his room and picked up a couple of letters to deliver to the caretaker's room, just along the corridor from his own, 'How's things Fred? The heating was late coming on this morning. Better check the clock on the boiler.' He continued on to the kitchens, where the cook and her assistants were already making the dough for the rolls they baked each day and getting together the ingredients for the midday lunch. She asked if he could see the catering supervisor that week, about closing the kitchens on the other site. He told her to arrange the appointment for Wednesday.

8.50
Returning to his office, he greeted his secretary. 'Good morning, Mary. Have a good weekend?' He glanced at his pocket diary but the day looked relatively empty. 'Never mind,' he said, 'I'm sure plenty will happen to fill the day.' Derek Smith, his second deputy, came in and leaned on the table. Before he could speak, Mary put through a call from a social worker anxious to speak to Mr Mercer about one of his pupils.

'Can I ring you back because I haven't had a chance to discuss it yet with my senior deputy.'

She persisted.

'OK. Why's he been taken in? What sort of trouble?'

As she went on speaking, he scribbled down details on a scrap of paper, signalling simultaneously to Mary to bring him another coffee. Having finished on the phone, he turned laughing to Derek, 'Derek, how are you? I'll be with you now.'

Derek told him of various incidents that had occurred on Friday, while Mr Mercer was out. He described how a second year girl had threatened a teacher, lifting her fist to him when he told her off. 'How serious was it?'

asked Mr Mercer. Derek Smith replied, 'Very serious. My advice is you'll need to come down on her very hard. The staff would feel very supported.'

9.00

When Derek had gone, Mr Mercer went on sorting through the pile of post his secretary had put on his desk. He muttered to himself:

> Who the hell borrowed a van from Trevor at £34.50 and hasn't paid. It's got back to me anyway. Talk about everything coming back.

Derek Smith knocked at the door and brought an electrician in. Mr Mercer told him what needed fixing and went back to his post; some papers he put straight into the file trolley at the side of his desk, some in his in-tray; others he put in a pile for delivery later. He turned to a pile of sixth form reports and started signing them. He knew he would be working on these on and off all day.

9.30

The LEA adviser from modern languages (Jim Brown) arrived, together with the head of modern languages, Stan Smith. They had arranged to meet with Mr Mercer to discuss the future of modern languages in the school. He asked Mary to bring them all a coffee and they sat down in easy chairs around a coffee table in one corner of the room. Mr Mercer began the discussion by commenting on this year's exam results in French and German, which he thought disappointing:

> That's what I was concerned about—children not being properly prepared . . . I'm wondering if it's because you haven't got any graduate teaching in the lower school, affecting these kids . . . That could improve next year when we have all the third years with us . . . Choosing a top band of 80 out of 270 is bit different from out of 130. (He offered the head of modern languages additional resources to ease the situation.) If I cover you for this year, Jim (the adviser)—can cover next year . . . That will cover you two years and no humping books from one building to next. (He suggested that Stan would have to be more stringent in whom he allowed to do languages.) We've really got to look at this in terms of limited target teaching . . . I think people are coming more to that even in other subjects. (He suggested a two-year German course in the sixth form and a review of how children were assessed lower down the school. Stan showed some surprise at Mr Mercer's unusually receptive attitude towards suggestions he had made in the past with little success. The meeting ended amicably, with all three agreeing to pursue different aspects further).

10.35

Jim Brown and Stan Smith left, as Mary announced the arrival of Sid Ruggles, an elderly governor with whom Mr Mercer had formerly taught. Ruggles was angry that something concerning the head had been omitted by the chairman from the agenda of the previous governors' meeting and asked for it to be added to the agenda of the next.

10.45

Mr Mercer went to the staffroom where his senior deputy, Roy Thomas, was giving out notices to staff during their break. It was very crowded and Mr Mercer stood at the back listening. When Thomas had finished, he added that three heads of department had not yet submitted their capitation requests; 'If I don't get it today, *I'll* allocate it.' He wandered around chatting to different teachers then returned to his room.

11.00

There he continued signing the sixth form reports. Thomas, Smith and Meg Evans, the other deputy, joined him for the senior staff meeting, which he had requested that morning. They sat round the large table at one end of his room, the deputies chatting while Mr Mercer finished what he was writing. They began by discussing the imminent teachers' action.

> I've explained to the AMMA rep. four times what totting means. He's very unclear ... you have to be extremely careful about offering it to an NUT person first ... I don't think you need worry too much about the lower school. Sid has the powers of laser beam eyes. He'll watch them walking round the park for forty minutes from his eerie ... we'll have to send a letter to parents ... OK. That's that one. Lunches. You know we've had a complaint to the paper. It's good copy. (He told them he'd invited a reporter in.) Right that's that one. Yes. What about Mary (head of lower school) ... You know she can't officially be put on a time-table because she's a candidate for redeployment. (The senior deputy said he didn't know and had timetabled her in.) If you publish it we'll have the unions on us. (He went through other teachers who had requested redeployment.) We've only had two applications for the biology job. We're only allowed to advertise in a restricted part of the local bulletin. I could ring staffing and say we've only had two. Both women, and I must have a man into this department. (The deputies agreed 'if only to break up the tea and cakes cabana'. Mr Mercer asked if they'd consider what to do if the huts weren't ready for next term. He checked the contract to see if the builders were doing what they should.) Well I tell you what, the painting at the lower school is the fastest thing since Concorde. (Thomas told him he'd met an ex-pupil of Mr Mercer's on Saturday, who remembered him as 'old Thrasher, a good bloke'.)) I can remember these kids straight off. They were a good group of kids. O.K. folks. (He asked the senior deputy how the timetable was going.) You've got to leave two rooms clear, in case these bleeding huts don't come.

12.15

The meeting finished and Ray and Meg left. Derek remained behind to accompany Mr Mercer on his tour of the school boundaries checking that no children were taking a short cut by jumping over the wall, through a neighbouring garden into the street. One or two people living locally had complained to him about this and he was determined to catch the boys and get them to apologise personally. They sat in their car for twenty minutes by the wall, ready to pounce but the only head to appear, disappeared just as quickly when its owner spotted Mr Mercer's car.

12.35
They went back into the school and to the canteen, where Mr Mercer chatted with the dinner ladies, as they got his meal and specially saved cheese and biscuits. He took it to the upstairs canteen, shouting at some children on the way to pick up litter from the floor. He sat at a table with his deputy colleagues and two other teachers, who finished their meals and left. The room was filled with noise from the children grouped at adjacent tables, eating their lunches. On the way back to his room, Mr Mercer looked into the boys' toilets and chased two youngsters out into the corridor.

1.10
He asked Mrs Regan to make some tea for himself and Smith and they sat and chatted in his room about what had happened the previous Friday, when a second-year girl had struck a teacher.

1.25
Mr Mercer took the tea cups back to the office and stopped to ask the head of music about the advertisement for a new teacher in his department. He caught the head of sixth as he went past, to check that some sixth formers were willing to help out at the parents' evening on Wednesday after school.

1.35
Back in his room, he waited for Ron Baynes, the head of the remedial department to arrive for his appointment. Baynes was annoyed at Mr Mercer's attack the previous Thursday on the whole staff for being unpunctual. He told him, 'You shouldn't lecture all of us on the sins of a few.' Mr Mercer laughed and went on to the next topic. Baynes' request to distribute a questionnaire to some staff, in relation to a pastoral course he was attending. Mr Mercer was sceptical about whether anyone would be bothered to fill it in, but agreed to Baynes going ahead.

1.55
Baynes left and the phone rang. Jim McDougall, head of a nearby Catholic school and a personal friend of Mr Mercer's, wanted to discuss the possible transfer of a boy from his school. Mr Mercer was reluctant because the boy sounded like trouble, 'and he's not our area, though.' Derek came in and checked the map while Mr Mercer was talking. It was left unresolved. Derek asked about the boy he had brought along to be disciplined, 'can we deal with the boy now? Goodies and baddies. It will only take you five minutes.' While he went to fetch the boy, the phone went again. A teacher from another school was enquiring about the home economics vacancy. Mr

Mercer gave her details of the job and pointed out that he could only appoint on a fixed term contract.

2.05

Mary came in one door with some letters to be signed and Derek brought the boy in through the other. In turn they shouted at and soft-talked to the boy until a tear appeared. Mr Mercer gave him some tissues:

> 'Here wipe your eyes. I can't stand to see him blubbing. Shall we give him another chance?'
> Mr Smith responded. 'You're the headmaster, Mr Mercer. You must decide.'
> Mr Mercer (to the boy): 'You'll be here first thing in the morning, to tell me you have apologised.'

When the boy had gone, Mr Mercer expressed surprise that he had cried so quickly. Mary came in to say that two teachers who had witnessed the event when a teacher had been struck by a girl, were outside waiting to see him.

2.20

They came in and Mr Mercer took them through the details, taking notes of everything they said:

> What do you mean she was throwing punches? ... Flailing? Throwing punches? You've got to be very careful what you say in actual fact. Was she flailing wildly or being fended off by Waters? ... O.K. leave it with me.

2.35

When they had gone, Mr Mercer asked his secretary to get the education welfare officer on the line. He wanted to discuss another girl causing trouble:

> Sally James, recognise the name? I've got to the end of the road with her ...
> She disappeared, down the docks, went in care, mother took her out, back here, effing and blinding to get herself out. Her mother is in total agreement with her being put on stage 5 if it can be done because it's quite crucial. There's been four cases since last Friday. Mother's on her own, there's a desparate situation and the girl needs to be somewhere not on her own. I've got another Stage 3 which may be a sticky one ... You haven't anything on her yet. I'd like to arrange for her to go to the other site ... Going back to Sally James, I've taken a lot this week but we're reaching the point where I'm not going to take any more. Mother is pleading with us to keep her until something can be done ... If I put her out and something happens to her, where the hell are we going to be? Hell, you know what it's like, so the kid knows she's won and beat the system ... I can't see her lasting here, Ted. Where's that? Whose in charge of it ... kids up there? What's his number? Right. Failing that I'll have to go through the procedure ... That would be a good idea. She'll be out of this area ...

2.40
Mr Mercer sat at his desk, signing the letters Mary had brought in. Then he started working through the rest of the sixth-form reports. Mary came in with a message from the NUT and NAS representatives, could they come and see him at three to discuss the incident with Michael Waters? Without looking up from his forms, Mr Mercer nodded and went on writing.

2.45
Mary put through a call from the head of one of the lower school sites. He had heard about the Michael Waters incident and wondered what the outcome was going to be. Mr Mercer reassured him that he would keep him informed.

2.50
Mr Mercer went on signing and filing.

3.00
The NAS and NUT representatives arrived. They made it clear to him that the feeling in the staffroom was that the girl should be suspended. Mr Mercer said that he could make no decisions until he had seen the girl's mother and considered all possibilities. The representatives left, stressing that he should realise how threatened staff were feeling.

3.15
When they had gone, Mr Mercer asked Mary for some tea and returned to the paperwork on his desk. He asked her to get the chief inspector on the phone and moaned when she said he wasn't there, 'I can never get hold of him.' He asked her to try the head of lower school but he was unavailable too. Ray Thomas wandered in and perched on the desk. Mr Mercer told him what the union representatives had said. He discussed what he should do when the girl's mother came in next day.

3.30
He went on marking sixth-form reports and signing sickness notes which staff had brought him.

3.55
He rang Meg Evans to get more details about Sally James; then rang the community unit where it had been suggested Sally could be sent. They agreed that she should spend a day up there the following week, to see how things worked out.

3.40
He asked Mary to get the file out on a metalwork teacher who was leaving, so that he could use the reference already written. He flicked through a publisher's brochure, advertising a new legal guide for heads. He decided to send for a copy. He glanced at and put to one side the agenda for the director's termly meeting with the county's headteachers. It was something he would go to but without much pleasure.

3.45
Mary switched the lights off in her office and left. Mr Mercer stood by the window watching pupils and staff leaving.

3.55
The school was quiet, the car park almost empty. Mr Mercer put some papers into his briefcase, switched off the lights, locked his door and left, to pick up his daughters from their school. After tea, he took the dog for its usual walk on the heath ('It's when I do all my thinking') then helped his younger daughter with some homework. He spent a couple of hours looking through the papers for the next regional CSE Examining Board meeting and sketched out a rough draft of the next governors' report. He finally retired at 11.30 to read the current large novel that he had begun in the holidays.

TUESDAY

8.30 Arrives. Opens post. Clerk brings coffee in.
Teacher in to say will be in on strike day.
Looks through references for music post.

8.43 Senior deputy in, chat about admission numbers.

8.46 Phone from parent about daughter having problems in school.

8.52 Phones second deputy for background information on girl.

8.55 Walks over to exam room to check all there.
Tells latecomers off.
Wanders around exam room.

9.10 On way back, calls in caretaker's office to discuss heating.

9.19 In room. Music teacher in to ask him to write certifying note for pupil.

9.20 Bursar brings strike notices in.
Head looks through post.

9.30 Second deputy in to report on boys in trouble. Leaves.

9.31 NUT representative in to report strike action plans.

9.34 Leaves. Head continues paperwork.

9.42 Secretary in about candidate for music job, who is on phone. Tells her to deal with it.
Asks secretary to get two other numbers.

9.49 Phone from officer (LEA) dealing with redeployment.

10.05 Back to paperwork and staffing figures.

10.07 Secretary brings in coffee and post-bag from the LEA.

10.15 Senior deputy in, puts paper on desk, leaves.
Head sorts through LEA post.

10.45 University department rings to ask to come and see the school's computers.

10.46 Researcher from ITV rings to ask if school can participate in a programme.

10.50   Goes to staffroom to listen to briefing notices.
Reminds heads of department to submit capitation request. Chats to staff.

11.05   In own room with AMMA and NAS representatives to discuss strike action.

11.10   They leave. Continues going through post.
Takes NUT post through to office and some post to the nurse and caretaker. Returns.

11.25   Head of lower school arrives for appointment to discuss career.

11.37   Leaves. Head signs court reports.

11.45   Goes out to bank.

12.10   Back at desk. Paperwork.

12.25   Lunchtime. Locks school doors after children have collected free school lunches. Turns off lights in canteen, collects sandwiches from dinner ladies, chats to them.

12.30   Eats sandwiches in staffroom with two second deputies and some part-time staff.

1.15   Unlocks doors. Back to room. Pupil shows him thank you letter.

1.29   Teacher in to complain about another school. Leaves.

1.33   Teacher brings latecomer in for scolding. Leaves.

1.35   Drinks coffee.

1.50   Paperwork.

2.00   Second deputy in about timetable.

2.02   Head takes boy over to exam room. Wanders around.

2.05   Goes to caretaker's room to find key for painters.

2.07   Back in room. Paperwork.

2.15   Teacher in to say will not cross picket line. Leaves.

2.17   Head of art in to report prize won in department.

2.18   Head continues working on staff lists.

2.30   Phone from staffing officer (LEA)
Paperwork.

2.40   Phone from senior deputy.

2.44   Secretary brings tea in.
Continues to work on staff figures.

3.00   Phone from other head. Chat about strike.

3.05   Continues working on staff figures.

3.10   Teacher in to say not going on strike.

3.15   Paperwork.

3.34   Phone to lower school for information.

3.40   Sorts through in-tray to decide what to take home.

3.45   Deputies in to say leaving early.

3.47   Girl in to tell him about her work experience.

4.00   Leaves.

A log of more extended events (more than five minutes) in the rest of Mr Mercer's working week

WEDNESDAY

8.30	Arrives
8.42—8.57	Discusses her career with head of lower school.
9.11—9.19	Chat with second deputy about pupils misbehaving.
9.20—10.30	Meeting in room with head of careers.
10.35—10.53	Chat with visiting governor, about next meeting.
10.53—11.02	Careers discussion with teacher.
11.03—11.15	Meeting with area catering office about closing lower school kitchens.
11.48—12.05	Chat with senior deputy about various topics.
12.05—12.20	Discussion with head of house about residential week.
12.30—12.55	Lunch in canteen with other staff.
1.15—1.35	Tea and chat in room with second deputy.
1.40—1.50	Goes through diary with secretary.
2.00—2.15	Looks round exhibition in art room.
2.31—2.41	Head of house in to discuss residential week.
2.43—2.49	Phone to teachers' centre about residential course.
3.01—3.21	Phone to head of lower school on variety of matters.
3.30—3.40	Paperwork.
3.46—3.55	Phone from head of lower school about computer software.
4.00	Departs.

THURSDAY

8.30	Arrives.
8.30—9.00	Coffee in room, goes through post.
9.00—9.20	Upper-school assembly.
9.20—9.35	Walks round site to inspect building problems.
9.55—12.00	Interviews candidates for caretaker post, with vice chairman of governors and LEA officer.
12.00—12.15	Chats with vice chairman of governors.
12.15—12.55	Lunch in canteen with staff.
1.00—1.45	Meeting with some heads of department.
2.00—2.15	Paperwork.
3.00—3.25	Takes post round to cook, bursar.
3.35—4.00	Chats in room to head of lower school.
4.00	Departs.

FRIDAY

8.30	Arrives.
8.40—8.55	Goes through post.
9.27—9.55	Discussion in room with head of sixth about next year's numbers.
11.00—11.40	Meeting with two deputies to make plans for strike day.
11.40—12.10	Walks around buildings.
12.30—1.15	Lunch in staffroom.
1.40—2.05	Meeting with union representatives about strike day.
2.35—2.45	Discussion in room with head of RE about study leave.
2.45—2.55	Paperwork.
3.20—3.35	To bursar's room to chat.
3.40—3.50	Chat in room with second deputy.
4.00	Departs.

A week in the work of Mr King

MONDAY

Mr King lived just a few minutes from the school in a small terraced house. He prided himself not only on knowing his catchment well but in being able to get on with and understand the working class parents and children among it. It was the same area from which he had come himself. He had been head of Aley Park for five years, having previously been its deputy for three years.

Aley Park is an 11-18 mixed comprehensive school with about 1400 pupils and 90 teachers. The sixth form has 83 pupils this year. It lies near the inner part of a large administrative city, serving an established working class community, as well as a largely immigrant and multi-ethnic area and the docks, where a significant proportion of residents are coloured and unemployment is high. The school consists of three main buildings, built in the 1960s with additions in the 1970s. Each building has its own school yard and the whole school is surrounded by playing fields.

7.30

Mr King drove into the school with his car radio on, listening to the news, through the empty car park and up to the main steps. The cleaners were at work, and he greeted two of them cheerily as he walked quickly through the foyer. He went into his room.

Mr King's room was small and crowded. One wall was a window, overlooking a grass rectangle of about 50 yards square, surrounded by a path and enclosed by buildings. In the course of the day he would usually knock on or open the window to shout—either at errant pupils, or to staff. Next to the window was a cheeseplant, the radio (which he listened to until about

8.15 in the morning), and a small filing cabinet which he could reach from his chair. His desk faced the door, which was often held open with a chock. Towards the end of our fieldwork, one of the craft teachers installed an electric 'enter' 'engaged' 'wait' buzzer-light for him—but the door remained open often. His secretary had a small adjacent room; Mr King would shout to her to request her to bring something several times in the course of the day. On the window sill and a table were clustered sporting cups, shields and trophies; and on a board were photographs of recent school activities.

There was a large safe, where a small amount of cash was kept (until his room was broken into, and the safe carried away in the school minibus and cut open on some nearby waste land). There was a store cupboard, where ties and other such items were kept, together with his black portable filing system with a file on each member of staff, and the school log. There were two glass-fronted bookcases, one largely full of old school logs going back about a hundred years; the other with various educational books and reports. On his desk, Mr King had a book rack, for his assembly books and *The Head's Legal Guide*.

He put the kettle on to make himself a coffee, the radio on to listen to the regional news, and lit a cigarette. He pulled some files out from the small cabinet beside his desk, got his 'staff' box file from his locked cupboard, and settled down to complete some forms for the LEA on particular staff. He carried on with his paperwork for about half an hour, when the caretaker, Tony, came in, for a chat, to discuss anything that was needed, and for his overtime sheet to be signed. 'Eh, you've had a bloody good week this week—thirty five pounds', Mr King said. Tony told him that he thought one of the boilers was not working properly, and Mr King told Tony where there was some graffiti which needed to be removed, and about some light switches which did not seem to work.

8.21

The deputy in charge of middle school, Dave Knowle, looked in. They chatted - about the graffiti, the youth wing, a particular pastoral case, and today's assembly. Tony returned with the mail, giving some of it to Mr King and keeping some of it for distribution elsewhere. Mr King opened the mail, chatting to Dave about the graffiti that had appeared at the weekend and telling him what was in the post: a letter to the head of classics; one on bio-technology ('I ask you, what is that'); and one from a publisher saying they intended visiting the school: 'They don't bloody ask you.'

8.27

His secretary arrived, and Mr King shouted out 'Good morning'. She came into his room and he gave her the letter to go to candidates for the deputy headship, and some mail which he had re-addressed to members of his staff. She brought in an order form which had been returned by the LEA; 'Oh, they don't do it,' said Mr King, 'I just thought I'd try it. If you want new plugs, you have to do it yourself'.

8.40
Mr Evans, deputy head in charge of lower school, looked in. He did not usually and Mr King told him that the photographer was coming for the Form 1 photo next week. In his view, photos were lucrative; 'They give me 60p a child regardless of whether they sell the photos, so that's one hundred and fifty pounds for me for nothing.'

8.44
The two deputies left together, and Miss Nixon, a needlework teacher, came in to ask him if he had signed the form for a school trip which she had left. Mr King ignored her at first, and continued turning the pages of his file. Still not looking up, he replied, 'I didn't even read it,' and asked finally whether it was a course. Only at the end of the exchange, when he said firmly, 'Well, as long as you don't impose a cover burden on your colleagues', did he make eye contact.

8.46
She departed and he rang Shirley, the chief clerk, to ask her for some forms for the advance account; she raised a couple of finance queries. While he was talking to her the head of craft came in for a chat, jokingly taking up his long-standing grouse about wanting promotion. Another craft teacher, Mr Wilson, looked in and asked the head if he was going to lower school assembly. He was and Mr Wilson said, 'Can you give out these certificates.' Mr King asked for a book rack for his desk and the young craft teacher said, yes, he had one he could have; he'd send it up. Mr King told him to make sure he finished the surround to the stage before the painters began there. The craft teachers left and Mr Smith director of studies, came in, shut the door, and asked Mr King about regulations on leave for funerals; his uncle's funeral was in London shortly. Mr King suggested that he just slip off, if he had no teaching.

9.07
Mr King picked up his Bible and assembly book, and walked over to middle school hall, shouting at dawdlers, latecomers and pupils around the pond. He stood outside the hall, solid and upright, with his hands in front of him on his books, watching the pupils file in. He told off one child who had no tie, and entered the hall after the last pupil. The theme referred to in a prayer and his address was homelessness. Mr King also led the Lord's Prayer and the hymn, and at the end swept out of the hall. He had a quick word with the teacher taking the Muslim assembly and shouted to late pupils to see Mr Knowle, the deputy in charge of middle school.

9.30
Back in his room, he lit a cigarette, singing the hymn enthusiastically to himself. His secretary brought him two cheques for signing, and he rang the office in another part of the school to ask Fred, the teacher who ran the adventure club, to get him the bill. The head of PE came in to give Mr King

a list of pupils who had been awarded plaques: 'Oh good, thanks, 'cos I wouldn't put it beyond some of the buggers to say they're due a plaque when ...' The head of PE departed, and the director of studies came in with a form about finance, 'and we ordered that Micro B monitor.' He left and Mr King rang the lower and middle school offices to ask them to send tie money up to him. He went out to the hall to look at the chairs there: he had been told some were missing. They appeared to be, so he looked in the adjacent music room and in an old cloakroom used for storage.

9.57
He returned to his room, to find a mother and her child waiting outside the room: a new admission. Mr King asked the boy if he was bright, and the mother replied, 'he is, but he hasn't worked'. Mr King said.

> I'd like him in tomorrow on his own, for a battery of tests ... intellect not knowledge ... 9.30 ... meantime, take that (options booklet) home, and a handbook ... it's no good ringing Sundown Boys ... sometimes we find other schools' tests are no good, we prefer to do our own, it might be they're just misbehaving at another school.

The mother said, 'I like that approach', and left with her son. Mr King shouted to his secretary for another coffee, and Jimmy, a PE teacher, came in for a cheque. Mr King told him that the chief clerk had the cheque book, 'OK, alright', said Jimmy and left. Mr King growled to Mr Judd, who was passing:

> Do you teach a boy called Ward ... Wall? Did he get 20 marks for maths? ... His dad rang, wanted to know whether he should get some coaching, in what areas ... I'm sure it was Form 4.

They chatted about Mr Judd's school trip yesterday. Next a teacher came in about a reference request for a pupil, who had put down both the head and the teacher as referees.

10.28
Mr King rang LEA staffing, about a teacher who claimed he had a year's contract when Mr King thought he was employed term by term. Mr Thomas undertook to look into it and clarify the matter. The deputy in charge of upper school came in for a chat—and told Mr King about his mother's deteriorating health. They had a cigarette together.

10.40
The break bell went and Mr King walked over to middle school to deliver the weekly news-sheets. He greeted several pupils on the way, and told off others. A teacher asked him a quick question, and he directed a visitor to the school from a puppet theatre, to the room she wanted. In the middle school office he joked with the education welfare officer and other staff, and

had a quick chat with the deputy head in the corridor outside. He looked
in to see the head of home eonomics, and bantered with her and some of her
colleagues.

11.08
He headed back to his room, collected a couple of books, and went to a nearby classroom for his first year history class: the medieval town. He had a
wall chart pinned up, and taught the class standing at the front, asking questions. He then set them some work to do—answering questions in the text
book, while he called each of them up in turn to have their books marked.
He frequently interrupted their work to tell particular pupils to be quiet,
sometimes engaging in banter the same pupils he had told off. He dismissed
the class, dropped off his books, and went for lunch, shouting at some girls
for dropping litter on the way.

12.16
He greeted the dinner ladies, and breached the queue to walk behind the
counter, into the kitchen, to serve himself. One of the cooks made him some
fried eggs. He sat at his usual table in the pupils' dining area, where he and
the other two deputies always ate their lunch—maintaining order around
them as they did so. Today much of their discussion was about what schools
were like when they were young. Mr King ate his lunch quickly, and set off
at his habitual fast pace to the youth wing—a building used by pupils at
lunchtime and as a youth centre in the evening. He sat in the midst of the
melee of table tennis, shouting pupils, and television, talking to the children
and drinking tea with Gerry Cousins, the Scale 4 teacher in charge of
pastoral care. They laughed about their eating and drinking after the PTA
Meeting last week, and exchanged gossip about a few teachers. Janice, the
school's social worker, joined them, and talked with them about a couple of
troublesome pupils, one of whom they were trying to get into an assessment
centre. Mr King and his colleagues interrupted their discussion to return
stray ping pong balls, go over to quieten some pupils down, and chat with
others. Mr King left them to walk around the yard; he believed firmly that
a major reason why the school had little trouble was because of the presence
of senior staff at breaks and the lunchtime. Two boys came up to him to
report others for misdemeanours; he struck two others playing pitch and
toss, and shouted at those playing with balls too near to the building. He
chatted with the head of biology, who had just been for a job interview, and
went down the back of the boilerhouse to what he knew as a smokers' corner.
On the way, he met a craft teacher whom he asked to buy him some
cigarettes while he was out.

1.27
Mr King returned to his room, and his secretary brought him a cup of tea.
The head of chemistry looked in:

Could you put some pressure on about the roof of the acid store ... you did put a requisition in?

Mr King got his book out and wrote a repairs chit. The head of art looked in to report that he had changed the display in the foyer; and the chief clerk came in to discuss her complaint about the lack of natural light in the middle school office. Mr King pulled out the file, and expressed sympathy; 'As you know, I try to do my best, I can do no more'.

1.48
The chief clerk left when Francis Jones, the English adviser, arrived; she had come for the interviews for the Scale 1 temporary contract post, for which three candidates were being interviewed. Mr King said that interviewing staff was one job he did not like doing. All three candidates came in, and the head explained the post, said a little about the school, and invited questions. All three candidates left and David, the head of English, joined them. The first candidate was summoned, and Mr King asked the first question: 'Perhaps you could tell us what you've done this year, apart from your four months with us ...' He asked a following question and then the head of English and the adviser took over. Mr King took his phone off the hook, after it rang for a second time. After the adviser told him she had no more questions, Mr King concluded the interview by asking the candidate if she had any questions. The candidate departed, and the caretaker came in to collect some cash to bank. The other two interviews followed a similar pattern, with the occasional joke—one candidate asked about extra-curricular activities, and Mr King laughed, saying 'it depends on what union you're in'.

2.50
Mr King buzzed his secretary for coffee and put his feet on his desk, having asked the head of department to run through his views on each candidate. There was little to discuss, and no disagreement. Mr King drank the stomach powder his secretary had brought him, they finished their coffee and the adviser went to get the successful candidate and to speak to the others. Mr King told her, 'on behalf of the director I should like to offer you the post. It's only a temporary contract for a year. Are you able to accept it?' He gave her some booklets and a timetable, and suggested that she might like to spend half an hour with the head of department, 'you'll get a contract from the Authority'. As soon as the head of department and adviser had left, he rang the deputy in charge of middle school to give him the new teacher's name.

3.00
The caretaker delivered books from the bank, and the secretary came in for a blank cheque, which Mr King wrote out. He rang the chief clerk to tell her about this. The director of studies came in and Mr King told him who

had been appointed to the English post. He rang the LEA buildings department about hand driers in the toilets, and painting the craft department, concluding the call, 'see you then, Alan, ta-ra, mate'. His secretary delivered some papers, and the head of home economics came in. They chatted about a school social event the previous Friday. A teacher rang in about some money; and a feeder primary head rang. The senior deputy came and joined the chat, which was interrupted by the secretary seeking clarification.

3.18
They all departed, Mr King to have a look around the school. He visited the swimming pool, and spoke with the teacher there, who told him that it was much cleaner with the new caretaker. He watched pupils playing games on the field, and then went into a class being covered—the teacher had left the door open. Mr King asked the teacher what the class was and left, to return to his room.

3.28
The education welfare officer, came in; and they chatted. The senior deputy delivered some figures on exam entries; and the caretaker came to report a repair. A new physics teacher asked for past 'A' level papers, but Mr King could not find them.

3.50
Mr King went to supervise his pupils boarding the buses, which he did every day at this time. While doing this, he picked up some litter, and spoke to the deputy in charge of lower school about three particularly disruptive pupils. He joked with and shouted at the pupils as they queued to pay for the bus.

4.00
Mr King returned to his room when the buses left, and completed forms relating to teacher applications. A member of the public phoned in to complain about some pupil's behaviour on the school bus; at this time, as was the case before 8.30 a.m., all phone calls came direct to the head. Mr King told him:

> No, I've got great sympathy for your problem . . . Get the number, that'll narrow it down a bit . . . Leave it with me. Mr Bridge, I'll see what I can do . . . Well, that's not our job, with all due respect, that's their parents . . . It's not really our job to bring the children up.

The caretaker called in to ask if he could remove a flimsy partition in the sixth form room; Mr King suggested he had a word with a particular teacher about it.

4.20
Mr King left his office, having a brief chat with the economics teacher *en route* to his car. He rarely took work home; and looked forward instead to

a drink later in the pub with friends, after the monthly church group meeting he attended and watching television before retiring at midnight.

TUESDAY

7.30	Arrives. Listens to radio, drinks coffee, sorts papers.
8.00	Rings maintenance about ceilings.
8.07	Greets painter coming in for instructions.
	Postman delivers mail. Opens it.
8.15	Teacher brings in receipt for curtains. Leaves.
8.21	Greets secretary.
	Teacher collects cassette and books.
8.24	Gives secretary letters for typing.
8.25	Rings deputy for information on boys. Not there.
8.35	Deputy rings back with information. Chats to other deputy.
8.38	Assistant caretaker in with keys.
8.48	Rings the county architect. Not in.
	Rings LEA about insurance for schools. Teacher greets him.
8.55	Rings teacher to say their room is being painted tomorrow.
8.59	Rings bank for new cheque book.
9.02	Teacher comes for cheques. Leaves.
9.07	Pupil brings him this file.
9.09	Shouts at pupil. Jokes with secretary. Rings the administrative office for the price of graffiti remover.
9.15	He asks a teacher to video the fashion show being held at the school. Shouts at girls.
	Strolls round corridors catching children not in assemblies.
	Jokes and chats with teachers.
9.31	Back in room. Tells teacher her hours the following term.
9.33	Rings the LEA to complain about broken windows.
	Teacher in to claim for school trip.
9.38	Has pupil in to discipline for slashing bus seats.
	Leaves
9.45	Rings photocopying clerk.
	Pupil in with deputy head. Head tells her off loudly.
9.55	Education welfare officer in to discuss pupil.
	Secretary joins in.
10.04	Pupil brings a chisel for the head to unblock the window.
	Does sums on calculator to get staff attendance figure.
10.07	Opens window with chisel in a classroom.
10.14	Talks in room to deputy head and education welfare officer. They leave.
10.21	Phone from another head to discuss redeployment.

10.24   Continues working out attendance figures.
          Signs forms.
10.28   Teacher in to discuss suspended ceiling. Leaves.
10.46   Walks round school during break.
          Goes to lower school staff room. Chats with teachers, shouts at children for dropping litter.
11.03   In room. Watches deputy tell children off for slashing seats.
11.06   Phone from the bus company about damage.
11.11   Teaches.
12.15   Back in room. Goes to youth wing. Greets community policeman. Tells child to fetch his lunch.
          Eats lunch in youth wing, chatting to pupils and staff.
1.45   Back in room. Tells boy off for smoking.
1.54   Rings adviser. Not there.
          Local county councillor brings in Asian student who wants teaching experience.
          Adviser rings back about teacher nominated for redeployment.
          Visitors leave.
2.12   Parents in to discuss their daughter's behaviour.
          Leaves.
2.35   Head of P.E. in with figures. Leaves.
2.42   Deputy head in. Chat about the parents who have just left.
2.51   Caretaker in with head's cheque book. Both leave.
2.52   Secretary in with papers to be signed. Leaves.
2.59   Phone from a feeder primary head.
3.03   Secretary brings tea.
          Rings LEA about the architect's specification. Science teacher in to tell him where the school can get tons of glass tubing free.
          Rings teacher to tell her five pupils will be late on Friday.
3.10   Takes a phone message for the head of P.E. about equipment.
3.17   Rings deputy about new child being bullied.
3.20   Paperwork.
3.45   Supervises bus queue.
4.00   Leaves.

A log of more extended events (more than five minutes) in the rest of Mr King's working week

WEDNESDAY

7.30   Arrives.
7.35—8.15   Writes governors report.
8.58—9.03   Parent and son, sent home from school last Friday, in.

9.20—9.34	Upper school assembly.
9.40—10.00	Patrols school; shouts at pupils for being late, dawdling, or uniform. Enters classrooms. Moans about graffiti, and rubs it off. Speaks to teachers. Enters staffroom.
10.35—10.50	To craft block to 'harass a few teachers'; and middle school.
10.50—11.05	Patrols school at break. Disciplines pupils.
11.07—11.42	Teaches first year history class.
12.17—1.24	Lunchtime supervision around the school.
1.44—2.12	Head of history in to discuss personal problem.
2.14—2.57	Chief clerk in to sort out invoices and account for year end.
3.45—3.55	Supervises bus queue.
4.45	Departs.

THURSDAY

7.30	Arrives.
8.41—8.47	Deputy head in. Discuss pupil in trouble yesterday/cover for football match/graffiti removal.
9.20—9.34	Lower school assembly. Sees parents of delinquent fourth year pupil who have been summoned to the school, with deputy head.
9.57—10.13	Teacher being redeployed from another school to discuss vacancy.
11.06—11.13	Disciplines pupils.
11.37—11.46	Deputy head in charge of upper school in. Chat about wife/a pupil's eyesight/request to leave school for quarter of an hour.
11.53—12.15	With redeployed teacher and head of department discussing post.
12.45—1.22	Lunchtime patrol: discusses one pupil with each of two deputies; discusses carpet with teacher; confiscates ball; deputy reports on visit to doctor.
1.30—1.37	Phone call in. Solicitor ringing about a pupil who has to appear in court.
1.41—1.51	Goes with caretaker to try to get lock off.
2.00—2.40	Teaches first year history class.
2.55—3.00	Rings LEA about a request to write a character reference for a teacher who is appearing in court.
3.05—3.32	Patrols school; visits classrooms; speaks to staff and pupils; deals with disscipline cases.
3.45—3.57	Supervises bus queue.
4.01—4.33	Meeting of senior staff.

4.33—5.05	Goes to watch school sport.
5.18—5.25	Rings chief adviser at home.
5.25—5.35	Fills in forms for temporary contract teachers.
6.40—9.00	School fashion show.
9.00	Leaves school for a drink with colleagues.

FRIDAY

7.30—8.19	Arrives.
	Paperwork: preparation for HMI inspection.
8.31—8.38	Opens mail.
9.15—9.27	Upper school assembly.
9.59—10.20	Meeting, previously arranged, with deputy, social worker and social services houseparent, about a pupil.
10.45—11.06	Supervises yard; chats, enforces discipline, cleans off graffiti.
11.06—12.15	Teaches William the Conqueror to first form.
12.15—1.27	Patrols school, chatting with teachers, caretaker, pupils, meals staff and having lunch with deputies.
2.18—2.56	Pastoral adviser visits. Discuss caretaker's resignation, vacant deputy headship, staffing.
	Exchanges gossip about the LEA.
3.04—3.10	Organises the collection of litter by pupils not doing games.
3.50—3.57	Supervises bus queue.
4.10—4.30	Paperwork for HMI visit.
4.30	Departs.

•||•

Heads and Teachers

•4•

Heads working with teaching staff

Chapter 2 described how heads' contacts with teaching staff formed the majority of interpersonal contacts during the typical working day. Here we consider those relationships from a number of perspectives: the distribution of contacts between staff; their formality or informality; and their purpose and content. We describe the general style of each of the four heads, in their relations with staff; what they saw as the tasks to be carried out with staff and the strategies they used.

The heads' contacts with staff constituted just under half of their contacts at work. There was little difference between the four heads in this respect. They differed, however, in which staff their contact was with; that is, how their contact was distributed between senior staff, middle management and junior staff. Table 4.1 indicates the percentage distribution of each head's contacts with different levels of staff.

The category of senior staff includes those staff whom the heads described to us as sharing their senior management functions—known in some schools as the senior management team. These are as shown in Figure 4.1.

With the exception of Mr Dowe, each head had considerable daily contact with his senior staff, although the contacts differed in amount and the degree of

Table 4.1 The percentage of each head's staff contacts with different levels of staff

| | | Headteacher | | |
Category of staff	Shaw	Dowe	Mercer	King
Senior staff	40	20	50	45
Middle management	40	48	20	22
Junior staff	20	32	30	33

The senior management structure in each of the four schools as their heads

er	Senior staff
Mr Shaw	First deputy head
	Second deputy head
	Second master
	Director of studies
Mr Dowe	Senior deputy head
	Second deputy head
	Senior mistress
Mr Mercer	Senior deputy head
	Two second deputy heads
	Three heads of lower schools
Mr King	Three deputy heads
	Three assistant heads of section
	Director of studies
	Pastoral co-ordinator

formality. Mr Shaw had a similar number of contacts outside of scheduled meetings with all his senior staff, whom he frequently described as a team and who met together daily as a group. All of these would come frequently into his office without an appointment and without first checking with his secretary. The ease of access also applied to all other levels of staff.

Mr Mercer's contacts with his senior staff were complicated by the location of the school on four sites, and what he described as the sometimes uneasy relationships between individual members of staff. We never saw him with all the senior staff together, even in scheduled meetings; and only rarely with the three deputies together. His contacts were mainly with one or other of the male deputies or the male head of lower school on their own; or the two second deputies together. Unlike Mr Shaw, the extent of Mr Mercer's contacts with individual senior staff appeared to be affected by the nature of his personal relationships with them. The three deputies and male head of lower school would come in without an appointment, though sometimes check with his secretary first. The other two heads of lower school always made an appointment, as did most other staff in the school.

Similarly, Mr King had considerable daily contact with some members of senior staff and not others. He saw much less of one of the deputies than the other two; little of the director of studies and much of the pastoral co-ordinator. As with Mr Mercer, his contacts with senior staff appeared to be determined in part by shared interests and liking.

Mr Dowe differed from the other three in having relatively little contact with his senior staff either informally or through scheduled meetings. He usually met (for about half an hour each morning) the senior deputy head to exchange information; and made contact briefly with the other two deputies, on average, less than once a day. He saw the head of lower school who was based on another site, a maximum of once a week when he visited the site for a morning.

Figure 4.2 shows that, as well as differing in the amount of daily unscheduled contacts with senior staff, the four heads also differed in the number of scheduled meetings they had with their senior colleagues. Mr Shaw, whose senior colleagues came frequently to his room throughout the day and attended his daily working lunches, also met with him formally four times in the week. The meetings took place in his office, in easy chairs around a coffee table, usually lasted an hour and covered a wide range of topics from small discipline matters to planning. If he had to cancel a meeting, it was re-arranged for the same week. On at least one evening a term, they met at his house for an extended meeting, as well as meeting socially outside school on occasions.

In contrast, Mr Dowe, who had few scheduled meetings with any staff, never held a meeting exclusively with senior staff. He chaired a weekly meeting of what was known in the school as 'the first XI', which had a rotating membership of middle management staff and a permanent member-ship of the deputies and heads of lower school. The school's senior council's brief encompassed both pastoral and curriculum matters, met monthly, was chaired by the senior deputy, and was attended by the head, all senior management, heads of department and heads of pastoral.

Both Mr Mercer and Mr King had frequent informal contacts with their senior staff, but only held meetings with them when there were specific

Figure 4.2 The pattern of heads' regular meetings with senior staff

Mr Shaw	Three time-tabled senior management team meetings per week. One senior management team working lunch a week.
Mr Dowe	Weekly 'first XI' meeting. Monthly senior council.
Mr Mercer	Meetings called regularly but at short notice with some senior staff to discuss specific issues.
Mr King	Meetings called regularly, at short notice, mainly to discuss specific issues.

issues to discuss; for example, during the teachers' industrial
we shall show when we discuss the style of each head's inter-
th his staff, the differences in preference for regular group
or individual negotiations with senior staff are additionally
reflected in their attitudes to both delegation and decision-making.

The variation between the four heads in the frequency and kind of their contacts with middle management and junior staff was still more marked. By
middle management we mean all those not included in the head's definition
of senior staff who were scale four or other heads of department or pastoral
heads. These teachers, for Mr Dowe, constituted by far the largest number
of contacts, although he only saw a small number—in particular those working with the sixth form, who were higher scale teachers. For Mr Mercer,
they constituted the group of lowest contact. Both Mr Shaw and Mr King
saw middle management staff as often as senior staff. These different levels
of contact can be attributed to a number of factors, some of which apply to
contacts with junior staff as well. The first of these is the head's availability
to staff at different times of the day.

Their availability for informal and formal contact with staff other than
senior staff depended on how they organised their own working day and the
extent of their movement around the school. We have shown in Chapter 3
that they all began and ended their days at different times, differed in the
amount of teaching they did, the number of scheduled meetings, and how
often they were out of school. These represent constraints on how often and
when they were available to staff. A common complaint from staff was that
headteachers were not available as much as staff would like. Each of the four
heads took deliberate steps to ensure some availability, as Figure 4.3 shows.

However, availability means available to all incoming demands, not just
staff, although only Mr Mercer used his secretary to control staff access to
him when he was in his room. With each of the other heads, staff entered
freely.

However, the reasons for the four heads' differing amounts of contact with
middle management and junior staff varied. The pattern of scheduled
meetings resembled that which we described in relation to senior staff and
is shown in Figure 4.4.

Mr Shaw was concerned that middle management staff should have a
ready forum in which to exchange information and express any doubts and
concerns. Thus the frequency of his formal contacts with middle management staff did not differ substantially from those with senior staff, although
they were generally more specific in content, as we shall show. His contacts
with junior staff were substantially less, something which he thought he had
taken steps to overcome. During the year he aimed to have every member
of staff coming to at least one of the lunches. He also held a 'house family
tea' for form tutors prior to report evenings, to 'build up camaraderie'.
Junior staff did come to see him in his room during the day, but less fre-

Figure 4.3 Heads' availability to staff (locations and time)

Shaw		Dowe		Mercer		King	
Where	When	Where	When	Where	When	Where	When
Entrance hall	Before school	Corridors	Beginning and end of school day	School yards	Lunch-times	School yards	Breaks and lunchtimes
Corridors	Between lessons	Walkabout	Rare	Canteen	Lunch-times	Canteen	Lunchtimes
School drive	After school	At home by telephone	Evenings and weekends	Walkabout	Daily	Walkabout	Daily
Walkabout	Rare	Room	During and between lessons	Room	Before school and during and between lessons	Room	Before school and during and between lessons
Room	During and between lessons	Lower school annexe	One morning per week	Lower school annexe (s)	Each one morning per week	Staffroom	Frequent
Room	After school	Staffroom twice per week	rare	Staffroom	Occasional		
Staffroom	Break time						

Figure 4.4 Pattern of scheduled meetings with staff (other than senior staff)

Head	All staff	Heads of department	Heads of pastoral	Other group meetings
Mr Shaw	Termly (addresses)	Monthly (chairs)	Weekly (chairs)	Daily working lunches with various groupings (hosts and chairs)
Mr Dowe	Termly (addresses)	Monthly Senior Council (attends)		Weekly 'First XI' (pastoral and academic) (chairs)
Mr Mercer	Termly (addresses)	Attends when invited	Attends when invited	Attends working parties when invited
Mr King	Termly (addresses)	Monthly (chairs)	Does not attend	Chairs working party on home economics curriculum

quently than other levels of staff. The scope of his contacts with staff was not noticeably shaped by his own personal interests.

The much greater frequency of Mr Dowe's contacts with middle management staff can be seen in the light of expressed interest in some parts of the curriculum and his practice of delegating a large part of the school's daily administration. The four staff in charge of the sixth form and the careers teacher had more interactions with Mr Dowe than his deputies. Their posts were created at the time we were carrying out our fieldwork and were an important part of his reorganisation of staff at the upper end of the school. Since he had previously carried out much of the work now to be done by the new post-holders, he saw himself as playing an induction role. Similarly he had close involvement with the English department. This was partly an extension of his own teaching commitment and academic interest; and partly in order to resolve problems which had developed in the department, and which had resulted in intervention from the LEA. Similarly, he had more frequent contacts with staff teaching general studies, which he also taught, having established it on the curriculum in spite of some parental opposition. Apart from these specialised contacts, Mr Dowe's interactions with other staff were not very frequent.

Table 4.1 showed that Mr Mercer's contacts with middle management staff were considerably less than for senior and junior staff. They rarely occurred casually, were usually by appointment and in order to discuss a specific issue. He did not attend the heads of house meetings; pastoral issues were delegated entirely to the two second deputies. He attended heads of department meetings only on invitation or if he had an issue he specifically wanted to raise. Otherwise, he dealt with them mainly on an individual basis, usually at their request. He had more informal contact with those staff, with whom he got on well socially, usually men. Although he sometimes referred to his own geography teaching backgroud, his response to staff from different departments was shaped more by individual compatability than shared curriculum interests. Since he disliked formal meetings, many of his contacts were by phone or as he walked around the school. He told us:

It gives a chance for anyone with problems to tackle me. It's a morale exercise.

The location of the school on four sites acted as a constraint, however, on his preference for an informal style, since visits to each of the sites were purposely arranged.

Mr King also favoured management by walking around and spent a considerable part of the day doing so. He was around the school a great deal and the pace of his interactions with all levels of staff was vigorous, both by phone and face-to-face. Throughout the day he would encounter teachers— when they called into his room, in the corridors and yards, or in their classrooms. There were some idiosyncracies in his choice of whom he interacted with; he never visited one of the three staffrooms with us. He described it as 'an NAS stronghold'; and was more friendly with some staff (particularly in the craft, design and technology subjects) than others. Although he taught some history classes, he did not show a greater interest or have more contacts with that department than others. A large percentage of his contacts with staff were with a few staff, whom he saw frequently. Generally, these were those he was on good terms with, rather than deputies, heads of department, etc.

It seemed to us that what the four heads were intending (with varying emphases) in their interactions with staff could be summarised under two main headings:

providing professional leadership (including guiding teachers in what and how they were teaching, and in how they handled aspects of pupil welfare; disciplining teachers and monitoring staff performance).

encouraging staff development (including selection, induction, promotion and training).

Additionally, a number of contacts with staff were in relation to general organisational matters; these are considered in Chapter 4.

First we shall consider the ways heads intended to demonstrate professional leadership with staff, specifically, those activities which can be included under the heading of curriculum leadership.

Professional leadership philosophies

Heads are in a strong position to shape the curriculum, since they have the resources and power to define what it might be, albeit in conjunction with all the other interest groups with which they must work. In interviews and conversations, all four heads credited themselves with having made substantial changes in their schools' curricula over the years.

They did, however, differ radically in their educational philosophies, particularly in relation to the extent to which their concern was distributed across the whole range of pupils or focused on a smaller group among them. As we show elsewhere, Mr Dowe took a strong interest in the more academic pupils in the school, concentrating the majority of his work with them on the upper end of the school. He described himself to us as a curriculum leader, and saw this as a central aspect of his job:

> I insist on running the curriculum as I want to run it. Obviously, I listen to people's advice, but ultimately that curriculum has to work according to the way I want it. The balance had to be right all the way through, and I'm willing to fight staff and I'm willing to fight parents.

In his broad overview, Mr Dowe had a number of important curriculum preferences: he was in favour of mixed ability teaching (with setting where and when the head of department deemed it appropriate), peace studies and a non-sexist curriculum. As the only one of the senior staff (apart from his senior deputy) with experience of mixed ability, he saw it as his primary responsibility to promote it, through the appropriate allocation of resources for it. He was also strongly supportive of a non-sexist curriculum, both in public statements and in selecting staff who would support his views. For example, his senior mistress took an active interest in this—within her professional association and in representations to the LEA, as well as at St Mary's. Mr Dowe supported her on this, and in particular her work with Women into Science and Engineering (WISE). At Senior Council, she spoke on WISE, concluding, 'I don't know whether the head would like to add anything.' He added:

> Yes. I thing we ought to get on to it ... We want to eradicate from their mind the idea that 'cos I'm a girl, I don't want to be doing CDT' ... it's all this thing about image-making ... opening of eyes ... and changing attitudes.

At the preliminary interviews for the deputy headship, Mr Dowe asked each candidate how they would remove sexist over- and under-tones from a school, and took a close interest in their replies.

He had his own conception of what constituted a balanced curriculum, which, despite opposition from parents, he had introduced into the fourth and fifth years: every pupil had to take at least one aesthetic or creative subject, at least one science subject, and at least one humanities subject; and in the sixth form, every pupil had to take supportive subjects like general studies, either at 'A' or 'O' level; ordinary alternative English, careers and recreation. Apart from keeping up to date with published reports on curriculum, his main source of knowledge about curriculum developments was through his work with various exam boards. Through his example as a teaching head, he sought to motivate his staff and keep them thinking and working as lively educationalists.

Mr King also described himself as the main force of curriculum innovation in the school, and was adamant that, although he first discussed proposals with his director of studies, neither the director nor any other of his staff had the ideas themselves. He favoured a flexible 'banding' system, including 'high fliers' classes, which he had introduced into the lower school three years earlier. He was firmly opposed to mixed ability teaching, because of the extra demands he saw it placing on both teachers and pupils:

> I do not believe it makes the children at the bottom end feel they're more equal because they're in a class with a child with an IQ of 110 to 140, who would finish the same piece of work in five minutes that they're going to take forty minutes to do. In fact, I think quite the reverse. It has a terrible social effect
> . . .

In practice, much of Mr King's energy was focused on the less able child. His approach to the most able was that they were going to do well anyway. He saw the day when 'O' and CSE exam results came out as 'what it was all about', but the 'A' level result day as giving him less satisfaction. He was a strong supporter of the new City and Guilds courses in the school, as he explained to a visiting HMI:

> I'm a great believer in City and Guilds ... their dads have done City and Guilds, they know what it is—they haven't heard of a CSE.

He was equally strong in his antagonistic views about a non-sexist curriculum and its relevance to the choices girls made among subjects. Similarly, he objected to positive discrimination in the form of special provision for ethnic minority pupils although his school was the one in his region with the highest proportion of coloured pupils. He was firm that the school should have no special policy for coloured pupils; he insisted that all pupils were treated the same. He was proud of his approach, saying that its test could occur any day, when he might have to deal with a racial incident. When longlisting candidates for the deputy headship, he said that he was not having someone with an ILEA line, and mockingly read from one candidate's application form that said 'schools should make a stand against racism'.

Mr Mercer's curriculum views closely resembled Mr King's on multicoloured education and banding, although he was more concerned than Mr King to promote a non-sexist curriculum in the school and had set up a working party to see how this could be done. The LEA's decision to close one of the school's lower school sites presented problems in maintaining the existing curriculum provision; on the other hand, the resulting staff and accommodation changes made it possible to consider curriculum innovation in some areas. He was seen by his deputies as preferring a traditional curriculum. However, the deputy head, who saw the humanities scheme as her initiative, expressed surprise at the head's acceptance of it:

> To give the head his due, he wanted the scheme and he chose it from alternatives. I didn't realise then it was a very *avant garde* thing for him to do.

He viewed modern languages, in particular, as a problem throughout the school. Having changed the school from streaming to banding in the lower years, and having changed French from a core subject to an option, he still saw it as creating problems, because it creamed off the brighter pupils and was diminishing in popularity. He was somewhat sceptical of many of the schemes for multi-cultural education in the school that he was asked to consider. Brayside LEA, more than Docklands, was intent on promoting multicultural education initiatives. The large number of children from ethnic minorities in the school meant that Hillsborough was seen by the local multicultural education centre as having special needs, for which it could provide appropriate staff.

While having good relations with the two community liaison workers who worked with the school, he did not appreciate some of the suggestions for a multi-cultural curriculum emanating from the centre. He told us, 'we (local heads) say "get out of the curriculum; concentrate your efforts on language". His main concern was to avoid racial tensions in the school, and he did not see curriculum change as a vital contribution to this. He would have preferred a totally integrationist policy, of the kind that Mr King was allowed to practice, but Brayside would not allow this.

Mr Shaw was fully committed to mixed ability teaching and stressed to candidates for teaching posts in the school that a similar commitment would be expected. Although there was only a small number of children from ethnic minorities in the school, he was keen to encourage more, so that, as he saw it, the LEA's multi-cultural education policies should be more relevant. He encouraged any developments towards a non-sexist curriculum.

Having acquired a unit for the school for children with special education needs, he was equally concerned to be able to demonstrate to parents that the school offered opportunities to extend the more able. He had instituted a programme of 'extended studies', the remit of which was still being debated. He disagreed with his senior deputy and the teacher in charge of the scheme, that it should be for high ability non-achievers first, then high ability achievers. In his view:

> It would go round the community that there's extra provision for children with special needs. We're in danger of becoming a lame dog establishment.

His concern was to maintain as broad a curriculum as possible. One of his main concerns was, he told us, 'trying to produce curriculum development in a plant which is growing old gracefully, with an absence of resources to equip it.' He found it 'frustrating when central government has got clear ideas of what we should be doing but no resources'. One of the reasons for his impatience with the LEA's attitude to some new initiatives in schools was Litton School's resulting inability to offer the same range of courses as the technical college:

> We'd have a marvellous sixth form if it wasn't for the tech ... it would be alright if they did what they're supposed to do, instead of being a glorified sixth form college.

Decisions taken at the senior staff meeting to discuss the organisation of the curriculum in the third and fourth years were thus strongly influenced by a concern to ensure maximum numbers for the sixth form. His membership of two LEA-based curriculum committees, the curriculum review group and careers advisory group, gave him opportunities to influence curriculum developments in both the county and his own school. He disliked what he called a 'humanities goulash' and described himself as 'anti-faculty, anti-integrating subjects, pro-mixed ability'.

Guidance of teachers

We see 'professional leadership' as encompassing individual guidance of teachers in what and how they teach and in how they handle aspects of pupil welfare; disciplining teachers and monitoring staff performance. Discussing curriculum matters with individual staff constituted less than a fifth of each head's contacts with staff (excluding contact with senior staff), although the discussions were usually lengthier than many other staff contacts. Mr Shaw most frequently discussed curriculum matters with individual teachers; Mr King was only observed to do this on five occasions during the period of our fieldwork.

In Figure 4.5, we illustrate the content of some of those curriculum contacts for each head. While Mr Dowe discussed curriculum matters with individual teachers almost as often as Mr Shaw, the discussions were more likely to relate to examinations and resource implications (particular staffing). They were often about subject content but rarely about how subjects were being taught. Similarly Mr Mercer, for whom slightly less than 10 per cent of his contacts with individual staff were about curriculum matters, focussed on some areas more than others, e.g., sixth form curriculum, CPVE. Mr King's discussions were almost exclusively about the practical subjects such as craft, art, P.E. We never saw Mr King discussing curriculum with a group of staff. We observed Mr Dowe to do this once (as part of the agenda of a senior council meeting); Mr Mercer to do this four times (at heads of department and a staff meeting); and Mr Shaw six times (at subject-based working lunches and heads of department meetings).

We never saw Mr Dowe, Mr Shaw or Mr Mercer monitor staff performance themselves by going into classrooms or asking to see work produced in class. However, we saw Mr King do this frequently. Mr Mercer occasionally went into classrooms to give a message and incidentally noted what was happening, but he had no procedure for following this up. Although the ground rules for procedures within his school were not always clearly defined, he saw one of his main tasks as keeping staff on their toes, through a vigilant watchfulness. For example, on one occasion, he told us:

> I think one of my staff is playing fast and loose, pretending to ring from home when he's ill but he rang from a call box the other day and we've been trying to get him at home and we can't.

Figure 4.5 Examples of observed heads' contact with staff on curriculum issues

Mr Shaw	Holds working lunches for commerce, PE, extension studies departments. Reviews with senior staff the effectiveness of the school's curriculum review group in the light of HMI comments.
	Asks heads of department to debate fourth and fifth year option choices in the light of reduction in first year entry and come up with ideas.
	Discusses syllabi with head of R.E. and commerce tutor. Holds meeting with those responsible for organising fourth year options to discuss future curriculum plans.
	Discusses his teaching contribution to the extension studies programme.
	Discusses feedback from inspector with head of careers.

Figure 4.5 (Continued)

Discusses content of fifth form course with youth tutor. Congratulates head of science on production of a new homework book.

Mr Dowe   Advises senior council of the value of welcoming CPVE for maintaining sixth form numbers.
Tells senior deputy ideas from an examining board on the active tutorial.
Allocates capitation to the benefit of any developments in mixed ability teaching.
Discusses the readability of course material with a head of department.
Discusses with a BEC teacher her role in drawing up its syllabus.
Discusses exam papers with head of department.
Discusses a parental complaint about the exam paper with head of German.
Discusses new PE syllabus with head of PE.
Discusses marking English papers with head of department.
Discusses new 17+ proposals just published with senior deputy.

Mr Mercer   Discusses PE syllabus with head of PE.
Tells heads of department meeting they must accept the sixth form pattern emerging from central government policies.
Tells heads of department to get on to exam board subject working parties.
Discusses the content of the life and social skills programme run by the school's youth tutor.
Discusses with community liaison worker the legitimacy of Urdu and Punjabi as language options in the school.
Looks in on art, craft workshop, home economics.
Discusses re-organisation of modern languages with head of department and adviser.

Mr King   Discusses exam results with head of department.
Looks in on art room, choir, dancing, PE, craft workshop, home economics.
Discusses craft teacher's refusal to submit schemes of work for HMI.

Mr Mercer then went through to the office and told the clerk on the switchboard to put the teacher through to him and find out where he was ringing from.

He went frequently into the classrooms when he wanted to speak to an individual teacher and looked through windows during his daily walkabouts. He often expressed a concern about classroom control, both in relation to individual teachers and generally throughout the school. This concern was the main focus of the three heads of department meetings of his which we observed; and he referred to the matter extensively at a full staff meeting.

Mr Shaw and Mr Dowe were unwilling to go into a classroom unless they had given the teacher concerned prior notice and we did not see them do so. Mr Shaw made reference to the need to get around the school more ('what I should be doing is getting around the school more, but it's very difficult') and reported that, 'after one senior management team meeting, we all went to four corners of the school to see what was going on'. The heads of department response was positive and it was agreed that they should debate it and report their responses back to the team. We only twice saw Mr Shaw 'discipline' staff. On both occasions, the teacher concerned offered an explanation of their behaviour before he had even raised the issue with them.

Mr Dowe relied on heads of department to monitor and evaluate staff. He did not himself enter classrooms to observe staff teach, because he was aware, and regretted, that they did not like this. His deputy had begun to do so, initially in relation to certain departments. Mr Dowe's chief criteria for assessing the effectiveness of the curriculum derived from his work as an examiner. This, he said, arose from his feeling that the exam system played such a central role in determining what went on in schools. He said that when he had arrived at St. Mary's he had thought that exam results were less than they should be; and explained this as the reason why he worked as he did, speaking with academic staff and teaching himself, 'to show the way'. The improvement in St. Mary's 'A' level results under his leadership vindicated his academic emphasis, he explained to us. In a discussion about his activities in relation to monitoring staff performance, he said that, ultimately, it was difficult for him to suggest any changes to a teacher or department's approach if it was getting the results—and thus satisfying parental expectations:

> Really, I suppose the only measure at the present time ... is what happens in August.

Mr King, in contrast, gave a high priority to keeping staff on their toes by his own presence. On several occasions we even saw him tell staff off in front of pupils. He commented:

> I can't stand the unprofessionalism of teachers much more. Most of them don't gave a damn. You have to keep a tight control over them.

To this end, Mr King requested six teachers in each section of the school each month to deliver their mark books to him, for him to see that they were up to date. Occasionally he made critical comments about them, which were relayed back to the teacher concerned by the director of studies. When the director of studies reported a teacher's response, Mr King smiled and said, 'that's a good excuse, I don't believe it'. The teacher visited him a little later to show him further documentation, 'just to prove that I do some work', she said to him angrily. Walking around the school during lesson time, he commented that he disliked staff covering the windows in the doors of the classroom, adding menacingly, 'and they know it'. In his view, it was a good management technique for staff never to know when you were going to drop in—which he often did, on certain teachers in particular.

The picture derived of heads' enactment of the professional leadership role was one of contrasting interpretation and performance. Staff often came to Mr Shaw to show him outlines of work or discuss course content. There were clearly defined procedures for discipline problems, which meant that he was often involved as advising and supporting staff, when a certain stage had been reached. Reminding teachers on an ongoing basis of the school's expectations of their behaviour and how things were done was a more common feature of his interaction with staff, than direct criticism. There was, however, no formal system for monitoring teacher performance in the school and we never saw him go into a classroom.

Mr Dowe's preference for delegating extensively to his senior colleagues and concentrating on particular areas of curriculum interest meant that he was more involved in guiding teachers in those subjects; he rarely discussed matters of pupil welfare. On rare occasions he had, reluctantly, to discipline staff. For example, he spent a considerable amount of time investigating parental complaints about specific teachers in relation to an alleged assault and an allegation that a teacher locked pupils in her cupboard. He told us that he was against telling off members of staff because they would always have their own way of getting back at him when he asked them to do something they did not have to. In his view, 'you can't countermand a head of department; I've tried to persuade'. Despite his professed concern for the whole ability range in the school, his primary contribution to the school's ethos was to underline its academic emphasis and make it attractive to parents for its academic standards.

Mr King was rarely seen to discuss curriculum with staff. Heads of department meetings consisted of the dissemination of information from the head; there was no discussion of issues. Likely LEA curriculum changes, such as CPVE, were passed on to heads of departments as information, with no commentary from the head or discussion by heads of department. In this sense, Mr King did not play the curriculum leadership role that the other three heads did. His main impact was on the school's ethos, by his setting a personal example to staff and pupil. To this end, he had a high number of contacts with staff and still more with pupils (substantially higher than the other three heads); and he was out of his room and around the school a great deal.

Mr Mercer's main involvement, as well as urging his teachers to think more broadly about curriculum matters, was in bringing to his staff's notice changes in exam board syllabuses, and the possible repercussions for the school. His main contact with staff on pastoral issues was through the two second deputies who kept him in touch with the progress of individual cases but rarely requested his direct intervention. His main concerns were to keep racial tensions out of the school and provide an education which would help the pupils get jobs on leaving. To this end, he was sceptical of some multi-cultural education initiatives; and favoured a vocationally-orientated curriculum for his school.

During our fieldwork, Mr Mercer had most contacts with staff in relation to staff development. Recent changes in the school's structure had necessitated the movement of staff and some had taken advantage of his offer to discuss their careers in the light of the LEA's redeployment programme. These contacts constituted about a sixth of his total contacts with staff. They amounted to less than 10 per cent of the other three heads' contacts with staff.

We have taken 'staff development' to mean processes through which staff are encouraged to assess and increase their job capabilities through counselling, extended work experience and the provision of advice and references. We also include the heads' approaches to selection and induction, insofar as they demonstrate each head's view of individual staff and their contribution to encouraging individual improvement and career progress. Figure 4.6 shows examples of heads' contacts with staff in relation to staff development.

Mr Shaw approached staff development in a systematic way. He considered selecting the right staff as the keystone to his and the school's success. Selection was carefully structured so that members of the senior management team were equal participants and could feel sure that they had chosen the right person. Since all pastoral appointments were internal, he

Figure 4.6 Examples of each head's contacts with staff regarding staff development

---

Mr Shaw   Discusses teacher's application for a deputy headship.
Commiserates with a teacher rejected by the LEA for an in-service training course.
Tells senior management team to listen in on phone conversation so they can learn what it's all about.
Encourages senior management team to go on courses.
Discusses early retirement possibilities with head of department.

Invites head of commerce on to finance committee.
Provides a model 'profile' for use by teacher not doing them correctly.
Holds meeting with senior management team to discuss staff movements.
Holds meeting to induct new staff.

Mr Dowe   Discusses future possibilities of work in the school with a temporary home economics teacher.
Discusses teacher's future role as a sixth form tutor.
Teacher asks if she can move to the remedial department.
Has friendly chat over phone with supply teacher about to start.
Teacher tells him she's applying for a post elsewhere.

Mr Mercer   Discusses with head of department possibility of one day a week release for training.
Plans his term's secondment so that his deputy will have complete charge.
Discusses with head of careers possibility of extending his role.
Discusses career plans in school with teacher who feels he is being blocked.
Advises head of department on what to say at a job interview for a deputy headship.
Discusses implications of changes in youth service for youth tutor's career and advises him.
Advises head of science on whether to apply for adviser's job.

Mr King   Suggests to teacher that she does administration in the library for eight periods next year.
Gives encouraging word to teacher about impending job interview.
Discusses teacher's application for a deputy headship.
Commiserates with a head of department turned down for a deputy headship.
Agrees to teacher going on a course.
Discusses with teacher the possibility of her taking early retirement.
Clarifies role with teacher by telling him what he should be doing.

saw it as necessary to ascertain that new appointees were willing to combine academic and pastoral responsibilities. Commenting on the high turn-out at report evenings and parents' expressed pleasure in their dealings with tutors, he attributed it to 'appointing staff who do their job properly'.

Once appointed, Mr Shaw took new staff through a day's induction programme. We observed the meeting he held to welcome six new staff to the school, in which a detailed exposition of the school's practices and expectations was combined with what he described as 'a tea party occasion to show they have all arrived together'. Staff development was central to his concept of a Maltese cross structure for organising the school's pastoral and academic systems. A model with different colour pegs represented the arrangement:

> All the roles in the structure are interchangeable. It's a tripartite system, with a head, deputy and senior teacher in each part of the system, which is made up of six mini-schools. There's a senior management team of five, with six teams of three, and each trio is in charge of two hundred and forty people. Everything is covered by these three people. It also gives a promotion structure within the school because promotion is not subject-linked. Mobility is maintained and all the pastoral posts are internal.

He saw the system providing, among other things, a basis for staff development, supported by the structure of the curriculum review programme which involved staff at all levels. By maintaining a continual dialogue with his senior staff he kept in touch with how individual teachers were thinking and feeling and, when appropriate, suggested or provided opportunities for further professional development.

During the year, he and his senior staff drew the attention of individual members of staff to posts advertised in the LEA circular, encouraged staff to go on courses and to get on exam board working parties and advised on presenting job applications. He told one young teacher, who had prepared a hasty application, 'stay up to midnight if necessary'. At the same time, staff were encouraged to join at least one of the school's curriculum-review working parties and to participate in a host of other school events. One member of staff who had been given special responsibility for an area of the curriculum asked the senior management team, 'Is my job staff development or staff exploitation?' Their response was that, when she wanted a reference, she would have had a chance to show what she could do.

After an HMI's visit, Mr Shaw reported to his senior management team that the inspectors had commented on the considerable emphasis they saw being put on staff development, and suggested to the head that he should take care not to over-burden staff. In the HMI's view, the curriculum review structure meant a generation of enjoyment and developing staff by cross-fertilisation but some enthusiastic teachers were carrying excessive loads. Discussing the HMI's otherwise glowing report, the senior management team agreed that they were in danger of always creating new things, and not allowing time for the consolidation period they had proposed.

Of the four schools where we carried out our in-depth fieldwork, Mr Shaw's, was contracting the least. This meant pastoral points could be used as the primary means of promotion in the school. To make decisions about the allocation of pastoral points, the head relied on feedback from the rest of the team on tutors' and teachers' performances. For example, at a senior management team meeting to discuss the tutor system, the head accepted his colleagues, rejection of his own suggestion that one tutor might be replaced. Some of part of every senior management team meeting that we observed was taken up with discussion about the movements and performance of individual staff, with his senior colleagues acting as a grapevine.

Mr Dowe's knowledge of staff was based on experience of working with them over the years; and informal networks which passed on information to him about other staff, which he considered told him as much about the teller as about the subject of the story. Commenting, for example, on a document produced by one of his senior colleagues, he said, 'I don't have to worry about this. It will work like clockwork. He's not a creative thinker, but utterly foolproof'.

His allocation of points and filling of posts, showed no signs of personal favours; it was based on the same formula as his allocation of capitation (see Chapter 7). He regretted being forced into the 'wheeler-dealing' of redeployment, at the behest of LEA officers and advisers who requested him to change the description of particular posts in order to make otherwise likely candidates ineligible or ill-qualified. He told us, 'It's terrible when you can't pick your own staff.'

Mr Dowe was occasionally rung up for 'informal' references. Whatever his loyalty to staff, he would at times make judgements about them which could have profound consequences. For example, he told one head that an applicant from his staff was 'not inspirational enough to be a head of department'. He encouraged staff to gain experience on both sites of the school, by pointing out it was in the interests of the school and their own professional development.

The need to identify people for redeployment and the number of staff on fixed-term contracts meant that there was little opportunity to observe Mr Mercer selecting staff. Mr Mercer commented a number of times on the constraint of only being allowed to advertise some posts locally and having to consider redeployed teachers within the LEA. For him, 'hunch is the important thing', and he relied on interviews and references to supply the necessary information to guide his intuition. His main concern was with whether candidates had the necessary academic qualifications and experience. He appeared less concerned to find people who 'fitted' the school as an organisation. He was pleased, for example, 'to have picked up a first class honours in maths' during the year but added, 'God knows what he'll be like'. He described the criteria for appointing a head of music as '... an academic background in music and a level of professional performance, energy and enthusiasm'. The interviews for this post (with five candidates in one day) were conducted by the head, the vice chairman of governors and the subject adviser. The two second deputies looked after the candidates during the day. There was no formal induction programme for new teachers to the school, although the second deputy was formally designated professional tutor. New staff were required to keep lesson notebooks, although Mr Mercer did not inspect these personally.

He saw staff development as a problem in the school, as a result of four separate sites.

> We had a staff development committee but it fell through ... The whole management structure folded because it became irrelevant to the new situation. We haven't replaced it because people were too busy last term to discuss it, having industrial action.

Until he initiated a series of interviews with individual staff about their careers, towards the end of the period of our fieldwork his involvement with staff development had been mainly on an *ad hoc* basis and usually in response to staff requesting references or advice on handling interviews. On different occasions he saw a number of individual heads of department about their future career plans, in interviews lasting from half an hour to an hour. He was not keen on the idea of staff appraisal interviews, however, having seen their negative consequences for the staff relationships of a colleague head in the Authority.

Similarly, he was concerned about the professional development of his senior staff colleagues, although generally regretted what he saw as their failure on occasions to seize the opportunities he provided. He was adamant that his agreement to a term's secondment for in-service training was as much to serve the interests of his senior deputy as his own:

> I talked it over with Ray and the other two deputies. It wouldn't do any harm for me to collect my thoughts for a term. It will be do or die for Ray. It could have a very advantageous effect on him.

It was his expressed intention to leave the whole running of the school to his senior deputy and not come in at all.

His concern with the professional development of his other senior colleagues was more uneven, depending on the quality of his personal relations with them. He saw them differing in the quality of their input and commitment and in their readiness to fit into the management structures he proposed; and saw himself as having to mediate between them and other members of staff, with whom they might be in conflict. For example, he told us:

> I'm seriously considering making Jane director of studies because Ray (the senior deputy) is sitting on her. She's done a marvellous job on the humanities block ... Ray is very poor at letting go, he's afraid to, so he just leaves Jane menial tasks. It means that we're not making the progress in curriculum that we should be, and Jane's got lots of really good plans which make sense.

During most of the year, Mr Mercer's discussions about the allocation of points were more with the county's staffing officer than with individual staff. The dominant concern was with meeting curriculum needs than individual staff development. The reorganisation of the school towards the end of the year made possible the movement of staff between sites and the use of points as a reward for individual staff performance. At the interviews he held with staff, in the latter part of the year in response to the county's request for lists of those requesting redeployment, he encouraged each teacher to express their views on where they saw their future. He then told each in a frank fashion, where their future in the school lay.

He wrote references on staff himself, without necessarily consulting the head of department concerned. When one head of department expressed annoyance that she had not been asked for her comments on a member of her department, he said:

> I reserve the right to make decisions and even not to ask the head of department. After all, when have you seen her teach? (The head of department said never, but she had seen the teacher's work.) Well, I've seen her around a lot. I'm very impressed. The policy is there's only one official reference from the school. Anything you write would be in a personal capacity.

On other occasions, he gave references over the phone, in response to requests from other heads. It was not a task he shared with other senior staff. His responses to staff's requests to go on training courses varied, according to how they presented the request and his respect for their work.

Mr King told us that interviewing staff for posts was something that he did not like doing. He only did so for staff lower down the school because advisers expected it. He accepted it as the head's responsibility for heads of department and above, and considered that 'there's not one duff one' amongst all the staff he had appointed. During the year, the school was mainly in a position of receiving redeployees. We observed him appoint a Scale 1, one year temporary contract English teacher, together with the head of English and English adviser. His approach was casual and he played little part in either the interviewing or decision-making. Induction was the responsibility of the director of studies.

During the course of our fieldwork a deputy headship, became vacant at the school; Mr King did all he could to see that his director of studies was promoted to the post. He told us that he would do all within powers to see that he got it and sponsored his application (and that of the school's pastoral co-ordinator up to the preliminary interview stage). At preliminary interviews, Mr King insisted that his internal candidate was the strongest; he spoke in his favour to the appointing committee of members of the Authority; and was extremely angry when another candidate was given the post. During the same appointment, he made it clear that he was reluctant to have a woman. In relation to another redeployment vacancy, he commented:

> I've got to be frank and honest. Whenever I have a vacancy I *always* try to appoint a man ... Often with women it's a second income, with a man it's his career, they tend to be more committed.

He demonstrated little interest in the professional development of individual staff and was generally offhand with requests to go on training courses, except on the part of some senior staff whose requests he encouraged and supported. Although a firm believer in monitoring closely what went on in the classrooms, he preferred to chat to teachers on an impromptu basis, while walking around the school, rather than discuss their performance or careers formally in his room. He saw his use of points to promote people as a way of rewarding good teaching performance. In the past, he had usually made decisions about the allocation of points with little consultation. More recently, he had begun to consult more with heads of department and, in one instance, allowed the decision to be made by a senior staff meeting.

•5•

Working with staff during the teachers' dispute

Increasingly in recent years, headteachers have had to question the extent to which they could take for granted duties performed by teachers in addition to teaching. As teachers have pointed to the ambiguity of their contracts, and the grey areas of convention have become the basis for industrial action, so headteachers have been forced themselves into an increasingly ambiguous role *vis à vis* their teaching colleagues. Though most heads have a similar pattern of contact with the teacher associations, the clear differences in their way of working with them only became exposed during our fieldwork and derived from their own perspective based in part on the history of their relations with each of the associations in the school.

Three ambiguities shape the relationship between headteachers and their staff during periods of industrial unrest. First, there are the ambiguities which arise when there is no contract of employment as to what duties are. Second, the headteacher's relationship with the LEA as the employer becomes more problematic when central government becomes another party to the employment, i.e., who the employer is becomes problematic and consequently the head's accountability too. Third, teachers belong to a variety of professional associations, each with differing stances on industrial action and employer-employee relations. The position is further complicated by the heads' membership of a professional association, influencing or reflecting their interpretation of the situation they face. In our survey of fifteen heads, and during our fieldwork with four of these, we were interested in the ways in which they handled their relationships with teacher associations' representatives. The interviews took place prior to the industrial action in 1984/86. We found then little evidence of anxiety or uncertainty among the fifteen heads about how they would manage their relations with the associations' representatives in their schools. Only one met with his school's associations' representatives regularly more than once a term. The rest met only when a specific issue arose.

In constructing a picture of their relations with the unions we were partly dependent on what the union representatives told us, as well as the heads' own accounts. Figure 5.1 shows the members of the four teacher associations in each school at the start of fieldwork.

Mr Shaw appeared to be the least affected by his personal relations with individual representatives or differing responses on his part to each of the unions' stances. On becoming a headteacher, he had joined the Secondary Heads Association, and played an active role in it. He told us, 'as you know, I am up to my ears in my own association, so I am sensitive to others'. Before the 1984 teachers' action, he described the school to us as 'a quiet school from the union point of view'. The three union representatives confirmed that there had rarely been problems involving unions in the school, partly as a result of the head 'playing everything by the book so well'. One of the representatives commented:

> He has rules so there can be no comebacks if there's an accident. It protects him against a court of law situation. Because he's an organisation man, he starts from that level; what are the problems, the possible legal complications, and organises it right through.

This picture of harmonious working relationships was sustained throughout the 1984 teachers' action, which we observed.

Mr Dowe had continued as a member of the National Union of Teachers on becoming a head. He also joined the Secondary Heads Association, but was not active and rarely attended local meetings. His strong affiliation with the NUT meant that, during the 1984 dispute, he saw himself on the side of the teachers, in supporting their action against both the LEA and central government as employers, to the extent of withdrawing his own labour. In the view of all three union representatives whom we interviewed, relations between them and the head were amicable, and there never had been any disagreements. His own NUT affiliation did not prejudice his relations with the other two unions represented in the school, and his contacts with them were as professional colleagues rather than individual personalities.

Figure 5.1 Teacher association membership in the four schools

Headteacher	NUT	NAS/UWT	AMMA	PAT	TOTAL STAFF
Shaw	31	15	30	1	77
Dowe	54	32	7	0	100
Mercer	36	27	29	3	95
King	28	37	5	0	90

Mr Mercer had formally been a member of AMMA and had joined the National Association of Headteachers on becoming a head, 'mainly for its strength in legal issues'. He said that his personal friendship with the NAS/UWT representative meant that he always knew ahead of time what the NAS/UWT were going to do. The NAS/UWT representative told us:

> I see him every day because of my departmental hat. There was a time when relations got bad, for six weeks when we were working five hour days. But as long as he knows exactly what's going on and can make provision, he doesn't mind ... we have a very cordial relationship.

Mr Mercer found it harder to keep track of the NUT who had branches on each of the school sites and with whose representatives he had a history of animosity. Relations between the head and the NUT had continued to be difficult since strike action two years previously, when, according to one of the representatives:

> ... the NUT rep gave him a public slanging. It was the fact that it was public that angered him.

Contacts with AMMA and PAT were unproblematic and he had relied on these in the past for support when others had taken action.

In spite of Mr King's once professed aspiration to office in the NUT, of which he was still a member, his relations with union representatives in the school were generally strained. He was also a member of SHA, occasionally attending local meetings, but was not otherwise active in the Association. He described his relations as uneven:

> AMMA hasn't been to see me for five years, the NAS twice. The NUT, being my representative, tends to be more informal.

During the year, when contacts increased as a result of industrial action, previous undercurrents of difficulties with one of the unions came to the fore and Mr King's general dislike of union interventions in school affairs became more manifest.

During the fieldwork and apart from issues to do with the teachers' industrial action, we rarely saw the four heads together with the union representatives, in that capacity. Figure 5.2 shows the issues which they or the representatives mentioned as necessitating contact.

The prevailing climate of headteacher-union relations was reflected in the repercussions of the tactics used by each of the unions in the four schools after April 1984. The action included: withdrawal of some NAS/UWT members for parts of the day; all out action on specified days in particular LEA's by the NUT; withdrawal of cover after one or more days by both unions; refusal to invigilate exams during free periods; and not staying after

Figure 5.2 Issues reported by the heads and union representatives as requiring contact between them, prior to our fieldwork

Headteacher	Issues mentioned
Shaw	Strike action
	Redeployment
Dowe	Pupil-teacher dispute
	Strike action
	Heating
	Parent-teacher dispute
	Deputy head visiting lessons
	Falling rolls committee
Mercer	Redeployment
	Lunch-time supervision
	Whether teachers should bring their own children into the school
	Strike action
	Profiling
King	Strike action
	Teacher assault by pupil
	Dispute with teacher over discipline
	Heating
	Teacher-governor disagreement on detentions

the end of normal school time or running lunch time activities for pupils. AMMA and PAT remained aloof.

The repercussions for each of the schools differed. Mr Shaw kept the school open during lunchtimes, and some lunchtime activities continued with staff who were members of AMMA. Weekly pastoral working lunches continued with a diminished attendance; heads of department meetings after school were cancelled. A meeting of the friends of the school's finance committee went ahead, as Mr Shaw explained:

> I must contact staff members about the friends distribution meeting, who'll feel they shouldn't be there. It's important that I see them personally to explain. If I cancel the meeting, distribution will be put back but I don't want them to think I'm ignoring their situation. The nuances are important.

The school remained open, although it was necessary to send groups of children home at times. In order to ensure that some reports were written, he approached the matter carefully with staff, soon after having written a letter to parents, in which he declared his support for what the teachers were doing. When considering how to tell staff when to have the reports in, he pointed out:

> We must soften the directive. We've got to be gentle with them. We can't be too prescriptive, can't write a letter and then turn around and beat them with a big stick.

Similarly, in order to ensure the presence of a head of house at a suspension hearing, he had a word with the NAS/UWT representative, to avoid jeopardising 'a reasonable *bonhomie* atmosphere'. Throughout the action both he and other senior staff referred frequently to the 'well-oiled machinery' of the school which ensured minimum disruption to its activity.

The impact was more noticeable in the other three schools, all of which closed for lunchtimes except for free school meals and sandwiches. All lunchtime and after school activities for both pupils and staff were cancelled, as were many school trips, where cover was not available. Mr Dowe's firm support for the teachers' action, including taking strike action with his NUT colleagues on two occasions, brought him some 'goodwill' in return and all reports were completed as usual. Mr King's school was most affected by the NAS/UWT's refusal to invigilate any school exams, an action which angered the head, and led to the breakdown of relations between him and the union. In spite of the action, the school fete and award ceremony were still held, but many teachers were absent from these events.

The teachers' action made it necessary for all the heads to make decisions about whether to send large numbers of pupils home, which pupils, for how long; and how to organise classes for those who remained in school. They had to decide whether to remain open or close for lunchtimes; whether to cancel exams, clubs and trips; whether to continue meetings; and what to do about in-service training. Where AMMA membership was higher (as in Litton and Hillsborough Schools), the heads could rely on at least some staff being available for 'goodwill' duties, since the Association allowed its members to operate a conscience clause; that is, they could choose not to take action.

This was particularly useful to the heads, where their senior colleagues were AMMA members, since it was not then inevitable that they would lose their support. One of Mr King's deputies, as a member of the NUT, withdrew from lunchtime supervision (to Mr King's disapproval), but the head was able to continue lunchtime supervision with the other deputies who belonged to AMMA. Similarly, Mr Mercer relied on his deputies to help him at lunchtimes, as well as those staff who were members of PAT, who had offered to help out. Mr Shaw reassured his senior colleagues that they should consider their union position first, but all four continued to carry out their normal duties (two were in AMMA, one in SHA, and one temporarily between unions). Mr Dowe, as a member of the NUT, took action alongside his NUT colleagues, but his deputy was an AMMA member and prepared to take over when Mr Dowe stayed out with his colleagues. Mr Dowe overcame the problem of lunchtime supervision by noting the NUT's advice that he could monitor the supervision to see that it was adequate, but not directly supervise any children during the lunch time.

Figure 5.3 outlines the occasions during industrial action in 1984 when we saw the heads meeting with one or more union representatives.

The tone of the encounters summarised above reflected each head's approach to the teachers' action. Mr Shaw's and Mr Dowe's contacts were mainly to exchange information and express support. Mr Mercer met with the union representatives to exchange information and sort out the details of arrangements, for which he took the main responsibility. He did not express support but remained neutral. Mr King's contacts were also mainly to obtain and give information so that he could make the necessary arrangements. He was, at times, openly critical of what they were doing, and eventually he delegated all dealings with them entirely to his deputy on the grounds that he wanted nothing more to do with them. Later he told us:

> There's some of the staff I couldn't establish relations with in fifteen years. I couldn't bear to look at some of them.

Both Mr Dowe and Mr Shaw were predisposed to support the teachers' cause, although they differed in the extent to which they were prepared to antagonise the LEA in demonstrating their support. Mr Shaw described his position:

> My policy is minimum damage to children and maximum support to the cause.
> I remain neutral. It strengthens my position with the unions.

Having made manifest his support for the teachers, while at the same time meeting the LEA's directive to keep schools open if possible, his main concern was to have full information from the union representatives about the precise form of action to be taken, in order to ensure the necessary organisational arrangements. Any irritations he expressed were in relation to inadequate information, rather than regarding the justice of the cause. When the directive came from the chief education officer regarding 24 hours notice for refusal to cross picket lines, he read it out himself to the whole staff, knowing that it would arouse some antagonisms. He was confident that there would be no objections from staff to the letter he had composed to parents, outlining arrangements and expressing support for the action:

> . . . because I always try it out on various dogs first and phrase things in a way that won't deliberately antagonise.

Figure 5.3 Four heads' contacts with teacher union representatives during the industrial action

---

Shaw:
NUT rep informs head of their plans of action.
Representatives from three unions meet with the head in his room to read through his letter to parents about the action.
Head addresses the whole staff, stating his support for the action.

Dowe:
Heads call in the three union representatives to see if they will be covering practical examinations.
NUT rep tells head of union decision regarding action.
Head suggests ways of publicising the action. NAS/UWT rep informs head of pattern of selective strikes.
All three union reps meet in head's room to discuss which schools have been chosen for strike action.
NUT rep informs head members cannot be made to go on after school hours with internal exams.

Mercer:
Head sees three reps about strike arrangements.
Head sees AMMA rep to explain 'totting up' system.
NAS/UWT rep informs head of their action plans.
PAT rep tells head that they will not be taking action.
Head reads out letter from the chief education officer regarding the action to NAS and AMMA representatives.

King:
NAS/UWT rep informs head they will not supervise practical exams.
NAS/UWT rep brings list of members out next day to head.
NAS/UWT rep tells head selective action is off but they are still withdrawing goodwill.
Head tells NAS/UWT rep that deputy is taking over all dealings with the unions.
Head tells NUT rep he does not want anything more to do with unions.

As a result of his cautious approach, staff appeared to accept his reasons for keeping the school open during the lunchtimes. As convenor for his own professional association, his involvement in discussions locally showed him, in his deputy's view, 'to be in the same boat as staff and fighting a similar battle'. His emphasis on maintaining good working relations with staff meant that he was less welcoming of clear-cut directives from the LEA. He told another head, who rang to ask his advice on the contractual implications of withdrawal:

> OK. I'll follow that up with the chief. I might ask about it unofficially first.
> If we get a clear cut, crisp decision, we'll be in a worse position.

While sympathising with the chief education officer's difficult position in an Authority where the education committee supported the strike, he considered directives to heads about what they could and could not do as potentially 'red rag to a bull'. He saw himself mediating between the LEA and his staff in a way which met his obligations to the LEA as a manager and satisfied his own commitment to the justice of the teachers' cause.

Mr Dowe had already been in conflict with the LEA on a number of issues. He wanted to help the teachers' action have a maximum impact on the LEA. He defended it at parents' meetings, withdrew his own labour, cast his NUT vote in favour of escalation, suggested ways of increasing the pressure on the LEA, and appeared on television supporting the action. There was no evidence of conflict in his relations with staff; they knew he was sympathetic. As with many other aspects of staff relations, he delegated most of the organisational arrangements during the action to his deputy. He did not expect guidelines from the LEA on how to respond during the action and, since he had relatively little to do with other heads in the Authority, did not use their responses as reference points.

We never heard Mr Mercer publicly express support for the teachers' action and he was angry when the NUT sent out a letter under the school's heading, outlining the reasons for their action. He told us that teachers 'have got a case even though I don't agree with the way they are supporting it'.

He took a tactical approach to the action. He kept a close eye on what individual staff were doing during the action, determined that all should be accounted for and that none should be allowed to take advantage of the uncertainties. He was concerned to demonstrate the limited effects of the action on the school's normal processes. When a parent wrote anonymously to the press, claiming pupils were being 'starved' at dinner times, he invited a reporter straight away to come and have lunch at the school, having first made arrangements with the cook. When a parent rang, expressing concern at the child getting wet when locked out at lunchtimes, he reassured her that he would personally ensure that no child got wet. This desire to minimise publicity for the effects of the action was at odds with that of the chair of governors, who advised Mr Mercer, if approached by the press, to say that he supported the strike.

Both Mr King and Mr Mercer regretted the failure of their respective LEAs to take a firmer stand. While Mr King openly admonished teachers for what he saw as the hypocrisy and immorality of their action, Mr Mercer issued warnings of what would happen if teachers failed to comply with LEA directives on notifying of absence. On one occasion he told them:

> If things don't settle tonight, I'll have to put pen to paper and issue a warning.

In Mr King's view, teachers had become increasingly unprofessional in what they were doing:

> I would think that I would be reasonable in saying most teachers see their job as very much a nine till four job and resent anything that impinges upon them, their life over and above that. Their professional commitment to children other than educational commitment is not as high as it was ten years ago.

'As soon as they become trade union members', he said, 'it's the end of the teaching profession as we know it'. He felt that they did not have a strong case:

> I'm the real socialist, the one with the interests of the working class at heart. I don't forget where I've come from. These middle class teachers don't understand that working class mothers go to work for bread, not luxuries.

The major issue was to whom they owed greater allegiance; the LEA or their staff. Both Mr King and Mr Mercer considered their responsibility as the LEA's managers to be more important than demonstrating support for the teachers' cause. Both considered some members of their staff to be in breach of contract at different times. Mr King was annoyed that the Authority did not take up his suggestion 'to instruct' NAS/UWT members to invigilate exams, when they would normally be teaching fifth and sixth year classes. Mr Mercer would have liked the Authority 'to take on' the unions over second day cover. He told us, and them 'as far as I'm concerned, it's a breach of contract'. When he told union representatives of a directive from the chief education officer, requiring staff to give 24 hours notice when they did not intend crossing the picket line, he refused to accede to their suggestion that, in the interests of staff relations, he should read it out himself to the whole staff. Mr Mercer sympathised with the LEA's concern that any rise in salary would mean sackings and Mr King expressed an awareness of this, and told other staff so.

Having reassured staff that individual consultation would replace the usual series of meetings, Mr Shaw found a welcome slowing down in his usual pace of work. Mr Dowe enjoyed the relative quietness of the school as an opportunity to get on with a considerable amount of marking; and commented, 'it's nice not to meet the PTA', one of his least favoured activities at that time. Mr Mercer described the dispute as 'a good time to push policy decisions through, no one to question them'. All three had been heads for ten years or more, and had had experience of earlier disputes. Only Mr King seemed to us more pressured during this time, although at the

secondary heads' meetings we attended, reports about individual heads suf-
fering as a result of the additional stress were common.

When LEA guidance was lacking, we saw heads turn to each other for
moral support and advice on how to act. Mr Shaw acted more as a mentor
to local heads. He advised sensitivity in dealing with the unions, consulting
them first, agreeing to them holding meetings after school, taking care not
to split a staffroom by naming people taking action.

As was his custom, Mr Mercer often rang headteacher colleagues when
there was a lull in activities and chatted informally about what was happening in their respective schools. He saw a colleague's breakdown during this
time as a warning not to take on too many additional responsibilities himself.

Mr Dowe, who generally remained aloof from headteacher colleagues in
the LEA, only once contacted another head about the dispute, that of his
neighbouring comprehensive. He was concerned that his school might be
singled out for NUT action because it was known he was sympathetic; and
was reassured to learn that this was not so. This was in contrast to his usual
expressed wish to make the action bite, a possible reflection of more concern
about the potential conflict in being committed as a head and to the NUT,
than he generally articulated.

Similarly, Mr King, apart from his usual attendance at the headteachers'
conferences where reactions to the dispute were discussed, was concerned to
discover whether the NAS/UWT were refusing to operate an exam timetable
in other schools. He rang five colleagues in the course of one afternoon and
discovered, to his annoyance, that it was not happening with any of them.

We have shown how each of the heads had a different view of the teachers
and their cause; and that it was incumbent on each to manage his school
through the action. All had to reconcile conflicting demands, from the
unions, the LEA, parents, governors, pupils. Whatever their sympathies,
when it came to specific action, they wanted a 'sensible' approach and
generally sought to reduce the disruption to their school. The reluctance of
the LEAs to specify closely the action headteachers should take gave the
heads the option of falling back on their own interpretations to determine
their individual responses. They sometimes modified these through discussion with their headteacher colleagues or at the behest of their own professional association. Generally, however, the overall direction was in keeping
with their approach to managing staff relations in more harmonious times.

•|||•

Other Work Inside The School

•6•

Working relations with pupils

We described in Chapter 2 the high proportion of time which heads spend on pupil issues. For some, teaching constituted the longest sustained activity. In this and in other aspects of their work with pupils, heads enjoy a strong degree of freedom. Consequently, we found great variation as well as common elements in this area.

In this chapter we look at the contexts for their dealings with pupils, how they make this contact with pupils, and how they keep themselves informed about pupils. We then look at each of the four heads' ways of working with pupils on the basis of how they go about three activities: teaching, taking assembly, and ethos-setting. Figure 6.1 shows some of the contexts we observed.

Mr Mercer, who did not teach, saw pupils either as a group in the formal setting of, for example, an assembly; or in passing in the corridors, between buildings, in the canteen or at the school gates. In these latter settings, contact with any one child rarely lasted more than a minute and was usually related to some aspect of discipline. Typical exchanges included:

Pick up that litter, girls. I'll be back.
We don't lean on walls and sit around like canaries.
Hurry up. You'll see your friends in forty minutes.
Boy, do your shoe lace up, right foot.
What do you think you're wearing? Have we changed the school uniform then?

The admonition was often accompanied by sarcasm. Two boys came through the door late for assembly.

Come on, Mr Price. Nice to see you. Where were you last week?

These reprimands were often followed by a comment to us about the failure of staff to supervise adequately:

Figure 6.1 Examples of headteachers' contacts with pupils

Mr Shaw:	Congratulates boys for helping disabled riders.
	Hands out distinction certificates in his room.
	Teaches a fourth year history class.
	Holds a working lunch with school council in his room.
	Tells boys off for knocking into the bursar.
	Supervises pupils boarding buses.
	Congratulates two boys on doing the lighting system for the school show.
	Interviews a boy wanting to enter the sixth form.
	Suspends three boys for assaulting a girl.
Mr Dowe:	Interviews fifth-year girl about her future plans.
	Interviews boy wanting to enter the sixth form.
	Teaches a study skills session to pupils entering the sixth form.
	Discusses university entrance with boy who's just got 'A' Level results.
	Tells off boy in corridor for wearing the wrong clothing.
	Pupil asks for time off to represent the region at tennis.
	Tells off sixth formers playing cards in common room during private study.
	Pupil informs head she is leaving the school.
Mr Mercer:	Inspects work brought to him by persistently late girl.
	Tells lost new boy where to go.
	Tells suspended girl to leave the premises.
	Catches truanting boys in the street.
	Tells boys off for being late.
	Takes a pointed instrument off a boy.
	Chats to sixth form girls at lunch table.
	Chases three boys out of the toilets.
	Takes a lower school assembly.
	Asks a boy if he has got a job yet.
Mr King:	Pupil comes daily for fish food for the fish tank in foyer.
	Sends pupil to fetch him graffiti remover.
	Confiscates 5p coins for school funds from pupils playing pitch and toss.
	Shouts two ex-pupils and a non-registered pupil off the site.
	Disciplines pupil with deputy.

Tells pupil off for smoking; sends him home with a letter.
Pupil arrives to collect minibus keys for a teacher.
Supervises rehearsal for school event.
Watches sport after school.
Tells off boy for uniform.

I'm worried about the number of children hanging around. I could make periods longer, but teachers defeat it by giving them a break.

Mr Mercer was often on the look out for potential trouble from pupils, watching from his window, waiting at the school gates, patrolling the streets around the school:

(From his window): Let's just intercept some intruders (ex-pupils) before they get too far.
(By the gates): I must get out to the back gates. We had some escapees yesterday ... I'm off to look at the wall. (To deputy head:) You cover the yard outside the dining hall.
(In the street): I'll just look in here (an amusement arcade) to see if any of our lot are in there.

He mainly saw children from the upper school where his room was situated, but encountered others fleetingly during his weekly visits to each of the other sites.

Mr Shaw differed from Mr Mercer in his contacts with pupils in three ways: more pupils came to his room for individual contact on discipline, welfare, academic and administrative matters; he had a regular teaching commitment (six hours a fortnight with a fourth year history group); and he was directly involved in all new admissions.

Mr Shaw had at least as many 'passing contacts' with pupils as Mr Mercer, although these were more likely to be in the corridors between lessons (rather than at lunchtime); and on the road outside where children caught buses after school. Passing comments to pupils were mainly to do with school dress and being punctual:

Come on, you're holding everyone up. Take your coat off.
I told you yesterday to get here on time. A detention.

In making contact with pupils he described himself as 'making them remember the school has still got a head'. At the end of the day, he commented, 'I'm going to do my bus look, so if anything happens they know who they are dealing with'.

This intention to make children aware of who was in charge was reiterated in his induction speech to new staff:

> Be very tough with them (pupils) to start with. We're not a difficult school, but we have some youngsters who are opportunist. Be very formal, firm, even to the point of being rigid. I want them to get the message the first time they meet you that you are the boss.

He gave a similar reason for doing new admissions himself.

> Why do I think doing admissions is important? It's looking at what's coming in and it's important they see what's at the top of the institution they're coming into.

In these ways, he had contact with pupils throughout the school, from first years to sixth form, and across the ability range.

Mr Dowe dealt almost entirely with pupils at the upper end of the school. He told us:

> I don't really know any kids below Form 5. Except for very serious things, I leave it to the heads of (the two) lower school.

He visited the lower school which was on a separate site for a morning less than once a week; when we accompanied him there, he spoke to no pupils. His contacts were mainly through teaching and the individual careers interviews he had with each fifth year pupil. He did this, he said, 'to identify those who need help in various ways ... to make sure they get the information'.

Mr Dowe also took it upon himself to interview any pupil entering the upper school. Occasionally this would be to the fourth or fifth year, more usually the sixth. He would discuss their subject choices, explain the other courses they would have to follow, and the school's expectations of them. Sometimes this would be done in the company of their parents.

Mr King provides a contrast. In the same time span, for example, Mr King had about twice as many contacts with pupils as Mr Dowe. Mr King was out and around his school much of the time, and interacting quickly and loudly with large numbers of pupils while there.

Before the school began, Mr King spent most of the time in his room. Even this early he would sometimes bang on his window, or open it, and shout at misbehaving pupils. He usually attended an assembly and would often speak to pupils when going to and from the hall. He observed pupils queueing and filing into assembly, and told some to remove badges, to take their hands out of their pockets, and to hurry up. Sometimes, if he was not attending an assembly, he strolled around the school to catch late pupils or pupils trying to miss assembly. After assembly, and at other times of the day, he stood to observe pupil movement, issuing orders to offenders to hurry to wear correct clothing, or to otherwise modify behaviour. He would also have a joke or brief chat with some pupils.

Mr King taught eight periods (out of forty) a week to classes lower down in the school and the bottom band of the fifth year. At some stage of most days, and sometimes more than once a day, Mr King walked around part of his school during lesson time. He entered classrooms to pass through them, to convey a message to a teacher or, quite often to interrupt a lesson for no apparent reason other than to greet the teacher. In classrooms at these times, he sometimes told a pupil off for current or past behaviour, or engaged in friendly, jokey banter with a pupil or two, usually the more deviant boys.

At lunchtime every day, Mr King was out of his room and around the school. He and some of his senior staff (the deputies, and the director of studies) were the only staff to eat their lunch in the dining hall with the pupils; other teachers ate in a small room on their own. For the benefit of two new senior staff, he said at a meeting of his senior staff:

> Senior staff here aren't encouraged to use staff rooms at break and lunchtime ... there are arguments for mixing with staff, but in large schools like this, you should be around the school ... That's how we've always operated here ... I think it's important the kids see us around ... I think that's part of the reason why we have it quite quiet here.

After eating his meal, he would then spend the rest of the lunchtime in the yards and in the youth wing. In both, he would interact with a large number of pupils. He also spent all of every morning and afternoon break in the yards. He saw this as central to the discipline and control of the pupils. He spoke to more boys than girls; to few Asians; and mainly to boys who had been in trouble in the school.

His contact with pupils was not confined to the school, a consequence of his community involvement. He greeted some Aley Park pupils in the local park one evening; the next day, one of a group of pupils excitedly asked him, 'Sir, is it true you were down Park street last night?' Mr King replied that he was, and was sorry he had not had time for a game of pool with the pupil. On one occasion when we were with him, he even met pupils in the pub, and often encountered them in local streets and shops.

Keeping informed about pupils

Mr Mercer delegated most of the responsibility for discipline and pastoral care to his deputies. The co-operation of other staff in providing information about pupils to enable the head to appear as though he knew them individually was, therefore, important. Since most parents appeared to approach the head in relation to disciplinary matters, he used the grapevines mainly for information on children who were misbehaving in some way. The deputy head responsible for boys' discipline came into his room at least twice a day to report on any recent misdemeanours both inside and outside the school; who was on remand, who was being released, and who was coming back to school. The deputy commented:

> The head wanted me as someone who he knew would deal with all these sorts of things thoroughly on a daily basis.

The deputy responsible for girls' discipline kept him informed mainly of those cases which might be brought to his attention by others anyway, rather than reporting on a regular basis. She commented:

> There are so many cases in a day like that. The head doesn't know at all what I do. He doesn't want to know, just the name.

The senior deputy kept him in the picture about the achievements and mobility of groups of pupils, rather than individuals, except for those sixth formers seeking university entrance.

In contrast, Mr Shaw's involvement in matters relating to pupil welfare was high, and he often dealt with pupils himself. A flow of information was ensured, in part, by the weekly pastoral lunch where individual pupils were discussed by house heads, the deputies and the educational welfare officers. It was also facilitated by the daily lunches with deputies. During the course of admitting a new pupil, he always explored fully with them their interests, both inside and outside of school, and followed up immediately anything identified with the staff concerned.

Mr Dowe knew about only a small proportion of pupils, mainly at the upper end of the school. Most matters to do with pupil welfare were delegated and he only saw parents about a pupil in extreme circumstances. His information came mainly in the context of the advisory role he enacted for fifth and sixth form pupils. He advised pupils on university entrance, and he had a great deal to do with Oxbridge entrants.

In his sixth form teaching and counselling, Mr Dowe got to know a small proportion of the school's pupils—the academic, arts sixth formers. Through parent evenings, lessons, chat after lessons and outside the classroom, he knew some pupils well, and played a pastoral role in relation to them. This also served the function of keeping him informed about particular pupil culture, aspirations and values.

Mr King's heavy personal involvement in all aspects of pupil welfare meant that he had considerable knowledge of a large number particularly those who misbehaved. He had no formal system for discussing individual pupils with others, but his gregariousness and ubiquitous presence ensured that there was little about them that he did not know.

The types of contact with pupils reflected each head's different interpretation of his role in relation to teaching, taking assemblies and ethos-setting. By ethos-setting, we mean the extent to which they were directly involved in shaping pupil behaviour through activities involving discipline and rewards. The emphasis put on these activities is shown in Figure 6.2.

The main contrast, in terms of teaching, was between Mr Mercer, who had no fixed teaching commitment, and Mr Dowe. In a lecture at the local university, Mr Dowe said:

> If teaching is important for teachers, then it should be important for senior management too . . . no use sitting on your backside in your room pontificating to teachers about how to teach . . . All my deputies teach about 16 out of 40 periods. I myself teach nearly half a timetable.

At the time of our fieldwork his commitment was to the top of the school. He told us that previously he had concentrated his teaching effort on the remedial department. Outside the formal timetable he taught an 'O' Level Latin class; and he also taught 'A' Level classical studies, English, and general studies. He was the only person teaching Latin and classical studies in the school; he had one set in each year of the sixth for English; and he was one of a multi-disciplinary team teaching general studies, again in both years of the sixth form.

His general studies teaching took place in various classrooms—the school did not have a base room system—on such topics as the media; this was with less academic and science pupils, as well as arts pupils. If he was showing a video, his English class would be held in the old library. He described his teaching as a 'luxury':

> Obviously I have to pay for that by taking time out of school in order to catch up on the admin. That's why the table's such a mess always.

Figure 6.2 Heads' activities involving pupils

Activity	Mr Shaw	Mr Dowe	Mr Mercer	Mr King
Teaching	Rare	Frequent	None	Some
Taking assemblies	Rare	Rare	Frequent	Frequent
Disciplining pupils	Frequent	Rare	Rare	Frequent
Rewarding/ praising pupils	Frequent	Rare	Rare	Rare

He was academically involved in the subjects he taught, reading and keeping himself up to date. The exam results achieved by the pupils he taught were good. He said that he spent quite a lot of time preparing for his lessons, particularly marking. He did his own photocopying for his teaching, and had a large number of pupil reports to write (one weekend in July he wrote 120).

He told us that he did not know how staff reacted to his teaching, 'they never say anything to me'. He thought that 18 out of 40 periods as a teaching load was reasonable, but found his load 'very wearing'. He saw his teaching as a combination of what he wanted to do and where he felt there was a need.

Mr Mercer had no fixed teaching commitment and, although he said to us that he was available for relief duties when necessary, he was never called upon to do this during fieldwork. At the beginning of fieldwork he had not taught for two years. Before that, he had taught games, but saw himself as a 'former geography teacher'.

> I miss teaching, but frequent calls mean I can't give a regular commitment. If I did teach, I would go in at the remedial end. It's the most difficult end. It wouldn't be fair to teach an examined subject because, when the results came through, teachers would immediately compare their results with mine, for better or worse.

He retained strong ideas about how teaching should be organised and often expressed the view that difficulties with pupils in the classroom were more the result of poor classroom management by the teacher than the pupils' behaviour itself.

Mr King taught 8 periods (out of 40) of history to classes lower down in the school, and the bottom band in the fifth year. He did no 'A' level or other sixth form teaching. In lessons, as in other situations in the school, Mr King shouted a great deal; in the neighbouring room one could clearly hear his every word. He directed more attention to white and male pupils than to Asians and female pupils, and was more familiar with their names. As well as speaking to the class, asking questions, and using wall charts, Mr King set his pupils work, while each pupil was called up in turn to have his or her book marked. While this was going on, Mr King kept up a friendly but generally aggressive banter, mostly with the more unruly boys in the class. Mr King did no preparation for his teaching and did most of his marking during the lesson.

His main reasons for teaching, he told us, were to get to know pupils and to remain in touch with the classroom. When he became a head, he had had only a few years teaching experience.

Mr Shaw taught six periods of history a week to a mixed ability fourth year group, whose history teacher he would remain until they finished in the fifth year. He also contributed occasional sessions to sixth form general studies, and the extension studies programme. He took a great deal of interest in his teaching, preparing lessons carefully and using a variety of teaching methods and aids. Although he considered himself 'just small fry' within the history department, he kept up to date with proposals for changes in the history syllabus and regularly reviewed the content of his own lessons. As with most other activities, he held classes in his room, the pupils drawing up chairs into informal groupings around it. His relationship with the pupils was friendly and informal, encouraging continual participation and personal involvement. His attachment to teaching was threefold; his interest in his own subject specialism; his desire to remain in touch with classroom practice; and his concern to retain first-hand contact with some pupils.

School Assemblies

Schools have considerable freedom in how they interpret the necessity to have some kind of assembly; headteachers also enjoy the freedom to choose the kind of involvement they want in it. Mr Mercer and Mr King attended assemblies regularly; Mr Shaw occasionally and Mr Dowe rarely.

Mr Mercer attended one assembly a week on each of his four sites, leaving one morning free. The formality of assembly was emphasised by the head wearing a gown, and, by the fact that a pupil was dispatched to fetch him once the deputy head had ensured all were assembled in an orderly fashion. He always conducted assembly in the same way. He said that he thought out the short sermon either on the way to school or in his room just before assembly; the stimulus might be something heard on the radio that morning or a theme with appropriate biblical extracts. This was accompanied by a prayer, often picked at random ('"God is our refuge" will do today'), reading out any messages, sports results and delivering warnings. Mr Mercer commented on the lower school assemblies, 'these are the only times the kids there see me'.

In the assemblies, censure was more common than praise. Having announced some sports results, followed by some desultory clapping, he expressed annoyance:

> I'm grateful, pleased at all those who gave up their Saturdays to come in, it shows loyalty, a sense of belonging. They have some spirit and purpose. They are people who give up time for you. Show some kind of enthusiasm. You act as if it doesn't matter that 800 of you are applauding for 40.

At the first assembly of a new school year, he told them firmly:

> Now this is the only occasion we are together during the course of the week. You'll stand together, listen carefully, won't fidget or talk ... a lot of you are strangers to each other ... don't run out of school into a bus, don't settle old scores now you are all together.

He was concerned in assemblies to cover relevant themes in the course of the year. Responding, for example, to criticisms from staff about the implementation of multi-cultural education in the school, he said, 'I'd like to think at least fifteen of my assemblies this year had a multi-cultural content'.

On one occasion during our fieldwork, he used assembly time to present prizes to individual pupils. This was accompanied by expressed disappointment in the absence of effort in the majority. ('I was disappointed there was only one entry for the competition. So I'll tell you the answers'.) The winner was called out and told he would receive a £10 book token by Friday. Prizes to pupils nominated by staff in another competition were also handed out, though he did not shake hands with them or use their names.

Like Mr Mercer, Mr King placed much emphasis on assemblies as an important arena for personal ethos-setting. In assembly he played a central role: he entered after all of the staff and pupils had asembled. Although he wore a gown to other public events in the school, he did not wear one to assembly. The format was always similar: a prayer, the Lord's Prayer, a hymn, a sermon, and notices. Mr King led the prayers, sang the hymn with gusto, and delivered the sermon. This was on a topical theme for the day, drawn from a book designed for such a purpose. As well as delivering notices, he also gave out certificates for competitions or whatever had been won. After this, Mr King swept out of the hall before anyone else left.

Mr Shaw said that he took four assemblies a term but we observed him to do so only once. He arrived after the completion of the main part of the assembly, to deliver congratulations, prizes, and warnings about discipline. He did not wear a gown; and used a tannoy system each morning to relay messages from his room to each assembly. Personally addressing the assembly for new pupils to the lower school, he began:

> Welcome to the land of beginning again ... There are heaps and heaps of new things to learn and people to meet ... I will live mainly over there in the big school. From time to time I'll see you in assembly, have lunch with you, take a great deal of interest in what you're doing. I like it best when I come over to give things away, when you're doing something well ... I'm going to set you a challenge. Every one of you will have at least one headmaster's commendation ...

Much later in the year, addressing the same group of children, he said:

> Now I don't think I'll have to ask this question more than once again. How many here have now got at least one commendation?

Nearly every hand went up. At frequent intervals during the year, he read out lists of pupils to come to his room at a certain time. The reason was to receive distinction certificates, but this was not announced publicly since:

I don't like telling individual children off in assembly or commending individuals publicly. Although I use these certificates as an incentive method, I
don't want children competing. It's done in an individual achievement way.

Messages over the tannoy system were equally concerned with praising
where possible, and disciplinary comments were often preceded by a comment on positive behaviour:

> I'd like to thank all those involved in *The Sound of Music*, a superb team effort
> . . . All those taking part in exams I wish the best of luck.

> Finally, don't forget the point I started with. The place is looking much nicer.
> Keep it that way.

> Movement around the front of the school is much better. Thank you. But a
> few still think paper aeroplanes on the front lawn is fun.

Mr Dowe rarely attended a school assembly. He told us that he found the
expectations of him in such a situation a charade which he found difficult
to play. The one occasion we observed him to do so was the sixth form
assembly. One of the sixth form staff introduced and read a poem and then
led the Lord's Prayer. A colleague read out notices and spoke at some length
about exams, concluding, 'Mr Dowe has a few words to say'. Mr Dowe
endorsed what had been said, made another announcement, and departed.
The Senior Mistress concluded the assembly.

Being a figurehead

Finally, we consider the heads in their 'figurehead' roles particularly in their
reinforcement of discipline through rewards and sanctions. Here, more than
anywhere, the difference in their interpretations is most apparent. Mr King
was the most pupil-centred, moving between being 'one of the boys' with
pupils, and enforcing discipline: we saw him tell boys off for smoking, then
ask a pupil to go to the shop to buy him some cigarettes for his own use.
Mr Dowe was primarily a teacher-adviser, concentrating on academic and
career matters rather than pupil welfare. Mr Shaw was predominantly a
counsellor and provider of rewards, though supporting teachers in maintaining discipline through direct involvement with pupils whenever necessary.
Mr Mercer delegated much of both control and care to the senior staff. His
own caring approach to pupils was mainly in his dealings with others about
them, rather than face-to-face. Mr King clearly enjoyed his enforcement of
discipline. 'Shall I go and catch some smokers?' he would say to us. He said
that there was a smokers' corner, but he did not go there too often or there
would be no-one there to catch. He was very firm with offending pupils. On

a number of occasions he shouted at girls until they cried. Sometimes he would join one of the deputies in shouting at a pupil. He also administered corporal punishment on a daily and unrecorded basis. He would strike pupils with a one metre ruler; twist their ears so that they were bent double and screaming; twist their cheeks; and hit them. Such punishments were meted out for being caught with cigarettes, playing pitch and toss, assaulting another pupil, being heard swearing, and so on. It was generally accepted by recipients as a legitimate punishment, although at least one parent wrote a letter of complaint to the director. Mr King also laughed and joked with pupils—often the same ones as he had disciplined. He also disciplined pupils who were being dealt with by the deputies if he came across them in or outside the deputies' rooms.

Mr King spoke of himself as having a 'pupil-centred style of headship'; he felt that this was resented by some staff. He was firm that the purpose of the school was to benefit its pupils and not its teachers. This approach was paralelled by his close links with parents. The high priority he attached to pupils as opposed to staff is exemplified by his leaving in the middle of an interview with two deputy headship candidates. The LEA officer and adviser continued the interview, while Mr King went to find a pupil who, he had heard, was ringleading a pupil strike; the rumour was tenuous, the strike never took place, and all of the deputies were in school at the time. On another occasion, Mr King met a pupil who had been sent out of her class by a teacher for misbehaviour. In mediating on this matter, he sided clearly with the pupil; he put his arm around her, spoke kindly to her, took her to sit in the back of another teacher's class, and then spoke harshly to the teacher.

Mr King saw himself as setting an example to staff of how to deal with pupils, as well as enforcing standards of discipline. He was as vigorous and energetic in his dealings with pupils as he was with parents. On occasions, he went further than just demonstrating an example. One teacher who was viewed as gentle with pupils was, quite unusually, shouting at a pupil, Mr King spontaneously congratulated him, and added, 'hit them too, then you'll be doing really well'.

Mr Mercer delegated most of the responsibility for disciplining pupils, as well as their pastoral care, to the deputies. He only became involved in pastoral issues if a deputy was away or if a final stage had been reached with a pupil in matters of discipline. On some occasions, the head and deputy would act out what they called their 'goodies and baddies' act. Mr Mercer commented to us, 'this will all be role play. Ron and I will cross question'. This involved the deputy shouting, and Mr Mercer questioning softly. The boy started crying:

Head: Here, wipe your eyes. I can't stand to see him blubbing. Shall we give him another chance, Mr Simmons?
Deputy: You're the headmaster, Mr Mercer. You must decide.

A merit system was only just in the process of being introduced in the latter half of our fieldwork. Responsibility for its implementation was to be mainly in the hands of house staff and the head's emphasis was as much on its negative as its positive effects.

> Can we make them (merits) mean something . . . ? A demerit takes away five house points from the child's total and is brought up in house assembly, which they don't like much.

On occasions, individual teachers tried to bring a pupil's achievement to the head's notice. The head's responses were inconsistent, and often directed not to the pupil him or herself, but to the subject of the pupil's achievement, for example, whether the school should take advantage of the county's special scholarships to Oxbridge.

In spite of occasional staff pressures, he was always reluctant to suspend a child, or lose a child into care or special education. He said of one girl:

> We've tried to carry her from the first year, even though she's a pain to other staff. I'm proud we've kept her in a normal school. Many teachers would have preferred to see the back of her.

Although we did not often see him praise pupils, he told us that the most pleasurable aspect of this job was being with children:

> Bringing the good things they do to the attention of the outside world and getting the reflected glory.

In the same vein he took pleasure in the fact that a high proportion of children leaving the school went on to some kind of employment.

During the year, we often saw Mr Shaw praise individual children, as well as rebuke them. When pupils came to his room to receive their certificates, his emphasis was always on personal contact. He used their names, shook hands and, by using a code on the corner of the merit cards, was able to comment on their personal progress.

When fifth and sixth formers came with leaving certificates to be signed, he would enquire about their future and comment positively on their performance.

> Congratulations. I gather you've got something special lined up. Splendid. It's all going for you.

> How did you enjoy the course? I'm just sorry you're not staying on with us. Never mind. Good luck.

> Great. Some marvellous comments there (on report card).

Often teachers would send children to tell him something they had achieved. To two first years, bringing details of money they had raised on a sponsored swim, he said:

> I'd like to help you make it up to the £100 mark. Thanks very much for all you've done. It's a jolly good cause.

He congratulated two other boys on winning a £250 prize in a competition; and praised the efforts of some others in devising the lighting system for the school play. He described the reward systems operating in the school as ensuring that he did not just see 'high-fliers'.

> Every child who wants it can have a record of achievement file. Very Victorian. It might be for being there 100 per cent of the time. Or for effort, an achievement grade.

Even when children were sent to him for disciplinary purposes, or were coming as new admissions after being suspended from another school, he was as likely to point out to them their good points as their faults. At a suspension hearing on a girl who had covered the school's toilet walls with graffiti about staff, he took photos along to ensure that the seriousness of the girl's misbehaviour would be clear, and then added her good points. Stern warnings were alternated with comments on what the pupil could achieve and the onus put on the pupil's shoulders to take responsibility for his or her future conduct. Before dealing with an individual pupil sent to him to be disciplined, he would always check with the head of house or form tutor first (and sometimes the parent) whether there was anything he should know and what would be the best way to approach the child. In one case, the head of house told him that the boy got upset if shouted at. Mr Shaw commented, 'that upsets me too'. When the boy came in, his approach was gentle, reasoning, explaining possible repercussions.

> Who is the only person who can stop this happening? (He got a pocket mirror out). Would you like to see a picture of the only person who can stop it? (He held it up to the boy).

On other occasions he gave the child the option of signing a contract (agreeing to behave well in future), often after having used what he called his 'loud-soft' approach (speaking first loudly, then gently). The contract was a new idea, 'never tried it before, I don't know how it will work'. He repeated it with others. Overall his emphasis was on what pupils were capable of achieving, rather than their negative qualities.

Mr Dowe dealt with pupils on some discipline matters, though not on a regular basis. In his patrols of the corridors and grounds, he would tell off a number of pupils for wearing the wrong clothing—ties, shoes or trousers, usually; or, occasionally, for being late. It was unusual for Mr Dowe to shout at pupils, or to express anger. After noting one pupil's name on his cheque book cover, he said to us:

> He's one of our more troublesome characters. In the end you have to turn a blind eye.

Sometimes he would instruct the pupil(s) to go and wait for him outside his room; or to come and see him after school that day or before school the next. He told pupils to keep quiet while public exams were on, getting very agitated as he rushed from one noisy place to the next one, saying 'sshhh'. On a few occasions, Mr Dowe was very firm with pupils; he would wag his pointed finger at them as he angrily rebuked them. He occasionally raised his voice in his room when telling pupils off. It was not, however, a central part of his style. After one pupil left, he apologised to us for his 'histrionics'. He explained to us that he found it difficult taking himself seriously when performing this role and, inside, often sympathised with the child. On another occasion when he was attempting to stop a pupil activity by shouting, he said to us, 'I wish I had Dick's voice for that'. (Dick was the very vocal head of a nearby working-class comprehensive). He did not enjoy detecting misdemeanours; it was neither his *forte* nor style. Whilst he certainly never failed to perform his duty in this area when required, it was not one he approached with relish, or one on which he spent much time. A small number of discipline cases were sent to Mr Dowe, as opposed to them being found by him. These were all situations where parents were already involved, and sometimes related to teacher complaints as well. One pupil in particular frequently met Mr Dowe in this context; Mr Dowe was gentle but firm with him, though failed to heal the rift between the pupil and one particular member of staff. Most discipline matters, however, were dealt with by year tutors, a deputy, or the senior mistress.

Summary

Each head enacted a figurehead role. This was achieved through contacts with individual pupils and groups of pupils at different times and for different purposes. Each had developed either formal or informal mechanisms for receiving information about pupils, both *in toto* and as individuals. As with other areas of their work, there were marked differences in how they went about their work with pupils. Contacts with pupils were mainly in assembly, when teaching, while supervising and disciplining or giving rewards, congratulations or praise. Mr Dowe eschewed assemblies and made most contact with a limited range of pupils through teaching and counselling on career choice. These, together with exam results, also provided him with his main way of knowing how they were doing academically.

Mr King's omnipresence around the school also gave him a degree of omniscience, making him less dependent on information from other sources. Contact through teaching took second place to supervising, disciplining, and, generally, ethos-setting in assemblies, school yards, corridors and at a multitude of school events. Maintaining good relations with pupils had a higher priority than maintaining good relations with staff. Rarely seen to praise pupils, Mr Mercer was more involved in controlling their behaviour through his watchful presence at different times of the day and in different locations. Being seen to support staff in their attempts to control pupils had a higher priority than being a direct influence on the pupils themselves. He relied heavily on his deputies, to whom most responsibility for pastoral matters was delegated, for verbal feedback on the progress of individual pupils. He was more directly concerned with pupils in special circumstances, both academic and personal. Mr Shaw spent as much time counselling pupils as disciplining them, providing praise more than sanctions. Teaching and assemblies were only part of an overall strategy for ensuring knowledge and concern for the welfare of every pupil, about which he was kept informed through a system of regular meetings and reports.

•7•

Dealing with routine administration and finance

The level of administration distinguishes senior jobs in schools from other teaching posts. In this chapter we look at what the four heads did as routine administration, and how they did it; that is, the systems they had developed and their working relations with administrative support staff.

The distinguishing characteristics of heads' administrative and financial work are that it is turned to by heads when there is a hiatus in other activities; it is what we found heads most likely to be doing when they were alone; and it is seen as never-ending. Much may appear trivial, but it was important to the heads, both in terms of the time taken to do it, and the extent to which they considered it something they should do themselves.

Clearly, as with so many aspects of the head's job, there is tremendous scope for delegation, which reflects choices which the head is making. Mr Dowe, for example, delegated the mail (rotating between each of the deputies and the senior teacher each term), buildings, DES and LEA statistical returns, and much of the administration of finance. Mr King, on the other hand, carried out a large number of administrative tasks: for example, he himself wrote out and sent in to the LEA repairs chits, sold calculators to pupils, dealt with individual invoices and completed statistical returns. Both Mr Mercer and Mr Shaw had bursars whom they saw daily and to whom they delegated responsibility for a large number of administrative and financial matters.

Much administration consisted of sitting at a desk with a pile of paper, with a view to working through it and sorting it out:

(looking critically at a full in tray) It's been allowed to pile up over the last week or two.

Just to prove I've turned over a new leaf, I'm going to file.

(holding up an empty in-tray) It gives me a greater thrill than almost anything else.

One day at 8.45 Mr Mercer commented, 'right, let's see what's in the post'. Later that day, at 1.45, he said, 'right, that's the morning's post done'. In between he had seen a variety of people, dealt with a number of issues and rarely spent more than five minutes without interruption on administrative tasks. On another occasion when he had no appointments, he spent a whole afternoon from 1.30 to 4 p.m. at his desk, dealing with the post and sorting out his files. During that time, there were twelve interruptions, so that at some points the activities only lasted one or two minutes.

We found slightly different patterns in *when* the four heads did their administration. Mr Shaw did not begin to look at his post until after 9 a.m. and then only for five minutes. He rarely had the first period free, and so throughout the day administrative tasks were fitted in between appointments or other demands or while waiting to get through to people on the phone (he found the loudspeaker phone useful in this respect since it left his hands free). At the end of the day he was always in school until after 5 p.m., finding this a useful time to catch up. He pointed out:

> The other advantage of doing paperwork at this time of night is one can do it relatively uninterrupted.

Mr Mercer began his day by going straight into the general office to collect the post and then started opening envelopes at his desk, sometimes spending half an hour on this. He would return to these at different points in the day, particularly between 1.15 and 1.45 after lunch, and then, depending on appointments and interruptions, on and off throughout the afternoon until 4 o'clock when he went home.

Mr King arrived at school particularly early, usually before 7.30, and spent much of the quiet period before many other staff arrived on administration. The post was delivered to his room, and he had dealt with most of it by the time the school day began. Usually he was out of his room at break and lunch times, so was not doing any paper work then. Occasionally when he returned to his room after supervising the bus queue he would tie up a few loose ends. Mr Dowe did least administration of the four heads while in school; he delegated substantial amounts, and said that he did other work at home in the evenings. He did a small amount periodically through the day, except for the substantial amount of time when he was teaching and the half hour of lunch time when he went home.

Before considering the range of administrative tasks we shall discuss the systems they had developed for doing routine administration. Mr King made considerable use of a number of filing systems. Locked in a cupboard which opened off his room was a portable filing system with a file for each member of staff. As well as individual details, Mr King recorded in this staff absence data and staff attendance at school functions such as the carol service and award ceremony. In a similar vein, during the teachers' industrial action he recorded the number of lessons lost per class per subject. Beside his desk he had a mobile filing cabinet with about twenty files in, and he often pulled these out. Other files—less confidential or less used—were kept in cabinets in his secretary's room next door. She organised and accessed these.

Mr Dowe had a filing cabinet in his room, but he rarely used it. We never saw him use the staff file it contained, for example. Most of his files were in the administrative office across the corridor; and, generally, he relied on the staff there to find him what he wanted.

Mr Mercer had two systems for filing administrative materials; a large stock room next to his office—I've a fabulous system in here. I can find everything first time'. We observed this to be true. He also had a mobile filing trolley which he had only recently acquired:

> This new filing system is much better. I can see it easily and move it around and have reduced the number of files.

He had started cleaning out his files for the first time in five years and had thrown out as much as he felt he could. He also had a large collapsible shopping basket for files to be worked on at home, which he filled particularly on Fridays. In his secretary's office, adjacent to his, were more filing drawers, for which she was responsible and he was often irritated when she was uanble to find something quickly.

Mr Shaw had his own system for filing papers, which consisted of an old brown suitcase, which he called his 'despatch box', a set of drawers behind his desk ('my rats' nests'), as well as filing cabinets in the main office, to which he had immediate and frequent access. The despatch box and drawers were used for papers that were relevant to groups of staff and to be distributed by him personally at the many meetings he held in his room. For example, a drawer was pulled out for the pastoral working lunches and the contents worked through with staff and distributed. Anything in the post relating to these task areas was put straight into the appropriate drawer, to be dealt with with the staff concerned—e.g., court reports, health and safety notices, supply teacher applications.

Mr Mercer had one phone giving him a direct line out. ('thank God I've got my own line. You can never get a line out'), and another, through which his secretary channelled all incoming calls. He told us, 'I've graded the calls'. He insisted on having some extra points installed 'so I can move around the room', and regretted the absence of a loudspeaker phone: 'at least it would keep my hands free'.

Mr Shaw had a loudspeaker phone. Most calls were put straight through to him from the general office, although some came through on a direct line, which he occasionally used. He did not use his secretary to intercept calls. On occasions he would ask the general office to get a number for him.

Mr King had two phones: an internal one, and one for outside calls. To phone Mr King an outsider had to get the general office, who put the caller through to his secretary, who intercepted the call before putting it through to the head. To make an outside call he would shout to his secretary to press the button on her phone which put the switchboard line through to his phone.

Mr Dowe's phone system was similar. Occasionally he was frustrated because the line was not connected to his phone—but he made relatively few calls. His incoming calls were put through from the general office, and staff knew not to interrupt him while he was teaching.

All heads said that certain administrative tasks which required a longer period—such as writing governors' reports or staff references, or staffing figures—were taken home. For example, after a day spent trying to work them out between other activities, Mr Mercer said, 'I think I'll take the staff figures home with me this weekend'.

Mr King rarely took work home. Mr Dowe loaded his attache case every evening, and accounted for most of his evening work as being related to his examining or on the phone—mostly to parents or his deputy. Mr Shaw always took work home. Mr Mercer took work home mainly at the weekends.

Each head organised his work differently in relation to clerical and secretarial staff. Mr King saw his secretary frequently. She worked in a small room next to his. A small proportion of his visitors went to her first. When he wanted a phone line, some information, to give some typing, or a cup of coffee, Mr King shouted to her. From her arrival at 8.30 until her departure while Mr King was supervising the buses after school, there would be a large number of interchanges. He frequently phoned the secretaries in the other buildings, lower and middle school, often to ask them to pass on particular messages; and the chief clerk, who worked in an office in middle school. He had a regular meeting to discuss administrative, and particularly financial matters with her once a fortnight.

Mr King's dealings with his clerical and secretarial staff were a mixture of bonhomie and abruptness. On occasions he repeatedly ignored his secretary's questions, and started some other activity, such as shouting out of the window at a pupil. Sometimes he spoke to her harshly; once she shouted back, on several occasions she departed in silence, and on other occasions she protested. Despite this approach, he joked and laughed with her and the other ancillary staff, often in the form of friendly ragging. Secretarial and clerical staff were invited to, and attended, school functions, as did the caretaker; and Mr King's secretary came in to work on the morning when 'O' level results came out.

Mr King's frequency of dealing with his white-collar non-teaching staff reflected his high degree of involvement in administrative matters; he delegated relatively little. For example, he wrote many cheques himself and, as we have seen, personally sold calculators and ties to pupils. Nearly every day he made a request to the caretaker in relation to the latter's daily visit to the bank.

Mr Mercer's style of working with ancillary staff closely resembled Mr King's. His secretary's room joined his, and the door between them was usually open, unless he was with someone. She was in and out of his room throughout the day. Although his approach to her was generally amiable, he was often critical of and impatient with her. He regretted a number of times that the LEA would not let him appoint a personal assistant, but only let him advertise for and appoint a clerical assistant with shorthand. Often one command would follow another, 'shred this ... file this ... get so and so ... remind me that ... coffee please ... where's ...'. At other times he was jovial, asking her how the courses she was taking were going and telling her about his family.

Although he often described aspects of her work as unsatisfactory from his point of view, he did little to try and change her behaviour. As with teaching staff, he considered it 'a case of dripping constantly'. In both cases he saw their incompetency as something he had to put up with, rather than something which was in his scope to modify and change. In spite of his sometimes critical view of her, he relied on her extensively to act as a gatekeeper, filtering requests for his time and attention. All phone calls for him were put through first to her office and she would then check whether he was prepared to receive the call. Similarly all visitors, whether staff, pupils or visitors from outside, called in first to her office and she would note their request to see him if he was with someone already; or ask him if he would see someone if he was on his own. There where many occasions when, although not apparently busy, he would tell her to say he was not available and an appointment (often some days ahead) was made.

He also required her services in preparing the minutes of the governors' meetings, for which she was the clerk. He discussed in detail with her what she should include and omit; it was one area where he had apparently trained her in his own expectations, to withhold information where expedient. Her other main function was to provide him with coffee at least six times a day and tea at a set time in the afternoon.

Mr Mercer's relations with ancillary staff were generally amiable, although he was more formal with the bursar, whom he saw daily on practical and financial matters—orders for printing, renewal forms for bookings, coloured ink for his pens. Whenever he could, he took post round personally in the afternoons, always calling in on the caretaker, cooks, bursar and reprographic assistants and chatting. He saw himself as acting as a go-between for the reprographic assistants and teaching staff, about whom they would sometimes complain. He would always try to make them laugh when he called in their room, tipping his flat cap forward, chatting about the weekend.

Mr Shaw had daily contact with his secretary and the bursar as well as a regular weekly meeting, the works management meeting, which lasted up to 45 minutes, with the bursar, caretaker and matron (who also worked in the office). In his view, putting matron in a separate sick bay 'guaranteed sick children'; and this arrangement gave him additional help in the office. The school's general office adjoined his, with a communicating door. Although Mavis was considered the head's secretary, she did not work exclusively for him and he would sometimes give work to others in the office to do. He did not, in other words, treat her as his personal assistant. Coffee was brought once in the morning at 10.30 and once in the afternoon at 3 by whichever of the office staff was making it that day.

An important service that Mavis performed was with work resulting from his professional association. He told us that he preferred to do some things himself both to relieve pressure on her and because it was often more speedy. Conscious of what he considered to be limited resources in the general office, he tried not to use her as 'a housekeeper' to put his things away. In a similar vein, and knowing that interruptions were always likely, he preferred not to use a dictating machine but to write things out himself. Whenever she brought him completed work, he expressed pleasure ('Oh super. That's good'.) When we commented once on the quality of print on a letter he had sent, he said, 'that's a daisy wheel with a marvellous Mavis behind it. She's super, magnificent'.

His relations with the women in the general office were always courteous and affable, even when calls were misdirected or he was cut off. He would chat to them about their families (two had children in the school), holidays, and the job. When they felt that the demand from teachers was too high, he would intervene and say 'no more' for two days. He stressed the importance of recognising the quality of their support when inducting new teaching staff: 'we are really very blessed with non-teaching staff. They are all very helpful'. Similarly, he advised on not taking the services of the resources staff for granted:

> Resources are really red hot, they're spot on. She'll whack you over the ear with an extension lead as soon as look at you, if you don't return something. Their service is speedy, excellent, and inevitably people over use it.

He used the points allocated to him to ensure that the office remained open during lunch times and until 5 p.m. each day and during the holidays, which he saw as important in meeting the needs of the public. He expressed great annoyance when an official at County Hall said he had not realised the school was open in the holidays. He was aware of his dependence in providing this service, on the goodwill of the office staff, whose hours he arranged in this way. He justified the placing of one child on reception each day, in part, because of its value to the office staff; 'they don't object. They couldn't do without them'. When we asked him about how the office staff might respond to proposals for computerised records, he responded, 'we'll just have to get them hooked'.

His relationship with the bursar appeared to be a more formal. The head did not enjoy dealing with financial matters and delegated as much as possible to the bursar. Dissatisfaction among staff about financial aspects meant that he felt required to intervene more than he wanted. He saw the bursar, who had a separate office (won for him, he claimed, by Mr Shaw's persistence with the LEA) at least once a day; also at the weekly works management meeting. The bursar also acted as clerk to the governors' meetings twice a term.

Mr Dowe spoke to his office staff less frequently than the other heads. His secretary worked in the general office, across the corridor. Occasionally she informed the head that someone was wishing to see him or wanted an appointment to do so. She or one of her colleagues brought him real coffee at set times each day—at 8.30, 10.30 and 2.15. She would also see him on about three further occasions in the course of an average day, to receive typing or take a letter. He would ring the office on most days—perhaps to ask for a message to be conveyed to the caretaker (e.g. to ask for the heating to be switched off), to particular pupils (e.g. for detention), or to particular teachers (e.g. union representatives). These calls were brief and to the point. The secretarial and clerical staff than rang or ran around the school.

Mr Dowe delegated a great deal of administration, particularly of finance. We never observed him to write a cheque; and, although he signed payment authorisation forms said, 'I don't really look at them'. As with the substitution lists, the timetable, and buildings, a deputy (rotating the tasks between them) dealt with the mail; and Mr Dowe's secretary opened his. Sometimes he asked his secretary advice on how to complete a form, or who to get on to about something. 'See if you can find someone to address this to', he said, before dictating a letter about a health and safety complaint.

Occasionally Mr Dowe went to the administration office to dictate a letter or sort something else out. He also went there when he wanted to photocopy material for his teaching. On such occasions, as well as when they came to his room, he chatted with the clerks and secretaries—about contemporary issues; the weather; and so on. With his secretary, Mr Dowe was courteous and business-like. When she was ill, he enquired about her health; and when she came to work ill, insisted that she went straight home. He shared with his secretary his future career plans, and she advised him as to the exact meaning of an apparent offer of employment. She occasionally had time off for her work as a JP, and, in lieu of this, came in to work for a period during the summer holidays. When she was away, Mr Dowe said to us, the other office staff did not work so well.

Before going on to look at the content of the heads' administrative work, we consider briefly their relations with other support staff.

In common with the other heads, Mr King dealt with a number of other ancillary staff, the school nurse, technicians, and lunchtime supervisors. He would joke and chat with kitchen staff and with cleaners—they sometimes made him an early cup of coffee, chatted about their own children in the school, and one sought his advice on hymns for a wedding in her family. His relations with them were highly personalised, even paternalistic.

Mr Dowe was rarely seen to have contact with other support staff. He spoke on very few occasions with the school nurse; and very briefly with the lunchtime supervisors, when walking around the school at lunchtime.

Mr Mercer's approach to the kitchen staff and cleaners was similar to his approach to administrative support staff. Like Mr King, he cultivated a relationship with all in a way which meant they appeared to take pleasure in doing small domestic things for him (the bursar kept his special supply of coffee, his secretary re-potted his plant, the cook prepared him special sandwiches, the nurse advised him on his ailments) while he gave positive encouragement to their efforts in return. This was in contrast to what has earlier been described as the absence of positive reinforcements for teaching staff and his secretary. This focus of energy on keeping ancillary staff happy appeared to reflect his concern with the successful day-to-day running of the school rather than its wider educational objectives.

Mr Shaw was equally praising of all other ancillary staff in the school, although he had less to do with the kitchen staff than Mr King and Mr Mercer. This was in part because the cook had stopped coming to the works management meeting:

> She used to come to Monday meetings but her hours were cut so much she doesn't come now.

He did not deliver any incoming post personally, rarely walked around the school, and had delegated most of the dealings with the kitchens, so that he only became involved when there was a crisis. For example, the senior teacher reported to him that a war was brewing between the dinner ladies and kitchen staff about whose job it was to put out tables. He immediately arranged for the county catering organiser to come in, as a matter of urgency.

Having discussed how the various heads organised their work with administrative and other support staff, we now turn to the content of that work; the nature of the administration they did. This work falls into three categories: the post; finance; and other administrative tasks. We have already described how they dealt with incoming post. Our discussion of their involvement in the school's finances is based on what we observed, rather than formal structures.

On a daily basis, finance was a major area of Mr King's administration. The administrative officer, who worked in another building, was responsible for the advance account, but Mr King was closely involved: he communicated with her most days, to arrange, for example, for some cash he had to be banked, for for a particular department's allocation to be charged. He met her for a longer period towards the year end to clarify that there was no over or under spend. He also undertook some of this financial administration himself. Often staff, pupils or his secretary would come and ask him to write or sign a cheque. On one occasion he personally counted several hundred bank notes, which had been taken at a school event the evening before. He sent and took bills over to his administrative officer, and would respond to her queries—perhaps sorting them out himself, say, by asking a teacher if a particular invoice related to his materials. He kept a cheque book and box file relating to finance in his room, and would often use these. In his safe he kept a certain amount of cash which he received from pupils to whom he sold ties and calculators, and he would arrange for this to be banked periodically. The caretaker went to the bank every day for the chief clerk, and would often collect from or deliver to the head before or after his visit there.

He delegated considerably to the chief clerk, but closely supervised her work. Previously she had been his secretary, and she was acting chief clerk while the clerk was absent with a serious illlnness, and so she was not altogether familiar with the job. Nonetheless, he left much to her. Signing the invoices for stock, he said, 'I don't really look at them. The chief clerk checks they're all right'. In general, though, he delegated little administration, preferring to get things done himself and thus, he told us, know they were done and know what was going on.

On a number of aspects of school finance, Mr Mercer worked with his bursar e.g. petty cash, lettings. Some aspects were also shared with staff e.g. capitation, trips, accommodation; and others with the committee responsible for administering the school bursary fund. The bursar would call briefly in to his office once or twice a day, to inform him of, for example, a letting request or a bill that had arrived. In the afternoon, he would often call in on her office to discuss any administrative issue that had arisen. When the youth tutor enquired whether he could carry a small float of petty cash for sales in the youth club, Mr Mercer was adamant that everything must be done through the bursar. He was keenly conscious of the scrutiny made of a school's finances by the LEA's auditors and was concerned not to be out of step in any way. He told the youth tutor:

> I feel very strongly on petty cash because it is very little used in the school. I manage in school on a hundred pounds termly. The auditors are very hot on this ... I wouldn't buy darts from a kid because you don't know where they've come from. That's my professional mind at work. I won't allow anyone in the

school to have a cash float because I think that's very difficult for the auditor ... The bursar is very adamant about financial control. I'm subject to the same and I'm glad, as when you're dealing with public money, you're accountable.

A formal system existed through which staff could submit requests for capitation but he was generally unimpressed by the ways in which they used it. He saw them as inefficient in submitting requests, unable to take a whole school view of the distribution of finances and over-concerned with protecting their own departmental interests. Going through some capitation requests he had just received, he commented:

> Look at the way two different heads of department treat them ... I'm checking their capitation totals against what I know is available. Some are ridiculous as usual, three aren't in. If I gave commerce the whole of the school capitation less 5p, she would want to know what I'd done with the 5p.

He appeared to respond differently to departmental requests, treating some less formally than others. When the head of lower school needed new computer material, Mr Mercer responded that '£100 is no problem; tell them to put it straight through me'. During a discussion with Mr Mercer about departmental matters, the head of craft commented to us, 'we have a unique situation; I don't keep capitation, I just spend until he tells me to stop'. To another unit head, Mr Mercer commented, 'just sit on your capitation at the moment, we can spend it on audio visual materials'. When another less favoured head of department made requests for additional resources, he had no success until a visit from the subject adviser, when Mr Mercer became unusually congenial towards the department and promised money hitherto unforthcoming. It was offered as part of a deal with the adviser to help subsidise the department.

> I can sub you now straight away three hundred pounds. (to the adviser) If I can help, can you? (yes). That will cover you for two years and no humping books between buildings.

Decisions as to how money which was in Mr Mercer's hands should be spent appeared to be taken solely by him, after discussions with the deputies and, negotiations with individuals.

He was also responsible for deciding which school trips should be helped from school funds, another area for which there appeared to be diverse ways of arriving at the decision. A school bursary fund had been established three years before, the money in it being raised mainly by school events, rather than covenants.

> We don't use covenants. We've got one covenant for five pound. That's not the style for this school.

A staff member's accountant husband acted as the fund's auditor and its treasurer advised on how the money might be invested. The bursary committee comprised three parents, two governors and four staff, meeting once a year to consider the distribution of funds. Mr Mercer, however, made decisions about when and how the money should be used to finance school activities.

> I have £2000 a year from the fund to spend at my behest. I have a prize for the best newspaper article to one of these community newspapers. And I'm giving small prizes to the lower school for finding out facts about the school founders.

When a tutor told him that they might have to cancel an already booked residential week because of insufficient numbers, Mr Mercer refused to agree to the school subsidising it. His response appeared to be based on scepticism about the efficiency of the member of staff's arrangements for recruiting for the week. He told the tutor:

> You've got to think of raising six hundred pounds. You've left it late to get the money in. You should have got it in half term before the weather changed.

Later he told his deputy to cancel the week even though the £300 deposit was still to be paid. He was similarly impatient with another tutor's request for a new minibus for the school, even though this tutor took full responsibility for servicing the existing one in his own time.

As well as the school's bursary fund, there was a charitable trust to which the senior teacher was responsible for making submissions for 'needy causes in the school'. Mr Mercer commented:

> It means we can often give a family a hundred pound. Sometimes we insist that we administer the money.

Mr Mercer also supervised and signed the cheques for any sums raised by the school for charity which he reckoned in the last three years to have been about £10,000.

In summary, Mr Mercer delegated responsibility for the school's day-to-day spending to the bursar, who kept him regularly informed of cheques going in and out of the school. He had considerable control over the distribution of capitation, which was influenced by personal friendships as well as the more formal system for departmental requests. He also made decisions about payments from the school's bursary fund, using the committee as a source of advice about investment rather than spending.

Mr Shaw worked closely with the bursar on all aspects of finance but found it a difficult area to delegate. His deputy said to us:

> He gave me capitation to do for the first time last year, but it still went back via him to the bursar, not direct.

During the fieldwork he was told by the county that the school was £5,000 overspent. His response was to find ways of monitoring spending more closely and of ensuring that there was not further slippage. He formed a finance committee of himself, the bursar, the senior deputy head and a head of department whose business experience he respected. He described the purpose of the committee thus:

> I've brought up the idea of a committee to give the bursar more power in monitoring how departments spend money. I would like you not to sign order forms in advance. They submit to us. We keep an account of what's been committed. We ought to have a rubber stamp made indicating to suppliers that they can only supply goods to the amount on the order forms. That's how we get slippage.

He insisted on retaining this mechanism for stopping the part-order problem, even when the other committee members pointed out the complexities of departmental spending:

> What I did was go through (the figures) and decide there's too much red, too much overspending over the years. Life is too short for *pro rata* working out, so we've got to start from scratch. I've started to see people to tell them what I've allocated. The main thing is to build in the control mechanism.

He was concerned at the mechanics for handling the new system.

> That takes us to the second stage where my expertise dries up. What's the best way of us working this committee so we're not inundated by paper?

The others advised using a computer, to which he agreed.

> When it's going on computer you can just send it to me for signature, as a growling gesture. I feel morally bound after our warning from the LEA.

Each departmental request appeared to be considered on its own merits in consultation with the senior management team. At the finance committee meeting, the staff member referred to a feeling among staff that some departments had not been cut back and that those who worked hard at not overspending would suffer at the expense of others. Mr Shaw's response was, 'that's why we've got to have the committee, to stop that'.

One feature of the school which Mr Shaw saw as softening harsh financial blows was a thriving enrichment fund which, although not to be used for anything the county should supply, could be used to meet requests from any teacher, to extend the pupils' educational experience. Staff were given the responsibility for submitting individual bids to the enrichment fund's committee, who met twice a year to distribute money. Decisions about how the money was to be spent were taken by the committee, not the head. Mr Shaw attributed the success of different teachers in obtaining funds in many instances to the quality of their submission. He explained the system to us:

> Bids for the enrichment fund came in every six months. All hand in bids by the right time. They know you can't cut the cake unless you know who is coming to the party. They don't always assess accurately though.

After one meeting of the committee, he told the senior management team:

> Some didn't present so well and lost out. We ought to look through them as a group.

As with many other aspects of the school's organisation, procedure for gaining resources were clearly defined and consistently adhered to. An enrichment fund meeting for new parents at the beginning of the year was given a high priority. He made sure that, after each new admission which he did himself, the parents' names were added to the list, to be invited to the evening. He described this as a fundraising event, organised primarily as a social occasion. ('Out here parents can see what happens with their money. In there will be the hard sell'). A very successful covenanting scheme meant that funds were considerable and a wide range of activities could take place as a result.

While Mr Shaw's main concern was that the money should be spent on people, he also encouraged staff to seek financial support for equipment and accommodation from other sources, particularly advisers. At a heads of department meeting he announced 'a free offer from the Authority and anything one is offered we don't turn down'. When one head of department produced a new homework book, he was allowed extra funds to run off copies; and the book was held up as an example of what money would be made available for, if the quality was good.

Mr Shaw made financial decisions in consultation with others and on a basis of equity. A request for resources was judged, not on who presented it but on what it was for and how the request was presented.

Mr Dowe had little interest in the mechanics, or administration, of finance. Occasionally he signed cheques or invoice authorisations, but did no other financial administration. He had, however, devised a formula whereby capitation was allocated. This involved multiplication of numbers of pupils and lessons (in each subject), including a weighting for the year group (e.g. more for sixth form classes). Heads of department, he said, were aware of this system. As well as this, he kept a few thousand pounds aside for his and his senior deputy's discretionary use—to support projects they favoured: staff were encouraged to make bids for this cash. The school fund, however, was controlled by the finance committee, of which the head was not a member; its chair was selected by the staff. He liaised between the PTA (which raised several thousand pounds a year) and teachers—who, again, were encouraged by Mr Dowe to make bids for this money. Finally, he controlled the headmaster's fund, made up from various sources and also occasionally topped up by the PTA. Mr Dowe used his discretion in its use—for example, to finance a pupil who was not financially well off to go to a university interview.

Summary

During the course of the school day Mr King carried out a large number of brief administrative tasks—alone, with others, and on the phone. Mr Dowe, on the other hand, did little administration. Mr Mercer discussed routine administrative matters with the heads of each of the three lower school sites either on the phone or during the weekly visit to each of the sites; he also did a great deal in his room. Mr Shaw shared administrative work with other staff; and was distinctive in his reflection on his administrative systems. Although, like the other heads, he was often interrupted during periods when he had no scheduled activities, he was able to sit quite often for nearly an hour, dealing with paperwork at his desk.

Routine administration constituted a high proportion of time for all the heads, except Mr Dowe, who mainly delegated. All saw it as a daily chore, to be worked through gradually throughout the day whenever there was a hiatus between other activities. They all took some pride in the systems they had personally developed to deal with administrative matters and, with the exception of Mr King, regularly took what they described as more substantive administrative tasks (e.g., writing governors' reports reading exam syllabi and reports, preparing documents for distribution) home. Mr King arrived very early and did these before the day began. They differed in the amount of contact they had with different members of the school's support staff, and in the use that they made of their secretaries. Mr King's and Mr Mercer's use of their secretaries was frequent, exclusive and demanding. Mr Dowe, having delegated much administration, had the least contact with his secretary. Both he and Mr Shaw avoided making exclusive use of their secretaries, requesting rather than demanding help, and doing some things themselves, rather than overburden the office staff.

In financial matters, Mr King chose to handle many aspects himself, consulting occasionally with his chief clerk. In spite of having a bursar, Mr Mercer also kept a close daily watch on the school's financial transactions. Mr Dowe had little interest in finances. Mr Shaw worked together with his bursar on a regular basis to allocate resources and monitor spending, but delegated as far as possible daily financial transactions. While all four heads

cultivated good relations with other support staff, as a necessar
tion to the daily running of the school, Mr Mercer and Mr King ga
emphasis (in terms of frequency, length of contact, and stated prefe
to this task than Mr Shaw and Mr Dowe, who assumed amicable relat
without continually seeking them out.

•8•

with buildings

The physical fabric of the school is an essential part of the head's responsibility involving liaison with the LEA, as well as close working relations with the caretaker and other support staff. All four heads acknowledged their responsibilites in this area, but each went about the task differently. Mr King and Mr Mercer maintained a high personal involvement, spending a great deal of their time on building matters. Mr Shaw used a scheduled weekly works management meeting as the primary forum for discussion; and involved the bursar and caretaker in meetings with officers from the LEA about the school's buildings. Below we show how three of the heads took a close interest in maintaining the buildings though the interest was expressed differently.

For Mr Mercer, inspecting the buildings and following up anything associated with their condition was a high priority. As soon as he arrived in the morning, he checked the heating, called in at the caretaker's office and followed up any problems. During our fieldwork, the many buildings were undergoing extensive repairs and redecoration, creating additional problems such as burst pipes, rubble, and scaffolding. Mr Mercer enjoyed talking to the builders, maintenance and delivery men and always went out to meet them or discuss progress. He frequently commented to us on the state of the buildings, during the year. Indeed, it was often the first thing he said, when we arrived. He was simultaneously concerned about the disruption to pupils and staff by the constant presence of builders; relieved that alterations and repairs were underway; and pleased at the opportunity to demonstrate his interest and knowledge in the practical aspects of the school's fabric.

On his frequent visits to staff in other parts of the school he always inspected carefully the state of the fabric, parts of which were more than fifty years old. He responded as energetically to the physical challenge of closing one of the lower school annexes as to its organisational consequences. Having been involved once before in closing one school and moving to a new one, he felt he was well versed in the appropriate procedures. If anything went wrong in any part of the building (for example when the freezers tripped out in the home economics section) he was as likely to follow it up himself as delegate it; and to do so promptly and enthusiastically. He made occasional reference to his awareness that it was not an entirely appropriate way of spending his time:

> The question is, although I know I shouldn't be doing it, who does? If any one else rings they haven't got the clout.

He was on friendly first name terms with the supplies officer at county hall whom he rung frequently, in pursuit of furniture and fittings.

He enjoyed getting things done more cheaply, through personal contacts and often implied he would not mind doing it himself. He told us that decorating the house and repairing the car were relaxing activities for him at home. He suggested to the head of sixth, whose area was not due for painting:

> Your common room would cost £900 to paint. What I've suggested is that they leave us some paint and get the sixth form to do it.

On occasions, he mended things himself, repairing the light on his door and the internal extension phone. He enjoyed showing other staff how to deal with practical problems such as overriding the heating system, ensuring doors were locked with special types of bolts, and mending the fire alarm.

On one occasion the science laboratory was flooded out where the builders had not mended the roof properly. In the same way as he felt he had to keep a watchful eye on staff, he felt he had to be vigilant about the workmen sent in by the contractors:

> They send kids out to do the contractors' job and before you know it you've got a couple of yobbos chatting up the girls.

Mr Mercer enjoyed good relations with his caretaker. The caretaker's room was the first room along the corridor from his own and he invariably looked in and stopped to chat if anyone was there. His contacts were frequent. When he learned that the caretaker, Terry, was leaving, Mr Mercer commented, 'I'll probably lose the best caretaker in the county'. Terry had a house attached to the school but had recently bought his own and asked to give up the tied house. The county refused to let him do this and insisted on him continuing to pay rent. At the same time, a new deal had been introduced in which caretakers were paid on a sessional overtime basis, not hourly as before—which represented a reduction in payment. As a result Terry resigned. Mr Mercer fully supported Terry's reasons for resignation, which he used in his own letter to the LEA:

> Good ammunition with the LEA ... I want to prove in my letter that unless the caretaker begins at three in the morning, there's no way he can clear up after lettings.

A new caretaker proved unsatisfactory and left within six months. Throughout, Mr Mercer compared him unfavourably with the previous caretaker, and expressed unhappiness about the deteriorating state of the buildings. Throughout the year he was constantly negotiating for new caretakers, as there was always a vacancy at one or other of the sites. He described managing ancillary staff as a problematic area of headship and one in which he would like more training. He attributed the new caretaker's early departure in part to his own attempt to introduce regular meetings and systems of checks. He told us:

> When I asked him to check on what's in every room and report every Monday, he didn't like it.

When he had only the two assistants to work with on the main site he suggested:

> It might be a good idea if we had a regular chat like this every Monday.

They were keen to do so, saying, 'we'll put our moans to you and you can to us!' He was most at ease with the caretakers and cleaners, showing always a personal interest and involvement in the nitty-gritty. To a request for screwdrivers, he said:

> I'll get a set of screwdrivers and screws for you. I'll pick them up from a hard-ware shop. If I buy an electric drill all the staff will want me to buy them one.

He did, however, promise to do so. On another occasion, when the assistant caretaker was away, he went to check the cleaners himself, at the end of the day. He appeared to take great pleasure in sitting in the caretaker's room, chatting and joking with the cleaners as they come in, knowing most of their names ('New boss today! What's your surname Mary, I should know'), and handing out the rubbish bags and bleach. He commented:

> Actually, sitting here, I find out everything that's going on. The toilets hadn't been cleaned for a week. There's thirty cleaners.

After half an hour of doing this, he handed over to one of the cleaners, telling her, 'that's called delegation'.

The other two main areas of preoccupation involving Mr Mercer's frequent contact with the caretaking staff were break-ins and burglar alarms; and broken pipes and heating. During most of the year we were in the school, builders were making extensive alterations with burst pipes being just one of the repercussions. On two occasions he discussed with the caretakers the fact that the police had been called in at the weekend because of break-ins. He told us it was a frequent occurrence to be rung up by the caretaker at the weekend because the burglar alarm had gone off; he would always come in.

Mr King's approach to his school's buildings and plant was very similar. Members and officers of the Authority credited Mr King with having improved the physical environment of Aley Park enormously in four years. He saw it as important: 'if I had a bursar or deputy doing buildings I wouldn't know what's going on'.

Walking round the school he picked up large quantities of litter, expressed concern about blocked gullies, noticed that the screws on a door's hinges were loose, had an eagle eye for graffiti, and went to check the boys' toilets when the smell from them was noticeable in the corridor. He put a lot of energy into doing repairs and making acquisitions for the school economically. He knew that the local glazier charged half the price of the LEA direct works section, so he would always try to get the LEA to let him get them to do a job—the need for urgency being one ploy to achieve this end.

One evening Mr King himself painted a wall: a bit of a corridor which had been plastered but which was not due to be painted. He knew that if he stuck to the LEA procedures, each room in the school would be painted, in his estimate, once every 30 years; so he paid former pupils to do the work, in cash. After the painters had been, several windows could not be opened so Mr King sent a message to the craft department requesting a chisel, and when this was delivered, he personally went to loosen them. When the school bell failed to work he shouted to the caretaker for a screwdriver, unscrewed and opened an electrical box, used the phone to trigger the bell and watched the exposed switch to see if it tripped. He explained to us, 'when they put this system in I had a good look at it so I know how it works'. Later he discussed the problem with an electrician who was fixing it. Similarly with the boilers, he was proud of his knowledge of them. He would often remove graffiti with a rag and solvent himself. When a deputy head reported to him that the boys' toilets were blocked, Mr King got his rod and went and cleared them.

As well as doing this work himself, he encouraged some other staff to do the same—the caretakers and craft teachers. The caretaker had set up a small workshop, and the head occasionally asked him to do small jobs he had noticed. He asked craft teachers to build bird tables, fit a surround around the stage, put up shelves, notice boards and so on—which they did.

Frequently we observed him completing repairs slips. He rang the LEA maintenance section about work to be done, and discussed the work with operatives. He also checked their work when in progress or completed. Teachers came to ask the head about carpets, curtains, chairs and desks— the problems they were causing, their replacement, their purchase and their storage. Sometimes he was personally involved in counting and sorting out chairs. He told a teacher to ring the parks department for some flowers for the platform for the award ceremony (having gone to the greenhouse himself to look for some he could 'pinch'). He instructed the caretaker to pick the apples on the trees. One indication of the significance he attached to this work, which also shows something about how he achieved his ends, was that he always asked the LEA officer in charge of buildings to school events—and he often came.

In the course of the day, Mr King always saw at least one of his caretakers; sometimes he spoke with them nine times in a day; about five times was average. He had three caretakers, the head and his assistant, who both had modern, detached, two storey houses with gardens on the site; and a day caretaker, who worked every day (unlike his colleagues who did duties, or shifts). Mr King appointed all three staff to their posts during the course of our fieldwork. The previous head caretaker had resigned, after Mr King had gathered some evidence about stock shortages: his replacement was promoted from assistant; the day caretaker to assistant; and a lunchtime supervisor was appointed day caretaker. On the day of the middle one of these three appointments, Mr King called the two caretakers to his room, and told them:

> I've just made the two most important appointments in the school ... if you two let me down now, I'll come down like a ton of bricks ...

On a number of occasions Mr King told officers of the Authority how good his caretakers were. He said to the caretakers' supervisor:

> I told the Director ... best caretakers ever, the last three months.

Mr King called on the head caretaker when he was off duty on a number of occasions, because something had to be done and the caretaker on duty was already busy. They did not seem to mind this. He visited their gardens to see their dogs and chatted to them in the yards at break. When there was a school 'do', such as the carol service or award ceremony, the caretakers would be invited and attended.

Good relations with his caretakers were evident in their flexible and conscientious approach to their work. They were quite happy to carry out minor repairs—they set up a bench and workshop for the purpose. His close interest in the physical fabric of the school was continual. On some occasions when the caretakers reported a difficulty, the head himself went off to try to sort the matter out physically—a lock they couldn't get off, for example. The caretaker delivered the mail to the head's room in the morning; and went to the bank every afternoon. Over these, as well as the more conventional caretaking matters, interchanges between the head and caretakers were highly amicable. When the caretaker brought his sheet to be signed, Mr King said, 'Eh, you've had a bloody good week this week ... thirty five pound (overtime) ...'

In contrast, Mr Dowe delegated supervision of the school buildings and plant to one of his deputies, and was glad that he was not more closely involved in this area. In the course of all our observations we only saw him involved in one matter, in which he had a particular interest: the heating. First thing in the morning he sometimes checked the rooms in his building, shutting windows and switching off heaters—'doing a caretaker's job', as he put it. On another occasion he told the caretaker that the school was using a lot of fuel; and on several occasions he rang the caretaker to ask him to turn the heating off.

His interest in this matter was well known to his staff; he rang the office once to ask one of them to find the caretaker and to get the caretaker to contact him, and in response to their comment laughed, 'no, its *not* to ask him to turn the heating off!' We never saw Mr Dowe signing repairs chits, ringing the buildings section, or being involved in the physical fabric at all. When he passed a maintenance worker who was fixing a door Mr Dowe did not acknowledge him. He spoke to the caretaker on some days, but more often did not. He was always courteous and the caretaker apparently co-operative.

Mr Shaw demonstrated his ongoing concern with the state of the buildings in a systematic way. He was constantly alert; when going from one building to another, he often commented to us on the state of disrepair. He met weekly with the works management team. He was on friendly first name terms with the LEA's estates officers, who called in frequently. He would have ready for their visits a list of things that he wanted to discuss and they would tour the building, together with the bursar.

Mr Shaw's main concerns were the health and safety implications of any disrepair, their appearance to the outside world and utilising to the best effect existing facilities and any others that he could persuade the LEA to provide. He explained to new staff:

> Our principal problem is that the buildings weren't properly designed for a comprehensive school. We don't have social areas ... Health and safety is very important. If you do see anything faulty let me know.

In his view, '£50,000 spent on this school would make an enormous difference'.

We never saw him carry out any practical task himself, though he carried the details of all the buildings in his head. Once, when he was returning from London and driving past, he noticed chairs and litter piled up outside the building, and rang the deputy to ask why and to check that there had not been a riot. On another occasion he expressed annoyance that a letter was missing from the school's sign outside the entrance. He was also concerned at the school's need for internal decoration. He told the estates officer.

> I'd like a lick of paint on the boys' loos this summer. I'd like to start the new year with the boys' toilets looking decent. Not the ceilings just the walls where there are markings.

On another occasion he said, half jokingly, that he'd like the clerk of works to come and have a look at a crack in the wall of his room:

> When it's exposed will it be painted? (laughing) It's a prestigious area to the school and I wouldn't want a great mess just for a crack in the wall.'

He liaised closely with the caretaker on all aspects of the building, meeting him regularly on Monday mornings and whenever the caretaker called in to ask about a specific problem such as the state of the furniture store, litter bins, leaking radiators, or collecting desks from another school. We rarely saw Mr Shaw seek the caretaker out, though he was always concerned to consult the caretaker first before agreeing to any commitments which might burden him. He followed up any dissatisfaction with the grounds or buildings expressed by the caretaker or other staff with the appropriate person at county hall, first inspecting the problem. He relied on deputies to keep him informed of any problems that he may have missed.

He only once expressed any criticism of the caretaker, when he questioned in front of someone else the boundaries of the job.

> I was very cross with Peter the other day when I asked the supervisor for an outside vacuum and Peter said it's not my job, it's a union thing. I was very cross. He used it for a political platform.

He was otherwise full of praise for how the caretaker did his job.

Summary

Mr Mercer and Mr King were closely involved, on a daily basis, in the maintenance of buildings, choosing some practical tasks themselves such as fixing lights and mending fuses. Mr Dowe delegated this task area almost completely. Mr Shaw took a close interest without becoming practically involved. He held weekly meetings with staff involved in 'works maintenance' and worked closely with them in pursuing the LEA. Three of the heads recognised care of the buildings as an important area of their work and saw it, more than any other issue, as one in which governors were likely to be most interested and helpful.

·IV·

Outside the School

•9•

Working with parents

Bush (1981) describes the head as occupying a position at the neck of an hour glass, mediating between the school and the outside world. Although not the only person dealing with individuals and agencies outside, much of this work falls on the head. In particular, the head occupies the key position to shape outsiders' experiences of the school.

What heads choose to do is likely to depend on their understanding of the appropriate and constitutional relationships of the school with outside individuals and bodies. We shall consider this in relation to four areas of work: with parents, with the LEA, in the community, and the educational world beyond their school. Heads, we found, adhere to different notions of the role of parents in the school—some seeing them as partners, others as clients. In the same way some maintained their relationship with their education authorities and governing bodies as one of active co-operation and some as indifference or even hostility. In their work in the community we found a broad spectrum, with some heads attributing a high importance to this part of their work, and others having only a nominal involvement. Similarly with their contribution to their profession beyond the school, we found some heads making a high contribution to the educational world, and others seeing such work as peripheral to the essential task of headship, which they defined as necessarily taking place within school.

Considering recent legislation—in particular, the 1980 Education Act—one might expect activity relating to formal accountability to parents to have become a more central part of the head's work. Whereas until recently there was little specific that schools *had* to do in relation to parents, the policy context today makes this work mandatory: the advent of parent governors and the publication of school aims and public examination results are specific ways in which legislation has brought parents closer to schools.

From the variety of contact we observed—individual casework and with groups of parents at school events—we were able to build up a picture of how each dealt with them. The patterns which each head displayed appeared distinctive and coherent. Only Mr Mercer did not see a parent on average at least once a day. Mr Shaw was unusual in that, as with most aspects of his work, he made explicit both to us and to parents and staff what he saw as the principles underlying his work with parents. Mr Shaw firmly adhered to notions of the school and parents being a partnership working for the education of the pupils. Mr Mercer's model stressed school ethos and control more, rather than the shared contribution of school and parents to education. Mr King and Mr Dowe both saw parents as a group to which they were accountable. Mr King articulated this quite explicitly, although the social composition of his catchment meant a relatively low parental involvement. In contrast, Mr Dowe's catchment included parents with high expectations of involvement. Mr Dowe accepted the legitimacy of parental involvement, but responded to this reactively rather than working in the proactive manner of Mr Shaw.

Mr Shaw

Mr Shaw's relations with parents were made explicit to new parents seeking their child's admission to the school, to parents with children in the school, to staff and to pupils. At the beginning of a lecture to the local university on 'Parental influence—a school perspective' he said,

> When I went to be a head in 1968, I took over from a head at the end of his career. I asked him what is your policy about parents. He said, 'keep 'em out'. It seemed one comment to end all comments on school policy!

His aim was to make parents see that 'the school cannot operate without parents'. To achieve this aim, he introduced the notion of a contract, to which every new parent's attention was drawn, in the handbook at parent's evenings and in individual contact.

One principle guiding his approach to relations with parents was a belief that parents were unable to be detached in the education process from the experience of their child. Responding to the Green Paper proposals for greater parental involvement, he said:

> If the governing body became parent dominated, do you think that the one most qualified to judge the quality of the sausage is the pig? Parents are part of the process ... look at any head's in-tray every day letters: from parents about my child. Parents don't have a corporate view.

The letter to parents in the school handbook was the starting point, setting out the relationship as a partnership, as shown in Figure 9.1. Mr Shaw's work with parents consisted of all non-routine admissions (i.e. pupils entering the school on appeal or after the start of the year), various open evenings (including those for reports, presentations, and fund-raising), and, most frequently, in relation to pupil discipline.

Figure 9.1 Extract from Litton School's handbook

RECIPE FOR SUCCESS

The secret of success at school is really no secret at all. Past experience suggests that pupils do well when there is a

PARTNERSHIP BETWEEN HOME AND SCHOOL

Whatever ability your child was born with, no boy or girl is going to do well unless conditions for learning and living are right.
Home and school each have something unique to provide.
HOME should provide:-

> RECOGNITION
> LOVE
> SUPPORT
> SECURITY
> ENCOURAGEMENT
> NEW EXPERIENCES

SCHOOL should provide:-

> UNDERSTANDING
> INSTRUCTION
> COMMUNICATION
> ENTHUSIASM
> PRAISE
> NEW EXPERIENCES

A six point plan for home and school alike. If each heeds all six, there are few bounds to your children's future success.

'Nothing in these notes setting out school policy precludes any parent requiring a different arrangement for their son or daughter. Such requests are always seriously considered and every effort made to accommodate them whenever practicably possible.'

He thought that it was unusual for a head to do admissions himself, and explained:

> Why I think doing admissions is important? It's looking at what's coming in and important they see what's at the top of the institution they are coming into. It means keeping control of the thing and, from an induction point of view, it means the basic is covered. And it is still an expectation on the part of parents that they see the head.

With any new admission, he insisted on seeing both parent and child and explaining to each carefully and with the use of visual aids, how he saw each fitting into the school. To a fifth year girl from another school, applying to transfer to the school's sixth form, he said,

> Nice to see you. No mum and dad? We don't usually do admissions without parents. If your mum and dad want to meet me, I'd be very happy to see them.

Admission interviews lasted from 10 to (more frequently) 45 minutes. Information about the child emerging in the interview was immediately communicated to relevant staff. Additionally, all new admissions were entered immediately into a day book, 'so I can invite the parents to the right open evenings'.

When the schools' department sent a new pupil to the school without telling Mr Shaw first, he rang up in anger:

> Mr Shaw: I'll ask you a question. Did you have any dealings with Mrs Round last week on appeal? It's all gone badly wrong. We got the wrong girl. Why wasn't I rung on Friday?
>
> Office: We didn't know you were in.
>
> Mr Shaw: We man the office throughout the holidays. Some idiot at county hall told them the wrong thing. I'm going to go bananas on this.
>
> Office: Please let me finish.
>
> Mr Shaw: A child dumped on my doorstep when we're very busy and can't give them proper service. It needs a top priority dealing. We are always open and we have our communications properly organised. We have five people starting. We got the name of the child wrong. She got sent off in the wrong direction just because you didn't know. I'm very cross. Thank you. (He rang off).

At the open evenings, whether for reports, presentations, fund raising or other social events, the concern with the school as being in partnership with parents was always evident. For example, each year an enrichment fund evening was held for first year and other new entrant pupils' parents. The head's main concern was to convince parents of the importance of their agreement to make an individual covenant to the enrichment fund. Each parent was greeted by children as they arrived, and introduced individually to the head. Then, on the platform with other members of the enrichment fund committee, he became the entrepreneur, seeking to elicit their money without betraying the educational ethos of the occasion.

> I'd like to start not with the fund but with your boy or your girl . . . they are the centre . . . virtually nobody leaves with nothing, a tremendous tribute to both the children and to the staff . . . this means a lot of activities beyond the boundaries of the school . . . we could have called the enrichment fund the experience fund. We are trying to bring into youngsters' lives as much experience as we can . . .

A fifth year parents' evening was equally carefully arranged, with the head alongside his deputies greeting people and showing them where to sit. He sat among the staff at the front of the hall, facing parents, and the deputy head acted as master of ceremonies, introducing the head as the first speaker.

As in all his dealings with parents, whether individually or in a group, he emphasised the crucial part he saw them as playing in their child's development. At a similar first year parents' meeting, before the beginning of the academic year, he commented:

> ... You spent the first eleven years bringing them up in crucial ways. There is a sense in which they are going to be finished off here. (Producing a three-legged stool). This is my secret recipe of partnership for coping with an adolescent son or daughter. You, ladies and gentlemen, are the third leg. Without your love, tolerance, understanding, patience, the stool wouldn't stand up. If I had to say which was the most important leg of all, then I'd say it's your leg.

At the fifth year parents' evening, his emphasis again was on how parents could help their child and the school in formulating that choice.

> We think this is a very important year. You obviously do too or you wouldn't have braved the elements to come. Although every year your boy or girl has been in the school is important, if I had to nominate which of the years was most important, I'd say the first one and this one just beginning now ... If you can make the subjects being studied a family interest this can be a tremendous asset. I can assure you from my own experience in my own family, it's much more fun ... the more you can encourage, praise the results, the better.

Figure 9.2 An example of Litton School's advice to parents

The 5th Year
HOW PARENTS CAN HELP

Encourage work on all occasions.

Provide the best working conditions that are possible.

Tactfully monitor personal progress - uniform, time-keeping.

Contact school over any problem.

Make sure you come to all school functions during the year.

Your children will be grateful.

He ended with a display on the overhead projector, to demonstrate, 'You are the magic formula.'

He structured report evenings so that the parents saw tutors and year tutors rather than subject teachers. The head stood by the door to greet parents and show them where to go and what to do.

> We're training parents to the system, making sure it's thorough, a flow, showing them where to go.

From time to time parents came up to speak to him on specific issues relating to their child. For him, it was important that 'we're all in the school together, seen as a whole school team'.

In his dealings with parents over pupil discipline, Mr Shaw took time to explore with the parent the reason for their child's behaviour; counselling appeared as important as implementing sanctions. On the latter, he explained the procedure that was involved in disciplining the child. On one occasion Mr Shaw had to explain to a parent why a teacher had flung her son's bag on the floor, breaking a bottle in it. Having spoken to both the teacher and boy, he rang the parent:

Mr Shaw:	A small spot of bother with John this morning, I should just like to tell you about. Nothing earth shattering, just things went wrong...John didn't move his bag and the teacher forcibly smacked the bag on the floor and you can guess what happened. The orange bottle burst...clearly Mr Peters shouldn't have thrust it on the floor with that force.
Mother:	Yes, but I can understand it if he wasn't obeying him. He didn't know the bottle was in there. I didn't even...Don't worry about that at all. I just hope John has taken notice of what you say. This last two weeks he's been getting too big for his boots...
Mr Shaw:	Shall I tell you what it is...Growing up...It's a question of being strong and controlling him...He's got to go through it...with your consistent control there won't be any problems, he's not someone I associate with trouble.
Mother:	I will let him have his say before I tell him you phoned. Thank you very much for ringing me. I'm very sorry you had this trouble. Thank you very much for ringing me.

On two other occasions, the head was put in the position of mediating between an individual member of staff and parents. His concern, was to establish the facts on all sides. To a parent, complaining at length about her son's trouble with a science teacher over an exercise book, he commented:

> I don't know the details of it. I'll see the science teacher to get her view of it. You and I are both a bit removed from it.

When the parent suggested that the teacher owed her son an apology, he responded, 'I must speak to the teacher first'.

Most of Mr Shaw's dealings with parents on an individual basis were in relation to problems. Mr Shaw, though, had a 'cheer ourselves up' file into which he put congratulatory letters from parents; he saw this a a morale boosting exercise for staff.

Again, like the other heads, his contact with parents, whether positive or negative, provided feedback to him on staff. Unlike the other heads, Mr Shaw saw his school as in competition with others—in the private sector as well as other comprehensives—which contributed to the significance he attached to work with parents. He did not, however, appear to distinguish between parents; they were all responded to in a similar manner.

Mr Mercer

Mr Mercer's approach was consonant with the fact that he did not see the school in competition—and was therefore less concerned to go out and attract parents to the school.

> They can choose but they all come here. There's no competition. We lost two
> last year to direct grant schools and one to a voluntary aided school. I just do
> a short introduction, then we let them look around the school.

His main concern at the meeting for the parents of new entrants was to explain to parents the rules governing pupils' behaviour and the boundaries of his responsibility for their children. The emphasis was on an instrumental partnership between school and parents, relating to ethos rather than more specifically educational expectations.

> Curriculum hasn't changed a great deal since you and I were at school. It's
> dictated by the examination system. So we do the usual things...We do wear
> uniform here. We would like all our children to wear school dress. At the end
> of the day, we've all been through this with our children, if there's no choice,
> it's quieter in the house.

The head encouraged parents to contact the school if they were concerned about anything.

> If you need to see us, it's far easier to ring or write and make an appointment,
> in case we're with a class somewhere or in another part of the school. But if
> you are concerned about anything, come in, for God's sake. We don't want
> lurid tales of what's happening going home. Children exaggerate.

Most of his contacts with parents suggested that they did feel able to contact him when concerned about their child; other contacts were in response to the school's need to discipline their child, when the parents would be called in. We only saw him with individual parents six times during our fieldwork.

Mr Mercer did not meet new pupils and their parents to admit them to the school himself, although he would sometimes be the first phone contact on the possibility of a child coming to the school. When he was contacted directly by a parent about a new admission the head's response was always the same: first he must check with the school currently attended by the child and then he would check against his own admission numbers. He did not check these himself, or have them with him, but delegated their monitoring to the senior deputy head, whom he would then consult.

Other phone calls were from parents concerned about their children's welfare. The head's response in each case was similar. He encouraged the parents to articulate their concern, and reassured them that he would take any necessary action. To the father whose son's wrist had been cut by another boy, he said he would fully support him if he wanted to take the matter further and suggested that he talk to the school policeman first. He consoled another parent, whose daughter had gone missing.

> Don't worry too much, they do turn up quite quickly...when she does get back, you and your wife come in with her and we'll see what we can sort out...I know, don't worry...it's the usual signs of rebellion that settle eventually. You can't choose their friends for them unfortunately. I'll make enquiries in school and get on to Mr Rawlings to see what's happening.

When Mr Mercer was observed with parents in his study, the issue was usually the disciplining of a child. On one occasion the parents had come along, at the head's invitation, to be present at their son's re-admission to the school, after he had been suspended. All three sat on hard chairs in front of the head's desk, while he spoke exclusively to the boy, warning him of the consequences of any further misbehaviour.

> Head (to the boy):   Do you want to be called a yobbo? I know you don't (act like one) at home. I know mum and dad won't let you...you're fortunate you've got parents who care for you and that's ninety per cent of it.'
>
> (The boy departs)
> Head (to the parents): Alright? See how it goes. Sorry you had to be dragged up again.'

The parents said hardly a word.

Mr Mercer saw parents as sharing a common purpose with the school; to control their children. Their possible contribution to the educational development of their children was touched on only in negative ways. Getting parental co-operation was consistently seen as problematic, whether to encourage children to stay on in to the sixth form and apply for university, to allow a child to be statemented to discover special needs or to ensure that any funds made available to their child were properly used.

He knew many parents in the locality by sight as well as hearsay, either because he had taught them when they were at school or as a result of his frequent forays into the streets surrounding the schools. Many of the shopkeepers had their children there. He would thus meet parents while buying cigarettes or a newspaper; or on Saturdays when he would shop sometimes with his wife in the area—he lived just over the catchment boundary.

His views of parents were based on information from the different grapevines to which he was party. Inevitably casual gossip with colleagues dwelt more frequently on the more sensational stories, of mothers who were 'on the game', fathers who were violent or in local ex-offender hostels and families in which parentage was uncertain and parenting non-existent. Only on rare occasions were parents discussed in the head's presence as positive contributors to their child's education.

In Mr Mercer's school, parents had a fairly low profile, which he attributed to the nature of the catchment.

> I'll never turn parents away. Often they demand to see me. I'll see them and then, having forewarned the deputy head, pass them over. There's a friends of the school who meet once a month. Few parents come to the meetings but they support functions like the Christmas fayre and school concerts.

He often described a distinction between his own experience as a parent and that of parents of children in his own school. When his own son was taking 'A' levels and negotiating university entrance, he became more involved in what his own school's sixth form was doing to help youngsters apply to colleges. He was insistent that sixth formers should come into the report evening with their parents, to help overcome what his head of sixth form called their 'parochial' attitudes.

Mr Dowe

Mr Dowe gave considerable priority to dealing with parents: rarely a day went by without him having some contact with parents. Parents who saw Mr Dowe fell into three categories. First, he spoke with parents of children who were about to enter, or were possibly to enter, the school, at its upper end—into the fifth or sixth forms. Such parents came to find out if their child could be accepted at the school, to learn something about the school, and, often to discuss options—generally 'A' level choices. These meetings were never less than five minutes, and sometimes nearly an hour.

Second, he dealt with parents of pupils who were in trouble at school—in other words, discipline matters. More of these were incoming rather than outgoing; they mostly consisted of parents getting in touch with the head because of their dissatisfaction with the treatment of their child by the school. In this way, the head became involved in 'awkward' cases.

Third, unlike the other three heads, Mr Dowe dealt with a number of parents who disputed aspects of the curriculum. He told us how, in the recent past, there had been serious parental dissatisfaction expressed by a vocal but small minority of parents over certain 'A' level results and over his introduction of a broadly based curriculum. In the second and third of these categories, the head was sometimes put in the position of defending his staff, or mediating between teachers and parents.

Mr Dowe seemed to deal with parents of three overlapping types. First, he frequently referred to 'Powdham parents'—by which he meant difficult, assertive, upper middle class parents from one part of the catchment. In his lecture to the university's education faculty, he referred to Powdham as 'near stockbroker belt'. On occasions he described a parent as 'typical Powdham' and contrasted a parent who had been very reasonable about a complaint with this Powdham model:

> If she'd have been a Powdham parent she'd have gone straight to a solicitor.

Another group, again not exclusive, were those who had unduly high expectations of their children's academic attainment. St Mary's was a school at which about 20 per cent of pupils had private tuition in their examination year. One of the matters Mr Dowe had to deal with was the reconcilation of parents to their children's ability. Mr Dowe was frustrated by the father of a pupil—who had been lucky, as Mr Dowe saw it, to get offers from polytechnics over the summer after 'A' level results—who then came back to the head thinking that he should be able to get the boy into a university.

The final category of parent was made up of parents who created difficulty: they defended their or their child's position, in situations where this seemed unreasonable, and opposed school policy. Mr Dowe said of one pupil he had found creating trouble that he had remembered that 'his father's a ranter'. Of another pupil's mother, he said to a colleague: 'hey, Mary's on the rampage again'. One parent defended his son having written that the school was a 'load of shit', on the grounds that in saying this he was acting as the spokesperson of a large group of pupils; and another rang up to protest about what Mr Dowe had said to her daughter when she was arriving at school late. In relation to this, Mr Dowe said to us:

> You can't even tell a pupil off for being late nowadays without getting a phone call from a parent.

Mr Dowe's knowledge of parents was based on a number of sources. As well as meeting parents as the head, as a teacher in the school he met parents—for example, at parents' evenings. The school had a year tutor system, and two deputies who played major pastoral roles; they and the tutors would often report, on an *ad hoc* basis, particular matters to the head. The school shared an education welfare officer with other schools; Mr Dowe was in touch with her about a small number of cases. Finally, of course, Mr Dowe often found himself dealing with parents he had already dealt with, and so had that base of understanding on which to build.

The importance Mr Dowe attached to parents was due to their status as a client group. Mr Dowe was concerned that parents should be kept happy. This does not mean that this took absolute priority; it did not. Indeed he often made moves in the knowledge of likely parental opposition. 'We've got to educate the parents', he said, Mr Dowe, though, remained aware—because it was pointed out to him so often—of the potential for parents to upset the school. In a similar way, he was aware that the school was in competition with the private sector at its sixth form level; he told one meeting that pupils entering the sixth form from elsewhere represented one and a half teachers' jobs. This did not mean, however, that he did everything to attract such pupils; on the contrary, he explicitly advised parents that the neighbouring school was just as good and more convenient for them.

However well informed and vocal the parents may have been, Mr Dowe was in a powerful position in that he knew that St Mary's exam results were good and that the school was highly thought of—more so than the neighbouring school. He felt that exam results were the key criteria used by parents.

Whatever his criticisms of them, Mr Dowe appreciated the need for both effort and clarity with parents, and found it a difficult area. In discussing a draft letter to parents with his deputy, he said, 'one has to be so precise to parents'. At a senior council meeting he stressed that the school should make clear to parents such matters as a new assessment system and the school calendar.

In interactions with parents, Mr Dowe was extremely courteous and co-operative. After a boy had been injured at school, seemingly due to the antics of another pupil or pupils, he said on the phone:

> When can you come in to talk about it, or would the phone be better...Can you come in the next quarter of an hour...The sooner you come in, the sooner we can sort it out.

On one occasion he was behind schedule and extremely busy. Two parents came to see him earlier than expected. Mr Dowe began: 'I'm glad you're early...'! On another occasion a parent had arrived without an appointment; a secretary told the head, who agreed to see him. Mr Dowe had never met the parent, nor did he know the pupil, but, in his usual polite and gentle tone, he invited the parent in, and to sit down. As he left, ten minutes later, Mr Dowe said to him that he was glad he *had* come up to see him, 'and if there's ever anything else... do come again'. This approach gave him prior knowledge of potential trouble and information about teachers; such interactions clearly reflected his belief in the legitimacy of parental involvement.

One distinctive way in which Mr Dowe treated parents was giving them his home phone number, which he did frequently and enthusiastically. At an interview with the parent of a prospective pupil, he said, 'one of the really important things is my home telephone number ... if you want a chat ... 'cos sometimes you can find there's changes have to be made'. He knew that parents were less likely to get hold of him during the day because of his high teaching commitment and wanted to ensure his ready availability.

The school's formal account of the role of parents is set out in St Mary's school prospectus.

> If there are any matters about which, when you have read this, you need to ask, I hope that you will not hesitate to get in touch with the school.
> Education is a partnership: pupils, parents, teachers belong to this partnership. The aim of the partnership is to provide the best education possible for all pupils in the school. For parents to play an effective part in the partnership, it is necessary for schools to remove the wraps of mystery which so often surround institutions.
> Your child will change while he or she is at St Mary's. Some changes will be induced by the steady natural development...Others you will induce...
> *Pastoral organisation of the school*
> You care for your children throughout the day and night. Teachers like to feel that they are acting 'in loco parentis' taking up the quality of your caring from the time your children cross our threshold.

The school had a strong year tutor system and, as discussed elsewhere, the head delegated extensively to deputies; including much of the school's dealings with parents. He would not necessarily be aware of letters, phone calls or meetings these staff had had with parents; though would be informed about some of them, in an *ad hoc* way. Parents he dealt with would be those who wanted to and found themselves able to see him, particularly serious cases, or parents of the pupils Mr Dowe taught. The head attended only a few feeder primary parents' meetings. His enthusiasm for the PTA varied. One school year he was disparaging about it, mentioning how its participants represented no one but themselves, that he had had to point this out to them; that he didn't mind the first bit of meetings, but got fed up listening to discussions of 'whether to have red or white wine'. During the industrial action, he was very pleased that he could miss the meetings. The following year, he found the PTA easier to work with. In both years, whatever his private opinions, he exuded an air of interest and enthusiasm at its meetings.

Mr King

Mr King had a similar level of contact with individual parents; but he had fewer letters and phone calls, and more face to face interaction. He also attended more meetings of groups of parents: all of the feeder primary meetings, every parents' evening, the annual new parents' evening (for parents of pupils about to enter the first year), and the Friends of Aley Park—a broader version of a PTA, including parents of ex-pupils, and other supporters of the school.

Mr King's dealings with parents were frequent, partly because he answered the school phone until the secretarial staff arrived at 8.30, and from 4 p.m.—he would receive calls from parents wanting to inform the school of the absence of their child that day; or to express concern that their child had not yet arrived home. He dealt with these briefly but politely. In common with the other heads he also dealt with parents on discipline matters. It was not unusual for a pupil to be sent home from the school for some act of delinquency, and to be told to stay away from school until his or her parents came in. Often such parents would see the head.

Third, Mr King saw parents who wanted their children to come to the school. Some were moving into the catchment, others lived outside it. Mr King spoke with them briefly, sometimes informing them that if 'it didn't work out' then they would have to return to their catchment school; and then sent them over to the appropriate head of school. Like Mr Mercer, during our fieldwork Mr King saw only one set of parents who were *considering* sending their child to the school; all of the others knew they wanted their child to come to the school. Mr King did not have to actively promote his school.

Mr King appeared to work with at least three typifications of parents. First, there was the respectable working class parent, for whom he had considerable regard. A parent of high social status was considering sending his son to the school, and Mr King said to us:

I couldn't give a toss (whether he does or not)...He'll be nothing but trouble. Give me solid working class parents any day.

Respectable working class parents constituted the bulk of those Mr King interacted with. Second, many of the parents of Mr King's pupils failed, in his view, to support their children. He spoke of examples in his own family, in the extended sense, to explain to us the centrality of parental support, rather than social class, to a child's educational attainment. Finally, Mr King had a particular view of Asian parents. He joked about their incomprehensibility, and about his having to have a pupil to interpret; and mimicked what they had done and said. His treatment of them was off hand in comparison with his interaction with other parents.

Mr King had a close personal knowledge of a particular section of his school's pupils' parents. He himself had been brought up in Aley Park's catchment area, and had been to school with the parents and relatives of some of its current pupils. He lived in the area, and was involved in a number of organisations in the community. For example, when at an evening meeting for 'new parents', Mr King invited questions, he indicated to one parent to ask his question, introducing him to the audience, 'this is Mr Gould, who I went to school with'.

Mr King was clear that it was the parents' job to bring their children up; he said this to parents and teachers. He understood the centrality of parental support to pupil progress, and *spoke* of a partnership. He repeatedly expressed his own and the school's accountability to parents—in a democratic rather than client model. Mr King was, then, firm in demarcating the very grey area, of parental and school role; and of his accountability to parents.

How then did he practise his relations with parents? He had a prominent presence in the community. His energetic approach to his job, his support for community organisations, and his own roots in the neighbourhood made him very well known. He met parents in many situations outside the school—in the supermarket on Saturday, for example. Many parents already knew him. He invited and encouraged parents to come to the school.

Aley Park's handbook begins with a note from Mr King to parents. This includes the following:

> We believe that education is a partnership between school, home and the community, and all our work is aimed at achieving this.

> We ask you, when and where it is possible to support our school to the extent of your ability, and to work with us for the welfare of your children.

This was his emphasis: on parents supporting the school, rather than the involvement of parents in the education of their children. He stressed his accountability to them. At the new parents' evening he said:

> I believe that parents are the most important part of the education system; and I believe that it's to you that I'm chiefly responsible.

He described the Friends of Aley Park—its equivalent of a PTA—as the 'most enjoyable part' of his work; he enjoyed having a drink in the pub afterwards with a group of its members. The Friends of Aley Park—with a hard core of about 30 parents—were mostly from the area where Mr King himself lived; they were respectable, white, working class parents.

In the high level of Mr King's involvement with the community, he appeared to do more than set an example to his colleagues; he not only practised leadership by example, but concentrated this area of work on himself. He was sent copies of all individual, as opposed to standard, letters by heads of (the three sections of the) school to parents; and thus kept himself well informed.

In common with the other heads, Mr King was concerned that his meetings with individual parents on an individual basis should be characterised by the parents' goodwill and support for the school. Although they might complain, they left in a positive mood. A pupil's mother and step-father had been asked to come up to school. Initially, the mother insisted,

> Shouldn't she be spoken to properly first. I've never known her to be cheeky. I think she's really understanding.

The stepfather expressed anger at her having been sent home in heavy rain for not having had a tie. Mr King went through the history of the case, and pointed out what he saw as the bad company she kept. He asked, 'what are we going to do to contain her in school for the next three months?' The mother replied, 'I think once I have a talk to her tonight, she'll listen'. The stepfather said that he appreciated Mr King's position: 'I couldn't do your job'; and they left on good terms. This was typical: the head stuck firm on the school's requirements, while sympathising with parents or urging them to exercise more control. The similar class background and social style of the head and parents seemed to enhance his acceptability to parents.

• 10 •

Working with the LEA

The second main area of the head's work outside the school is with the LEA. The relationship between the head and the LEA is not clearly defined, although aspects of it have been formally specified; the degree of specification varies between LEAs. Nowhere, though, is it defined in explicit and comprehensive terms. It is hardly surprising, therefore, that both between and within the LEAs the relationship is interpreted by heads in different ways. We discuss particular differences between LEAs below (Chapter 13) where we deal with LEA officers' and advisers' perceptions and expectations of their headteachers.

The relationship between heads and their LEAs reflects an ambiguous dual allegiance. On the one hand, they work with the LEA to promote the interests of the school, to get support for what it wants to do. On the other, they have to implement within their schools LEA policy—which, in extreme cases, may be opposed to their view of the interests of the school. Different heads find themselves facing different demands in this respect; but, even in similar situations, we found that they interpreted their role in widely divergent ways.

One of the greatest limitations on the autonomy of heads in their schools has been imposed by the contraction of the secondary school service, due to falling rolls. These have led LEAs to the position where they have to assume more co-ordination of the service, with a concomitant diminution of their schools' autonomy. Walsh's recent study of the management of contraction summarises this situation:

> Schools are less able to stand apart as independent. . . and the Authority is less able to let them do so. Cooperation, coordination and indeed direction is increasingly seen as necessary by authorities (Walsh, 1984, p.278).

This situation is well illustrated by an example from our fieldwork. Mr Dowe found the LEA intervening increasingly in his allocation of scale points; this had reached the situation where any promotion of a Scale 2 or above had to be approved by the Authority; this approval was not merely a formal ratification process. The LEA's rationale for this was that in a redeployment situation it was inappropriate for a number two in the biology department to be Scale 3 when in other schools the head of department was Scale 3.

Although all four heads were equally susceptible to pressures for the increasing involvement by the LEA in staffing issues, they responded differently. They each had expectations of the extent to which they were prepared to allow LEA policies to affect the running of the schools—or the scope they had for affecting that. They also had different strategies for dealing with LEA contacts.

At one end of the spectrum, Mr Dowe was firmly committed to what he, the staff, parents and the community saw as the interests of the school; he resisted any LEA policy which conflicted with this. Mr Shaw did not oppose LEA policy as firmly, but demonstrated a considerable concern with the interests of the school, particularly in maintaining initial entry numbers. At the other end of the spectrum, Mr King and Mr Mercer, in different LEAs, had the greatest allegiance to their LEAs; the managerial concerns of the Authority played a prominent part in their view of particular LEA policies and the individual interests of their schools took a lower priority. We shall consider the nature of each of the four heads' work with their LEA in turn, in terms of the content of their contact, and the nature of their relations with LEA staff.

All of them dealt with a large number of individuals in many departments of the LEA, including the staffing section, educational psychologist, catering officer, caretakers' supervisor, educational welfare officers, personnel, and buildings section. Additionally, they had contact with a small number of officers and advisers. Most of their contact was on the phone; their meetings were both at school and at the Authority's offices. The two LEAs imposed similar requirements on their heads: arrangements regarding staff redeployment and appointment, pupil resources, in-service training, catering, caretakers, admissions, educational welfare officers, the completion of returns, occasional days' holiday, and so on. Their emphasis, however, varied somewhat: Brayside, for example, pursued a policy on peace studies and multi-cultural curriculum, in which Mr Mercer, in particular, was caught up.

Mr Shaw described the relations between his school and the Authority thus:

> This is an independent school which is financed by the LEA. They set up the conditions for things to be done and trust the head to get on with it. They are not a constant intrusion. They do not poke or probe.

Unlike Mr Dowe, he did not see it as a conflict relationship, and was on a number of LEA Committees (e.g. ATCC, curriculum review group, careers advisory group), on which he worked directly alongside locally elected members and LEA officers. We only saw him in open opposition to the LEA on one issue: their decision to reduce his intake numbers. He had welcomed the unit in the school for children with special needs, which the LEA had offered in response to the 1981 Education Act; although for the unit to be effective he had to engage in constant dialogue with the LEA's Special Education Department, to secure adequate staffing and appropriate pupil placements. Although Mr Shaw was aware of becoming increasingly constrained in his appointment of staff by the LEA's policies on redeployment, he succeeded in keeping LEA involvement to a minimum. He prided himself in the selection system which he had developed over time which maximised the influence of himself and his senior management team, and was reluctant to lose that control. He even held potential governor encroachment at bay by convincing them of the efficiency and superiority of the existing system in which they were not involved.

He worked amicably with the LEA on supply staff (he saw Brayside as particularly generous in its provision), buildings and the Authority's suspension procedure, which rigidly laid down in a detailed way the steps to be followed before a child was finally suspended from school. It was usual for him to attend the hearing at county hall which would decide the child's future. LEA officers and advisers were invited to the school's public functions and, during the year, he showed his appreciation of their help when he could: for example, he arranged a buffet supper 'for those who have helped us at county hall'.

Mr Mercer, in the same Authority, was not particularly perturbed about the reduction in his school's admissions. At the beginning of fieldwork the LEA had already decided to cut the school's intake from 400 to 275 necessitating the closure of one of the school's sites and the reorganisation of the other three. He felt that he was over resourced, and that the slow rate of falling numbers over five years had made it possible to maintain the curriculum without much difficulty.

> It's been less traumatic here because we've had resources to absorb the drop.
> I've been looking forward to this.

He regretted, however, the lack of closer LEA support in implementing the closure proposals, particularly in relation to redeployment. He told us, 'The only representative from the LEA on all this has been our adviser'.

Staffing and buildings dominated Mr Mercer's dealings with the LEA. To keep the school running during a period of substantial changes required vigilance over staff numbers and movement, with regular cross checking with LEA staffing. It also involved considerable liaison with the different departments involved in supplies and maintenance. He saw dealing with the LEA on this matter as his primary responsibility and delegated little.

As the head of an inner city, multi-ethnic school, Mr Mercer was immediately affected by LEA policies on multi-cultural education and peace studies. A number of staff from the Authority's multi-cultural centre worked in the school, and Mr Mercer was on the centre's consultative committee. He had reservations about some of the Authority's multi-cultural initiatives and responded cautiously to their introduction into the school. Sometimes in his dealings with the LEA he chose to play a waiting game, for example, in relation to peace studies. He told us:

> Peace studies hasn't emerged in my school yet. I reckon I've only got to last until next May, until the Tories get in. Then we'll have war games!

However, he volunteered for a racism awareness course run by the Authority, since he considered it would soon become mandatory. Although sceptical of a number of aspects of the way Brayside went about things ('typical Brayside, all cloak and dagger'), he maintained harmonious working relations with them. Any doubts he had about their way of working were expressed privately.

Mr Dowe, in contrast, saw his relations with the LEA as far from amicable. He commented to us:

> I don't think they like my style. I think I'm a bit of a thorn in their flesh.

The basis of his attitude to the LEA was that it acted in its own interests rather than those of the school; and he had little respect for senior officers as educationalists.

> So they're very clever. If you say 'is there a policy...' they say 'no.' Yet it operates. If it was a policy, at least the heads' group could discuss it.

In his view, the LEA was unnecessarily obtrusive, for example, in appointments:

> I never had this in my last Authority, having to justify every bloody ad.

To Mr Dowe, LEA redeployment policies were 'an erosion of a head's right to employ his own staff'. He felt particularly annoyed about LEA interference in the allocation of points to reorganise his sixth form staff, and fought a battle over this for several months. On the question of redeployment, which affected St Mary's quite profoundly because its intake had been reduced substantially, he co-operated with the head of the other school in Seatown to oppose LEA policy which acted against the interests of Seatown. He felt that Seatown was 'in danger of being completely swamped by...the whirlpool' of the LEA; and went on:

> We want to get the Seatown voice heard in the education offices. I know I've been accused in the education offices of wanting to create a Seatown anarchy ...the feeling is that we're cushioned in Seatown. I don't think we are.

He took a similar stance in the consultation phase of the Authority's tertiary proposals—which, as he saw it, were undesirable because they would lop off his viable and effective sixth form, for an unproven gain.

Mr Dowe's relationship with LEA officers was characterised by conflict. When an adviser told him of who in the Authority would be interviewed for a post, he said to us, 'it's a bit arrogant of the advisers'. He described them as thwarting his attempts to reorganise the sixth form staff. He reported to us that after the disciplining of a senior member of staff, 'I didn't see the relevant adviser for a whole year'.

Mr King worked in the same Authority as Mr Dowe, but his relations with the LEA were cordial and close. He had four times as many contacts with officers than Mr Dowe, and these often involved a substantial element of chat in addition to the business in hand. In common with Mr Mercer, any caveats he had about the Authority's support for heads were expressed privately rather than manifest in his dealings with the LEA. In other words, Mr King was prepared to accept the Authority's policies and rules, and to work with its officers—and enjoyed the protection and benefit which accrued from this. His relationship with the Authority was one of partnership rather than conflict. 'It's not a bad LEA', he said. He made a point of inviting a large number of officers to social events at the school. He got on particularly well with the two officers with whom he dealt most, the assistant education officer (schools) and the school's pastoral adviser.

As well as contact with the Authority's officers, heads also deal with members of the LEA—mainly those councillors on their governing bodies. The four heads had different expectations of what governors could contribute to their school, and dealt with them in contrasting ways. Mr Mercer saw himself at odds with many of his governors, preferred to deal with them individually rather than as a group, and was not always confident of their support. Mr Shaw had frequent contact with his governors, and worked with them in governors' meetings to win their approval for what he wanted. Mr Dowe had very little contact with his governors, and only tried to use them to support his opposition to the Authority. Mr King had a close working relationship with his governing body, encouraged their involvement in the school, and had their firm support.

Mr Mercer circulated papers in advance to a selected few, avoided raising issues at the governors' meeting itself, and played down troublesome issues in the minutes. He dealt mainly with the vice chairman of governors, whom he respected and who called in frequently to see him between governing body meetings. Although sceptical of some of their motives, he valued good relations with governors. He told us: 'a head who can't handle his governors has had it'. Although he considered that 'the effect of governing bodies in this county is negligible', he also thought that 'the first thing any head has to learn is how to handle his governing body'. In his view the situation should be that, 'senior management make the decisions, the governors agree to them'.

For example, during the period of the school's reorganisation, he persuaded them that they needed a working party of four to work closely with senior management. He attributed difficulties to their apathy, and their ignorance, their political partisanship. The fact that we were unable to observe a governors' meeting at the school was, in part, the result of his concern that an outside observer might upset an already delicate situation.

When discussing other heads' problems with their governing bodies Mr Mercer considered himself both fortunate (in that his were less active), and successful in handling their demands. He was particularly fortunate, he thought, in having a vice chairman of governors 'who agrees with everything you do'.

His scepticism regarding the competence of some of his governors led him to take care in controlling the content and circulation of the governors' report. His secretary acted as clerk to the governors' meetings and he would afterwards indicate to her what should be included in and played down in the minutes. He gave a number of reasons for compiling the report and minutes in this way.

> if you make it too complicated the governors will get their knickers in a twist. The main thing about this lot is get your figures right. Some fool will spot any mistake.
> I can invent a governors' report without having to refer to much, I'm afraid, out of my head. I know what will keep them quiet.

He was not keen on all the governors having a copy of the governors' report.

> There you tread a tight rope because there's two staff governors. All this democracy has succeeded in doing is making it all more secretive. It's not confidential because things have been quoted to me from it.

In general, he regarded governing body meetings as a chore in which it was expedient to try and fill up the time as much as possible in ways which would avoid any confrontations over serious issues. When his deputy was due to take the next governors' meeting, in his absence, Mr Mercer promised him:

> I'll window dress the next meeting for you. Shirley will talk on Russia, that will take 40 minutes, and there's the minutes of the last meeting. I've put in a bit about leaking roofs and that will keep them sorted out.

There were issues on which he had different views from many of his governors. The county had stated that it would no longer give support on wearing school uniform in schools. Mr Mercer wanted his pupils to wear uniform and at the new parents' evening in July, he did not refer to its optional nature. He commiserated with other heads who said that their governing bodies were trying to insist on its abolition and said, 'I've been told by my chairman that he'd give me no support on them wearing uniform'.

Another area of disagreement was in the degree of support to be given to the teachers' industrial action. Mr Mercer considered a number of staff to have been in breach of contract and thought that the LEA should have taken a firmer stand against them. His chairman of governors thought differently, as Mr Mercer told us:

> I had the chairman down last Tuesday. I'd rung him to tell him we're having industrial action. He turned up at two, stayed until four. We went through things. He told me, if the press contact you about the strike, say we support the action and exams aren't affected.

Mr Mercer's own view was that he did not support the strike and exams were affected.

> As far as I'm concerned it's a breach of contract. My governing body passed a vote of thanks congratulating teachers for not affecting exams. What rubbish. They certainly did.

He was sceptical even of his governors' views on multi-cultural education, which the Authority strongly supported. In his view, his governing body did not reflect the community it served.

> I've got one black governor and he's Nigerian and got as little in common with my West Indians as I have.

When he did seek their support, for example in requesting a two day closure at the end of the Summer term to help with the movement involved in the closure of one site, he achieved it by 'doing a deal'.

On another occasion, his deputy told him that one of the other headteachers in the area was seen to be poaching on their catchment. Mr Mercer commented that he would have the matter brought up at the next governors' meeting. He felt strongly that the director of education should enforce planned admission limits within catchments and would use his governors to put pressure on if necessary. He saw their support as necessary when there was potential conflict with the LEA, for example when he had drawn up a new structure for the management of the school. In general, however, his relations with his governors were in contrast to those with LEA officers; with the former there was more overt conflict and less confidence in their support. In contrast, Mr Shaw's relations with his governing body resembled those he enjoyed with the Authority. He respected the views and efficiency of his chairman of governors, and expected to receive their support for most proposals. He described them as 'a head's principal supporters' club', particularly in his dealings with the LEA. He met with them twice a term. Prior to each meeting, Mr Shaw would ring the chairman and arrange to meet him to discuss the agenda. The chairman of governors visited the school on occasions to see other people and had a few brief words with the head in passing.

Mr Shaw claimed to base some of the way in which he approached handling his governing body on his own experience as a governor of the local technical college.

> It makes me aware of how I need to present things to my governing body, not to leave things as unclear as they do.

Observing him preparing for a governors' meeting, it was not apparent that he felt a need to conceal information from them. Mr Shaw never made any critical comments about them to us. Only once did he refer to possible conflict with them, when one governor questioned the extent of their involvement in appointing staff.

At governing body meetings, held in the head's room, he arrived half an hour before it began and chatted to individual governors as they arrived. Fourteen were present at the first meeting which we observed; nine at the second. The report to the governors was distributed to all beforehand and the school's bursar acted as clerk. Both meetings began with a presentation from a member of staff on some aspect of the school; on one occasion it was the extension studies scheme; on another, the community studies programme. The two deputy heads attended, as did the school's pastoral adviser. The governors asked a number of questions about the content of the talks; both seemed to raise issues of political significance. The first caused a heated debate on what should be the role of extension studies (by implication for brighter children) in a comprehensive school. Did it imply streaming and elitism? Mr Shaw let the presenters handle questions, interjecting at times. In response to the question directed at him, about allowing something to happen in the school by selection, he said, 'comprehensivisation does not mean uniformity', and went on to point out how pupils were selected for extra music tuition and special needs programmes. The governor who had doubts said that Mr Shaw had convinced him by putting it in the right perspective. The head also justified extension studies on the basis that parents often asked him what the school was doing with the more able. In the second, councillor governors were interested to know the ways in which political awareness was stimulated and handled within the community studies brief. When a governor asked about the political opinions of those taking the community education classes, Mr Shaw commented:

> I think it is a very important point Mrs Brown is making. In the wrong hands this could be very dangerous. If you have an activist, extreme right or left, it could be dangerous because there's no monitoring in the classroom.

Having dealt with minutes of the previous meeting and matters arising, Mr Shaw was then invited by the chairman to take the governors through his report. The main issue discussed at the first meeting was the Authority's imposition of what Mr Shaw considered restrictive admission levels. He then gave them a range of figures to show that the LEA's projected figures for the school were wrong and the potential impact on the school would be detrimental. When he'd finished, there was unanimity that he had destroyed the officers' case and the chairman of governors commented, that it was 'the most important thing we've discussed in ages'. The head suggested that *they* wrote a letter asking for a meeting between themselves and senior officers and suggested the proper channels for directing this. He thus won their support and promise of action on the issue.

He also asked their co-operation on pursuing with the land and buildings committee decisions which meant that the school would not be redecorated internally for some time, and in matters to do with the state of the grounds. He suggested that the governors inspect these themselves at the next meeting. The report stated:

> It is requested that these matters be taken up by governors at the highest level along with the repeated failure of the school playing fields unit to return the school's tractor.

For each item that he reported he had relevant documents, overhead projector diagrams and maps available. Much of the discussion of practical matters such as access to the school, buses and buildings, showed a detailed knowledge on the head's part of the locality. Each discussion took the form of a dialogue between the head and the governors, in which most of the governors joined. Their support was also asked for in seeking the co-operation of the leisure committee's long term planning to finance permanent provision for youth work activities in the school.

In reporting the local MP's interest in introducing TVEI into the school, he admitted his own bias in favour and criticised the county council for 'short selling children by not taking up resources'. The county council had decided not to participate in the MSC's TVEI programme. He added, 'politics apart, it is the legitimate task of any MP to take an interest in local schools', and asked if he could assume the governors' support for developing some school-industry curricular liaison.

The second meeting had a more controversial aspect, since at the previous meeting questions had been raised by a governor about whether they should have more involvement in staff appointments in the school. He told us:

> At the last governors' meeting, a governor started jumping up and down about no governor involvement in appointments. I told them it amounted to a vote of no confidence in me.

When the item was reached on the agenda at the next meeting, the governor was invited to put his case, which he did.

Governor: I would like to see this governing body carrying out the instruments of government, in participating in the selection of teaching staff in this school ... There's nothing undermining asking this but in all the schools I'm concerned with, governors have always played a part in selecting staff ... I've no reason to believe any appointment here wasn't right. I'm not casting aspersions on anyone ... I'm a professional railwayman ... I'm first to say teaching is a professional job but ...

Chairman: It would be right and proper of the governors to ask the headmaster to reiterate what does happen at the moment.

Mr Shaw put up a diagram on the overhead projector, showing staff involvement in making appointments in the school and saying that 'it is the most important thing a head has to do in a school'.

He provided a detailed description of current selection practice, emphasising the scale of the exercise, 'as a massive operation; we discuss it very fully indeed, we have been known to take the entire evening'. His strategy was to imply the extensive commitment of time which their involvement would require and the advantage to them of leaving it in the hands of the professionals. His approach was supported by the chairman of governors and the school's adviser, who was asked to comment on practices in other parts of the county. He said:

> Here is one of the most thorough procedures of any schools I have ever been involved in. The legality is O.K.

While registering that he agreed with the fairness of the present system, the governor who had raised the issue forced it to a vote on whether the governors wished to be involved in the appointment of teaching staff. The proposition was lost and the head remained free to continue the process that he had started some fourteen years previously.

They then moved on to another issue, planned admission levels, which the head presented as a battle they had fought and lost. He stressed to them that they would bear the brunt of its effects, as parents who were unable to get their children in to the school would take their protests to councillors.

> The figures of the school roll indicate the level of choice the school attracts in the community ... we're turning people away. The ultimate nonsense would be a new caretaker with eleven year old twins living on site. Technically there's only vacancies in the third year. The sixth form has a good staying on rate.

A governor, asking him whether they should advise parents to appeal, said:

> People out there don't realise what's going on. We're not as governors governed by you. You've got to do what you're told. We're not. We can put forward what we like. I think we can fight, and don't give up.

The head commented that he very much approved of governors who fought for the school. He had engineered a situation in which the governors had agreed among themselves to put pressure on the education committee, thereby showing how popular the school was. It was agreed that the head should draft a letter to the education committee. Mr Shaw responded:

> I will consult, chairman, with you whether my letter meets your requirement.

Having gone through other items on the headmaster's report, he then referred to the Green Paper on parental involvement in governing bodies and asked if they would like copies. Although there had been heated debate during the meeting, the evening ended as a triumph for Mr Shaw in that he had deflected a move towards more involvement in one aspect of running the school, selection, than he would have liked.

Mr Dowe's chairman of governors was a local councillor who was not prominent within his ruling Labour group. Mr Dowe was aware of his marginality, and of another one of his governor's greater centrality in the county Labour group. His governors were not particularly active in terms of the frequency and scope of their involvement, despite Mr Dowe's attempts to get them involved in his disputes with the LEA. In this, he saw his governors as a useful part of his strategy of opposition to the LEA. As part of his defence of the interests of the school, he opposed local authority policy in relation to a number of matters, notably resourcing. As he saw it, the LEA

> has been pulling the wool over members' eyes. Members simply haven't been told the effect of the policy on an individual school.

In his report to his governors—which gave a full account of the life of the school—his criticism of the (LEA) office was hardly veiled. Having referred to a departed teacher's replacement, his report added:

> Once again, I view with dismay the temporary nature of Mrs Robinson's contract. Indeed if county policy is maintained in 1985 we could have teachers from other schools on permanent contracts replacing in September 1985 both Mrs Robinson and Mr Hill, acclaimed above, who both won their places at St Mary's after interview.

Later, having described the poor state of windows, the heating system, capitation, computers and text books, Mr Dowe's report continued:

> Having said all this I feel selfish. Our Authority is suffering an accumulation of all its schools' woes. I feel particularly sorry, for our Director who has not been able to devote time to what, I know, he sees as his real priority, contact with schools. This is illustrated by the fact that in September I requested a personal interview with the Director to resolve certain unresolved problems to do with St Mary's. Such has been his workload that he and I have been unable to meet.

His report concluded: 'Let us hope that 1985 may not be as bad as most of us fear'. In this report Mr Dowe stated firmly his understanding of present resourcing and cuts. His governors, although not antagonistic towards him, were not galvanised by his words. Their only comment on the above quoted parts of his report was in the brief concluding remarks on the report by the chairman, who said, 'I wish I could put my hand on my heart and say I could see no further cuts', adding that it looked as if there would be, and explaining why. No one commented on the failure of the director to meet Mr Dowe. They showed little interest or involvement, although he reported several phone conversations with his chairman of governors in the evening. He felt that officers of the Authority mystified his governors when they raised matters. Also, he told colleague teachers that he found that, 'if I put certain crunch issues in my governors' report, county councillors shy away'.

Between the termly governors' meetings, Mr Dowe had little contact with his governors: we observed him contact them once—to inform them of what he saw as LEA incompetence. Whilst he was not critical of them, worked with them in a formal sense, and showed them appropriate respect, Mr Dowe had little to do with his governors, a situation which they appeared to find agreeable.

In contrast, Mr King's relations with his governors were frequent and friendly. His governors were fairly prominent members of the county council; they included the vice chairs of the education, social services, and finance committees of the county council. Mr King had once been a councillor and so he had had long term contact with his governors or their predecessors. In other words, he had been 'one of them', and was well known to them.

Mr King considered that he could more effectively control governors through his power to choose what went in the governors' report. He did not find dealing with governors difficult. He was willing for them to be involved in the school and actively encouraged this. He rang his chairman of governors, at home or at work, several times between each governors' meeting. During an HMI visit, for instance, the chairman phoned Mr King (after the latter had left a message asking him to phone back). Mr King said:

> Dave, I was going to ask you to pop in today … see the HMIs and have a quick chat would be nice, and to talk about the deputy … They haven't actually asked to see you … If you can't, is there some stage over the weekend I could have a chat with you?

He also rang the chairman before each governors' meeting; and during the industrial action the chairman rang his frequently. At the county heads' conference, the heads were asked which of them had been contacted by their chairman of governors enquiring about how the industrial action was going; only Mr King and one other said that they had been. Mr King even spoke to the previous chairman of governors, a member of the other political party, on several occasions—keeping him informed about the school. Another governor often stayed behind after meetings to discuss details of suspension cases; Mr King knew of his interest in this, was aware that he would always ask about suspensions, and said to us and others that such concern by a governor was good. Mr King always invited all of his governors to school functions: the carol service, award ceremony, fashion show and so on—and often laid on a buffet with drinks for governors and other high ranking visitors. His relationship with them was entirely co-operative.

Once, several of his governors, with other members of the Authority, visited Aley Park with the Shadow Secretary of State for Education. On this occasion, Mr King showed another aspect of his dealings with governors. He was asked a question relating to non-sexist curriculum, and gave an answer which emphasised attempts to practise positive discrimination and to break with the traditional gender stereotyping of particular courses. Yet Mr King's own view and practical commitment was to something much more traditional, as we discussed in Chapter 3. In common with the other heads, he used his relationship with his governors to add weight to his own policy preferences for the school, for example, in supporting City and Guilds. On the other hand, he was aware that a few of his staff had their own access to governors; he told us who these were, whom they knew, and in what context. He worked hard at maintaining good relations with his governors, involving them in the school's affairs wherever possible and encouraging their support for the school.

amount we found
For example,
other two w

Pres

• | | •

Presenting th
and wo
professional
the school

• | | •

Presenting the school and working professionally beyond the school

Some of the headteachers' work takes place outside the school; indeed, the presentation of the school to various parts of the world outside has been seen by commentators as an increasingly prominent part of the head's role (Morgan, Hall and Mackay, 1983). This work outside the school can be divided in two broad categories: first there is the presentation of the school to the outside world. Second, there are the head's own professional interests which go beyond his or her immediate school work.

Taking the first, working for the school outside the school, the work can be divided into three types. First, there is school paper work which is done at home, in the evenings, at the weekend, or in the holidays. Second, there is work in building up the school's public image. Much of this takes place in the community—the local youth centre's management committee or the feeder primary parents' evenings, for example. The third type of outside school work is the heads' contact with local colleague heads.

The heads' professional work which goes beyond school work falls into two types: local, and further afield. The local work of this order which we found included membership of LEA committees or working parties and in their professional associations. Moving to a regional and national level, three of the four heads were involved in professional associations and examining. Unlike some heads in our broader fieldwork, none of the four actively pursued additional careers outside of education—as artists, politicians or businessmen.

The heads were able to exercise considerable choice in what work outside the school they did. At each end of the spectrum, one was out of school for a day a month, another for one and a half days a week. As well as the amount we found considerable variation in the nature of their outside work. For example, two worked almost exclusively at a local level, whereas the other two were active members of national networks.

Presenting the school

All four heads saw public relations as important, both within the school and beyond its walls. They had a similar approach to the media. None saw it as a prominent, frequent or troublesome area; but all were aware of its potential as a cause of trouble, in some cases as a result of their own experience. As a result, they all put an emphasis in their dealings with the media on using them, rather than being used by them. For example, during the teachers' dispute, Mr Dowe diverted a newspaper photographer who had turned up to photograph children being sent home, to photographing exam classes being taught without pay by NUT members.

He told us that he did not really like dealing with the press, because he did not trust them. However, he was willing, for example, for them to take photos of him being weighed in as part of a sponsored slim; and wrote to reporters and appeared on television during the teachers' industrial action. When a prominent member of the Conservative party, a member of the education committee, wrote a long letter to the 'Seatown Times' alleging political bias in the local school (clearly St Mary's), Mr Dowe responded to his staff's anger by going to meet the writer. Ultimately, the letter writer sent a written retraction of his comments to the staff at St Mary's—which was pinned up in the staffroom. As it transpired, the allegations seemed unfounded, and no harm was done. Every stage of the matter, however, was treated by Mr Dowe with the greatest care, as a potential storm.

Mr King courted the press more actively, so that his school received much attention in the local paper, and Mr King himself kept a scrapbook for articles and photos. He spoke to the press about the industrial action—with interest and honesty, while refusing to give figures on the numbers of pupils losing lessons.

In common with many heads whom we interviewed, Mr Shaw had had bad experiences of the press in the past, and now treated reporters with caution. He welcomed them in on many occasions to describe the good things that were happening in the school (the acquisition of a new minibus; the school's presentation evening), and took up local television's offer to participate in some of its programmes. He was determined to avoid a repetition of the incident some years earlier when accusations by a pupil of her victimisation by a member of the school's staff were debated in the press, 'who were thoroughly nasty'. In his view, it had a considerable rebound effect on the reputation of the school, something which worried him deeply. In general, he thought his relations with the press were good, but he remained suspicious of them.

In many ways I see the press as a pain, there's no control over them, no
guarantee of understanding on their part. They are an increasing pressure.
They're there like a shot if anything happens.

When Mr Mercer was approached by the media, he welcomed them in,
believing 'it pays to be nice'. When an anonymous letter was sent to the local
paper, claiming that children at the school were starving, he invited the
reporter to come and sample the menu:

> I told him he can come up. He'd like to bring a photographer. It's not our
> aggravation. We might want a favour from him when the next stone throwing
> incident occurs.

He warned the cook that the reporter was coming, suggested adding a sweet
to the menu that day and arranged for a few 'sensible kids' to be around for
the reporter to talk to. The stone throwing incident to which he referred
occurred a couple of years previously and had resulted in the media 'bom-
barding' the school:

> As far as they are concerned all bad news is good news. They're on the
> doorstep as soon as anything flares up. I never say 'no comment', I always say
> something. Yesterday they rang me for information for an article on schools
> falling down because of lack of money. I welcomed them to come and look at
> the school. It's not been decorated since 1971 but it's not falling down. If I
> can do them favours I will. I don't want to create enemies.

He responded willingly to a request from a television company to use pupils
and parents from the school for a programme on consumer views of education. Thus, by co-operating with the media on issues which presented the
school in a favourable light, he hoped to hold at bay the media's more
threatening presence. It was an approach which all four heads shared.
   School events attended by the public, particularly parents, were another
channel through which the heads sought to promote the school's public image. They all attended these events, but differed in their involvement in the
arrangements. Mr Shaw was the most concerned about the school's presentation to the public. His deputy commented about him, 'to the head,
presentation is everything'. This was demonstrated in his own performance
and the performance he expected from his staff and pupils at the many
events organised at the school. He had a list of people whom he would invite
to these events; it included the local MP, LEA officers and advisers, governors and other community members, and representatives from local industry. On the occasion of the school's special anniversary, he put a high
priority on doing 'a number of different things appealing to different
groups', in spite of a less enthusiastic response from his senior staff. This included a 'thank you buffet' for all those who had helped the school at County
Hall.

Although Mr Mercer also saw school events as important opportunities to present the school in a favourable light to the public, he supervised the details of the arrangements less closely than Mr Shaw and played a relatively low key role. In common with the other heads, he was always present at these events, attending, for example, the school musical on all five nights of its presentation. He acted as host when appropriate, serving sherry in the interval of the school's concert, showing parents to their seats at the centenary celebrations, but his contribution was more casual than Mr Shaw's, less orchestrated. Whereas Mr Shaw invariably appeared at public events alongside his senior management team, often taking backseat to their contribution, Mr Mercer was usually on his own and clearly identifiable as the head.

Mr King, like Mr Shaw, attributed considerable importance to school events as social occasions for promoting the school's image. At these events he would invite a large group of supporters of the school—members of the PTA, the caretaker and his wife, senior education officers, governors, secretaries and staff—for sherry beforehand and a buffet meal with wine afterwards. Mr King was clearly the host on such occasions: apart from issuing the invitations, organising the event with the head of home economics, greeting guests on arrival, introducing guests to one another, and filling up glasses, Mr King himself paid for the wine on some such occasions. It was on his initiatives that there were floral displays on the stage and fresh art work displayed in the foyer. He personally supervised the rehearsals for some of these events. Mr King wore a gown on some occasions, introduced the carol service and sang a solo verse, and gave an address at the award ceremony. In common with Mr Shaw, his close relations with parents and governors ensured their ready support and willing involvement.

Mr Dowe played a much less direct role in promoting the school's image at school events. He was supportive of staff involved in these, but did not play a prominent figurehead role himself. At parents' evenings, teachers were in and near a school hall; Mr Dowe was alone in his study, available to parents, at the other end of the school building.

The other part of heads' promotion of their image or that of the school takes place outside the school. Three of the heads sat on committees in the community which their school served: Mr Shaw was a governor of the local technical college, and Mr Mercer and Mr King sat on youth centre management committees. Mr King also sat on the local Dr Barnado's and Community Concern committees. Mr Dowe's regular work in the area was confined to the joint falling rolls committee of his school and the neighbouring one. Mr Mercer was chairman of the school's old boys' association.

As well as being involved with particular organisations, most of the heads worked in the community in other ways. Mr Shaw referred to the need to cultivate the interest and support of the local Member of Parliament, to forward the school's interests. The MP had been impressed by the school's use of achievement files for each pupil, to record any type of progress; and had requested examples to show to the Secretary of State for Education. He was also interested in developing TVEI in local schools, and expressed an interest in developing links between the school and local industry. For his part, Mr Shaw was also eager to attract resources to the school and therefore keen to maintain the MP's interest.

> I recognise him as our MP. One needs to have tolerably good working relations whatever the political colour. It's a useful aid for secondary heads to get things done.

As a result of his own particular interest in careers education and his membership of the county's careers in-service training committee, he had established links with the training officer of a large well-established local industrial complex as well as with new industrial ventures in the locality. Membership of this committee also brought him in contact with other heads, teacher centre representatives, and the university. He saw potential advantages to the school, in terms of additional resources, as a result of cultivating these different sources of support.

As well as maintaining strong links with local firms, in case of future TVEI developments, Mr Shaw also had a network of personal contacts for possible work-experience placements for pupils. The school was very involved in the local community's twinning arrangements with towns in France and Germany and Mr Shaw had accompanied parties twice on official visits. He also had close links with the local parish church, which the school used on occasions. Members of the community, including a local bank manager, acted as trustees for the school's enrichment fund. Mr Shaw also had links with the Rotary Club (although he was not a member) which had made a video of the school which was used to present the school to interested visitors.

Mr Mercer's involvement with the community was not very different from Mr Shaw's. He knew, personally, a number of local employers and enjoyed contacting them either in relation to work experience placements for pupils from the school (he put a high priority on finding jobs for pupils) or to take up matters to do with the buildings and use of equipment. For example, he tried when possible to use local builders he knew rather than ones sent from the LEA. When there was a query about the cost of a coach trip, he contacted the coach company directly, as he was on first name terms with its boss.

> Let's ring up the coach company then. Nothing like striking while the iron is hot. Hello Tom (gave him all the details)...Get out of it. I know you go to Corfu for your holidays, mate, but think about the rest of us!...OK Tom, I'm sure you will. Ta.Ta.

On another occasion he composed a letter to local businessmen asking them to finance the school's Duke of Edinburgh scheme. He enjoyed drawing on this local business contacts—the local bank manager, and the garage owner from whom the school bought or rented cars at advantageous prices.

In common with the other heads, Mr Mercer was concerned to maintain a good image of the school in the eyes of the community. When the school's neighbours complained about children climbing over their walls, he stationed himself at strategic points at lunchtimes and after school to prevent pupils using these routes; made them apologise to the neighbours when caught and invited the neighbours to school concerts. In his view:

> The community has a no-nonsense attitude to the school. They have an image that there's a lot of help for kids in the school. They trust the school.

The community policeman called regularly in to the school and would chat with the head on those occasions over coffee. On his way on foot between buildings, Mr Mercer would call at the cafés and amusement arcades to see if any of his pupils were there. He did not trust the community as a place for the children too be loose in, and was unwilling to consider community service as a mode three option because this would release the children into it. He was concerned about truanting girls in particular, as his catchment included the city's red light district. This was reflected in his response, at an area heads' meeting, to proposals to turn schools in the LEA into community schools:

> I'm not really sure what we're aiming at. At one moment we're welcoming the LEA's support in being able to dispel intruders. Now we're saying let anyone in...Not all of us have such salubrious areas that we want to let anyone in. We don't mind the law-abiding ones.

His contacts with local employers were less formal than Mr Shaws', taking place mainly over the phone rather than in meetings. He expressed his disappointment when the deputy decided to discontinue an exchange scheme between teachers and a local firm, while industrial action was taking place. He wrote to the head of the firm saying:

> I'm sad to see the way (the visits) have fallen through last term. I want to continue the link regardless of industrial action and would be able to honour any commitments made.

He maintained contact with the local churches, including the Sikh temple, through the community liaison workers. As a member of the youth centre's management committee, he regularly met other community representatives from adult education and the church.

Mr King, of the four heads, was probably the most firmly embedded in the local comunity: this was personal as well as professional—he was a long-standing member of it. His earlier political activity meant that he knew local politicians well: two particularly prominent MPs had visited the school on a number of occasions, and he maintained close links with local members of the Authority.

As a local man, he was particularly well informed about, and sensitive to, local opinion about the school. Like Mr Shaw, he supervised pupils boarding the buses daily, and dealt promptly and firmly with reported misdemeanours on the buses. He saw that local pensioners were given free tickets to school events. Like Mr Mercer, he had close contact with local shopkeepers, and patrolled the street to the nearest shop on occasions. The local community was not something 'out there' which he had to work with; he was a part of it, and accepted the legitimacy of its concerns.

Mr King knew who the local employers were, but did not himself deal with them. He shared with Mr Mercer a preference for arranging repair work with local suppliers rather than the LEA, having a keen awareness of their superior prices and service. His contacts with the local Sikh community were largely delegated to his pastoral co-ordinator. He felt that they were prepared to make persistent and unreasonable demands on the school, but were not constructive or active when it came to actually doing something.

Like Mr Mercer, he had close contact with the community policeman, whom he met at least once a week. He joined Mr King for a drink on occasions, as an outside speaker he taught some of his classes, and he would stop for a chat—either around the school or by calling in at Mr King's room. Occasionally Mr King rang him at the station—and got an efficient response. As heads of inner-city schools, both Mr King and Mr Mercer were active in encouraging the community policeman's involvement in the school, as a preventitive strategy, as well as maintaining regular contacts with the police locally at committee meetings or social events.

In Mr King's case, such promotion of the image of the school in the community cannot be separated from his membership of that community. He saw his involvement, in his capacity as head of the local comprehensive, as an important presence: he saw himself as a leader in the locality. He felt that other people noticed his involvement, and appreciated it. His involvement also had a pragmatic aspect:

> And you get a lot of good results, you can get a lot of sort of spin-offs from it, you know—if you need any help you can ring up people and say, 'Look, I've got a bit of a problem, can you sort this out for me'.

By comparison, Mr Dowe was hardly involved in the community around his school. He was not involved in placing pupils with local employers, nor did he have any pro-active contact with politicians (beyond his governors). He did not sit on any community bodies or committees; and nor did he personally place repairs or other orders with local businesses. In short, despite his expressed commitment to community schooling and previous experience in that type of school, his focus as head of St Mary's was essentially within the school. He did, however, encourage his colleagues to work in the community—and would himself play a figurehead role where appropriate: for example, when the local chemical company sent some staff to the school as a contribution of the Girls into Science and Technology programme.

The third area of the head's work for the school outside it is their contact with colleague headteachers. Here we consider only their local contact; in the following section, where we discuss their professional work beyond the school, we consider their broader (regional and national) involvement in headteacher organisations. We consider their local contact with heads in terms of individual contact, heads' meetings, and their professional associations; and conclude with a discussion of the significance they attach to their collegial relations.

Much of the contact with individual heads was over the phone, although they met together at headteacher meetings and on committees. The reason for many of the phone contacts was staffing; asking if they had suitable people for a vacancy or requesting references on staff who had applied. For example, one head rang Mr Dowe about a history teacher from St Mary's who had applied for a head of department post. Mr Dowe advised him:

> No I wouldn't appoint her head of history, she's extraordinarily sound...she goes through the old approaches of teaching it...she goes through pages 1 to page 97 with a toothcomb. Sound, reliable, but I don't think she's inspirational enough to be a head of department. She gets good results...I can't fault her for marking books, preparing lessons, discipline, but she's not a head of department, she's a good number two...

The colleague grapevine was always used when local applicants were involved and sometimes to headteachers in other Authorities. Mr Shaw, for example, used his wide network of contacts to follow up external applicants for a head of history post. All heads put a great deal of reliance on this kind of referee.

Other phone calls related to pupils, often awkward ones, who were being transferred. On these occasions, the heads used each other for information which might not have been documented. They also used each other as sounding boards, to discover how a particular policy was working in another school—perhaps to use in their negotiations with the LEA. During the industrial action, in particular, there were calls to colleagues to see what the unions in their school were saying, and what responses the head was making. This was particularly important in the absence of guidelines from the LEA. Phoning a colleague head also provided an opportunity for social chat, in the course of the working day, something which the heads' partial exclusion from staffrooms otherwise made difficult.

They also met colleague heads at meetings and courses. Their contact was mainly at local heads' meetings: in one LEA all secondary heads met monthly at the teachers centre for about two hours; in the other LEA there were area meetings twice a term and a termly meeting with the Director. Mr Mercer also met about twice a term with a group of local heads, who considered their schools' close geographical location gave them something in common. Unlike the other three heads, Mr Dowe rarely attended any such heads' meeting. He was timetabled to teach at the time the meeting took place, but he always sent a deputy in his place. Other than close liaison with the head of the adjacent school on their shared problem of falling rolls, he demonstrated little need or desire for close affiliation with headteacher colleagues in the LEA. He was, however, both a member of Council and editor of the twice yearly review of his region's heads' body. He felt that this body's discussion of educational principles distinguished it from the LEA group, which he saw as concerned with day to day issues. The other three heads considered their meetings with colleague headss in their LEAs useful and desirable to attend heads' meetings for the social discourse they provided, as well as business, e.g., borrowing equipment, recommending staff, sharing information and experiences, deciding on concerned action vis-à-vis the Authority.

In each Authority, the LEA's headteacher conference followed a similar pattern. The chairman and secretary, elected annually by their peers, sat at a table facing those assembled; it was unusual for an absent head not to send apologies, there was sometimes a full complement, and attendance never fell below 70 per cent. Occasionally substitute deputy heads were present. At the Docklands' headteachers' conference, speakers—for example a neighbouring LEA's adviser on a curriculum initiative—were often invited; sometimes the guests would be senior officers of the Authority. We never heard outside speakers at Brayside's headteachers' conference, and never saw officers present. Joint meetings were held with them and the director of education, once a term. At both conferences, the few minutes before and after the main proceedings, and the tea break, were used for social chat or to exchange information—one head might ask another about a pupil transfer, redeployee, or LEA action over playing fields, for example.

In Docklands, the essence of the meeting, however, was the transmission of information from the Authority to its heads. Officers and heads debated the points being made, sometimes in a heated, but respectful, way. It was, however, very much the *heads'* conference. Any invited officers stayed only for the agenda item with which they were concerned. Brayside used the occasion exclusively for collecting heads' responses to LEA directives or current problems. During the industrial action, at both conferences, the heads spent some time planning their strategy regarding the LEA—and comparing notes on what was happening in other schools and what their colleagues there were doing. Often there was strong disagreement, in the case of the industrial action for example, because of different interpretations of their duty.

Both groups of heads arranged social events in the course of the year, involving spouses and presentations to retiring heads. Three of the heads made frequent contributions to the meetings, although Mr Shaw had an additional reputation among his peers as a mentor, perhaps as one of the longest-serving heads in the Authority and as one who 'had the director's ear' (although he did not see this as the case). He was also known as local convenor of his professional association and was, therefore, someone sought for advice.

Mr Shaw, as well as being convenor of the local branch, was on the national executive and several committees. This provided him with an interest beyond his school which, apart from its intrinsic satisfaction, gave him a extensive knowledge of what other heads did.

Regular phone contacts with other local heads and attendance at their meetings were two important sources of support for the heads in their work. In this way they got to know what others were doing, something about which they were otherwise very much in the dark. Their deputies provided another source of information about what was happening in other schools. The heads even expressed a discreet interest in how we, as researchers, found the others we were working with. They knew that other heads did things differently but were unsure about what and how; and even showed at times, some insecurity about how their own practices compared. What they knew of each other, however, seemed limited. Mr Mercer, for example, said, 'I don't know how heads manage who are regularly out for two days a week', while Mr Shaw could not understand how a head could run a school without the series of scheduled meetings which he organised.

Mr King sometimes compared his own performance with that of other heads in the Authority, with anecdotal knowledge of his colleagues. Only Mr Dowe remained rather estranged from his local colleagues and rarely sought their support and advice; although he was active in his broader, regional heads' group.

Working professionally beyond the school

None of the four heads' contribution to education was confined to a narrow concern for their school; but the degree of their contribution beyond this varied considerably in scope and extent. In Mr King's case, this contribution was largely local; Mr Mercer's spread to a regional level, and Mr Shaw and Mr Dowe had national as well as local commitments.

Mr King was the headteachers' representative on the management committee of his LEA's assessment centre for children with special needs. This involved him in a monthly afternoon meeting with the school's head, one of the centre's staff and several LEA officers. One reason for his involvement in this was to enable him to look after the interests of his own school more closely—he was in a good position to support or oppose a proposed course of action in relation to individual pupils who may have come from or be going to Aley Park.

As the head of one of the few schools within the Authority with a racially mixed catchment, Mr King was considered suitable for membership of the LEA's multi-cultural committee. This had been set up on the initiative of members of the Authority, though Mr King said that he did not agree with its general approach—and had told its members that their ideas would not work in practice. The committee met a few times each year. He was also a local representative in the regional schools' Football Association, and attended occasional meetings of that throughout the region. He also attended occasional lectures or meetings locally: for example, on child abuse at the neighbouring town's university; on an educational panel answering students' questions at a teacher training college; and about education at the local university.

Mr Mercer attended the director's headteachers' meeting for a day three times a year, as well as the area and district heads' meeting described earlier; sat on the LEA's multi-cultural education consultative committee, the management committee of the reading and learning resources centre, and on the committee of the youth club serving his school. Outside the Authority, he sat on the regional CSE exam board, attending this about once every two months.

Mr Dowe did not sit on any local committees, but had a high involvement in examining. His main commitment in this area was as representative of his local board on a subject committee of the Secondary Examinations Council, which involved him in meetings throughout the region.

Mr Shaw, like Mr Mercer, attended his director's headteachers' meetings, and was very active beyond his school both locally and nationally. As something of an expert on careers education (he had previously been a head of careers and had published books in this area), he sat on the LEA's careers advisory group and careers in-service training committee. He was also on the Authority's curriculum panel curriculum review group and, as local convenor of his professional association, on the ATCC, which met monthly. He was a member of the local technical college's governing body; and, stemming from his own religious affiliation, of the Free Church Federal Council Education Committee. He was an UCCA trustee, and on CSE council; and, taking up more of his time than any other outside school activity, an officer in SHA.

In some cases these outside activities were volunteered for; in others the body concerned had approached the head concerned. Clearly, heads are, or can put themselves, in a position where they are likely to receive such requests. Receiving such requests, choices have to be made; and the dividing line between a request to the head of the school or to the individual is often unclear. The patterns of professional work beyond the school displayed by the four heads demonstrate the choices that they have made. Mr King, the only one of the four not involved in examining, felt quite firmly that a head should be in the school as much as possible. He saw his outside activities as meeting expectations the local community had of its secondary school head rather than his own personal development needs; and for pragmatic reasons.

> You get a lot of good results...spin-offs...if you need any help you can ring up people...
> I find out things about the community that I wouldn't know about unless I went to these meetings.

Mr Shaw saw his work with his professional association in particular as stimulating, and improving his own work. He described it as 'a blast of continuing in-service training, much better than going on courses'. He made significant contributions to many of the activities he engaged in, and saw himself bringing useful knowledge and information back into the school. He was the only one of the four whom we saw discuss with his senior colleagues whether to take on a particular outside activity.

Mr Mercer did not see how a head could run his school if he was out for two days a week; and only took on what he saw as a necessary extension of his school work. It was mainly in the community, and with the LEA, although he too saw his attendance at the CSE Exam Board meetings as an important way of gathering information about current curriculum developments to feed back into the school.

In contrast, Mr Dowe was not involved with organisations in the local community; examining was the focus of his outside work. He saw this as an extension of his role as head, although separate. In his view, the content of schooling was so closely tied to the examination system that the latter largely controlled the former. An example he gave was of a teacher who, in his view, dictated too many notes and in other ways had a traditional teaching style, but whose pupils achieved good examination results. He was particularly concerned with preparing his colleagues for the GCSE, with its emphasis on criterion referencing and course work. In Mr Dowe's view, education meant more than exam achievement, but he felt there was little that he could do to change such a traditional teaching style when it was meeting parental expectations and pupil success. In other words, he saw examining as something outside the school which fundamentally determined what went on within it; and for this reason—as well as his own subject interest—was involved in 'A' Level examining and various exam boards' 16+ discussions.

Summary

In this section we summarise each of the four heads' work outside the school: working with parents, working with the LEA, presenting the school, and working professionally beyond the school.

All four heads described their relationship with parents as a partnership, both to us and in documents provided by their schools to parents. They were keen to get the good will of parents and to that end, welcomed parents into the school individually and at larger school functions, where they maintained high visibility. As well as welcoming parents into the school and discussing individual pupils with them, they saw themselves as mediating between parents and staff on contentious issues. Other than at larger public functions, they tended to see parents mainly in relation to 'awkward' cases, late new admissions, suspended pupils or pupils otherwise in trouble, and pupils with personal problems.

In spite of this common emphasis on encouraging parents to see themselves as partners in the school's activity, the four heads defined partnership differently. Mr Shaw responded to it as an equal partnership in which he encouraged parents to maintain a high profile in the school and involved them fully in any disciplinary measures regarding their child. He saw parents as providing important feedback on the school's effectiveness in a number of ways: bringing to his attention any classroom weaknesses and strengths, and demonstrating the school's popularity through choosing it in preference to other schools. Although he delegated a substantial amount of work through the clearly delineated pastoral system he used formal channels and informal grapevines to keep himself informed of what was happening. While not always taking the centre of the stage at public events, he was always clearly visible as the host and ensured personal contact with every new parent by doing any late, new admissions himself.

As in all his other work as a head, Mr King remained firmly centre-stage in relation to parents, often wearing a gown at public events, increasing his visibility. They were as likely to see him as other members of staff on visiting the school, as he enjoyed working with them. He saw the PTA as the most enjoyable part of his work. He saw some new parents himself, more out of personal interest than from a concern to attract more parents to the school, which he did not see as being in competition with others.

Mr Mercer welcomed parents in to the school, seeing them when necessary but not encouraging much involvement beyond that concerning their own child. Most of his dealings with parents were by phone, since the majority of matters relating to individual pupil welfare were delegated to his deputies. In common with Mr King he did not see the school as being in competition with other schools and did not therefore view parental choice as a gauge of the school's effectiveness, or become involved in new admissions. His contacts with parents were mainly over ethos rather than educational matters and any feedback he received from them tended to be about negative rather than positive issues. He described them as partners more in controlling their children than in educating them.

Mr Dowe, in contrast, was ambivalent about the parents' role in educating children. His close involvement and interest with older pupils meant that he saw parents of new entrants at the upper end of the school himself, so he could stress to them the range of academic choice. Parents of pupils in his catchment formed a vocal group, with a strong interest in curriculum matters. He resisted their attempts to become more involved in the curriculum at the same time as courting their children for his sixth form. Most other aspects of dealing with parents (other than disputes between teachers and pupils) were delegated.

Each of the heads expressed some concern about greater interference from their LEAs in some school matters: provision and allocation of scale points; greater involvement in appointments; and systematic curriculum review. Three of the four heads dealt on a daily basis with a wide range of individuals in the different LEA departments (mainly by phone). Their responses to increasing LEA imperatives were different.

In our discussion of the heads' relations with their respective LEAs during the teachers' action, we commented on their differing loyalties to their own staff and to the LEA. Mr Shaw remained pragmatic; Mr Dowe stood against the LEA; Mr Mercer and Mr King demonstrated their allegiance to the LEA. When matters of redeployment and selection were involved, Mr Shaw aimed to involve the Authority as little as possible, though having no choice about interviewing redeployed candidates from within the Authority. Mr Dowe went along reluctantly with the Authority's attempted domination of appointments in the school, as did Mr Mercer, though the pressure from this Authority was less. Mr King allowed the Authority to dominate the process in appointments at the lower end of the scale but tried to promote his own internal choices at the upper end. In both Authorities, moves were being made to reorganise schools as a result of falling rolls; Mr Mercer and Mr King accepted the Authority's reorganisation plans, which had little impact on Mr King's school but considerable repercussions for Mr Mercer's. Mr Shaw fought the Authority's decision to reduce his intake numbers but accepted defeat without resentment. Mr Dowe, in contrast, was singularly unimpressed by the officers of his Authority and particularly angry over redeployment and promotion procedures, despite having accepted the necessity of reducing his intake. All heads were critical of individual officers within their Authority and found some easier to work with than others. This partiality was only evident in their comments to us; their usual mode of working was cooperative and uncritical, although Mr Shaw once lost his temper over the telephone to LEA administrators whom he judged to have been incompetent. In their contact with LEA officers and advisers (several times a day in the case of Mr King, once or twice daily with Mr Mercer and Mr Shaw and least frequently with Mr Dowe) they were often involved in seeking additional resources for their school and used diplomacy rather than confrontation as their main form of communication. Additionally they cultivated officers socially, inviting them to school events, treating them as important visitors when they arrived in the school. While these three heads responded to the LEA as a partner in achieving the aims of their school (albeit a partner which sometimes did not pull its weight) Mr Dowe saw the Authority as opposed to the interests of the school.

Rather than identifying members of their governing bodies with the LEA, the heads saw them as potential allies in any battles they might have with it. Even Mr Dowe, who generally received little interest or support from his governors, tried to win their allegiance in his fight against the LEA's decisions about staffing at St Mary's. Both Mr Shaw and Mr King worked closely with their governing bodies, from which they had firm support. As in his other working relations, Mr Shaw treated his governors as partners in the process of running the school, ensuring the availability to them of comprehensive information and full opportunity to discuss any issues about which they were concerned. Thus he was able to rely on their support about uniforms (although the Authority did not support their enforcement), and buildings (requiring a number of modifications). In contrast, Mr Mercer in the same Authority disagreed with his governors about uniforms (they were in accord with the Authority's view); considered that they did not understand staffing issues; but saw them as useful allies in fighting for more physical resources for the school. In general, Mr King's governors reflected the views of the Authority, with which he was in broad agreement; thus, there was little conflict between them and he felt he could rely on their support, even if he was sometimes selective in the information he made available to them. He saw them as important allies.

Finally we looked at the four heads' involvement in work outside the school, including other professional activities. We showed how all four heads had a similar approach to the media, ensuring that they used them to the school's advantage before the media used the heads to the school's disadvantage. Bringing good things that were happening in the school was just one way of presenting a favourable image of the school to the outside world, alongside other events to which the public were invited. The main difference between them was in the extent to which they orchestrated the school's performance, in a way which ensured that the image they wanted to convey was the one given. Both Mr Shaw and Mr King took considerable trouble over the details of public occasions.

Each head had a different kind of involvement with the community served by the school. Both Mr King and Mr Mercer in inner-city, multi-ethnic schools, ventured often into the community surrounding the schools, although for different reasons. Mr King saw himself as part of the community, one in which he had grown up and with which he identified. Mr Mercer, who lived just outside his catchment area, was distrustful of the influences which the local community could bring to bear on youngsters in his school; his forays into the nearby streets and shops were equally to protect the youngsters from the community as the community from the youngsters. Both, however, enjoyed using personal contacts in the community to provide services more economically and more speedily to the school. Mr Shaw's relationship with the community served by his school was more formal, in part as a result of the school's situation some distance from shops and houses. He knew local shopkeepers and business owners and participated in many of the community's civic events. Although he did not see himself as part of the community, he encouraged his pupils' participation in community events and kept in touch with developments through his governors. His contacts with representatives from local industry were part of his longer term plans for bringing resources to the school, rather than for any immediate material benefits which might accrue. Mr Dowe had little to do with the community in which St Mary's was situated, although he lived just beyond the catchment. He saw his main concern as with the educational processes that took place inside the school. He delegated to others the responsibility for developing and maintaining networks of those who might be of help from outside the school.

In choosing to become involved in other professional activities, the four heads demonstrated relative autonomy in deciding how often they would be out of school and for what reasons. Mr Shaw was out of school more than the others. Mr King was out of school least, preferring to remain at the centre of things, with his finger on every pulse and visible at every turn. His other professional activities were limited to local commitments to community activities which would reinforce links between the community and the school. Similarly, Mr Mercer preferred to remain in school as much as possible, even though he enjoyed the diversion of external activities. In spite of extensive delegation, he saw control as centred around his own presence and only took on outside commitments where these were pressed on him rather than from choice. In contrast Mr Dowe saw his extensive examining commitments as providing him with the knowledge and stimulus necessary to fulfill successfully his educator role. Examining took a considerable amount of his time at certain periods in the year.

Many of these other professional activities involved contacts with other heads, locally and nationally. These contacts provided the four heads with an important reference group, particularly in the absence of anyone of the same status in their schools. Even Mr Shaw, who saw his 'senior management team' as 'one of the main protections against the isolation of headship', took pleasure in comparing notes with other heads. Only Mr Dowe eschewed attendance at the LEA's headteachers' conference and rarely contacted other heads by phone during working hours, except to provide a reference. For the others, the phone provided ready access to other heads' recommendations of staff and strategies for the different situations which arose daily. Similarly, the headteachers' conference held in each LEA represented a welcome forum to exchange views and experiences and create a united front against whatever group was currently threatening the heads' mode of operation—whether teachers, governors, the media, the LEA or central government itself.

·V·

What Others Say about the Heads

● 12 ●

The views of school staff, LEA officers and advisers

We have so far been primarily concerned to present a picture of headship based on our observation of headteachers doing the job. In this chapter we look at others' views of the heads with whom they work, on the basis of interviews with teaching and non-teaching staff in fifteen schools: and officers and advisers in nine LEAs.

The views of school staff

The purpose of our interviews with staff was to identify those aspects of headship which staff considered important. In each school we covered a spectrum of staff including some members of the school's support staff, in particular the caretaker and a member of the administrative staff.

Comments by staff described their perceptions of headship and the type of contact they had with their heads, distinguishing between their head's availability or accessibility; his or her approachability, by which was meant the extent to which the head is perceived to invite or avoid personal contact with rank and file teachers; and visibility, or presence around the school. Only two of the fifteen heads were described as readily available, easily approachable and with a high degree of visibility in the school. They were both seen as being in touch with both pupils and staff. It was clear from the other patterns of availability, accessibility and visibility that emerged, that a high profile in one did not necessarily accompany a high profile in the other.

Six heads were described as readily available but staff had reservations about how visible they were, or how easy it was to approach them or obtain a response. Their comments suggested that often they saw something in the head's interpersonal style which made social contact uncomfortable or problematic. The head's social ability to influence staff was seen as important to teacher morale. Staff seemed to refer to those attributes classically seen as constituting a definition of leadership, whether in its people aspect (i.e., the cluster of attributes often termed *consideration*) or as applied to the tasks which must be accomplished (i.e., the cluster of attributes often termed *initiating structure*).

In summary, we found four patterns of staff perceptions of the relationship between a headteacher's availability, accessibility and staff morale. These are shown in Figure 12.1.

When we interviewed the heads' senior staff colleagues, we asked them to describe the pattern of their contact with their head and how work was divided amongst senior staff. There were three patterns or working styles described: those heads who mainly shared major administrative tasks with colleagues (e.g. Mr Shaw); those who mainly delegated to colleagues (e.g. Mr Dowe); and those who mainly performed such tasks themselves (e.g. Mr King and to some extent, Mr Mercer).

Staff perceptions of the extent to which their headteachers consulted them as part of the decision-making process suggested three different ways in which individual heads consulted. These are shown in Figure 12.2.

In contrast, non-teaching staff were less concerned with formal consultative processes than with the extent to which they saw headteachers as giving them autonomy in their jobs. The majority of non-teaching staff were mainly uncritical of their working relationship with the head. Some

Figure 12.1 Staff perceptions of their headteacher's availability, accessibility, visibility and contribution to staff morale

---

Type A: are easily available, have an easy manner with staff who are not reluctant to approach him or her, are visible and present around the school, and know how staff and pupils are thinking and behaving.

Type B: are easily available and approachable but do not circulate enough around the school and know less well what staff and pupils are thinking and doing.

Type C: are available and may be highly visible, but lack *consideration* in their interpersonal style which makes some staff less willing to approach them. They are seen as not fully in touch with all staff. Mr Mercer and Mr King came into this group.

Type D: are not easily available because of other commitments. They are less visible around the school than staff would like, although thought by some to be in touch with how staff and pupils are feeling and behaving. Mr Dowe and Mr Shaw came into this category.

Figure 12.2 Staff perceptions of how far their headteachers take their views into account in decision-making

---

Type A: are seen to consult and take staff views into account when arriving at decisions, Mr Dowe is in this group.

Type B: are seen to consult but some staff feel unsure about the extent to which their views influence the decisions. Mr Shaw is in this group.

Type C: consult sporadically and are selective in whose views they seek. Mr Mercer and Mr King are in this category.

---

secretaries wished that heads would be more systematic in letting them know their whereabouts; but generally non-teaching staff considered they were given the right amount of freedom and support in their job.

Overall, the qualities which staff identified to us as important characteristics of headship related mainly to sensitivity and communication. They responded to their headteacher's degree of availability and accessibility, visibility, supportiveness, and knowledge about what was going on in the school. However much the value to the school of the head's outside activities was recognised, if the activities made him or her less readily available, or less of a visible presence around the school, then they were seen as detractors from, rather than enhancers of effectiveness. Staff emphasised the wish for heads to be present and direct contact. The proviso was that the head's presence be accompanied by approachability; that is, an interpersonal manner which puts staff at ease and makes them feel they are really being listened to and their views are likely to be taken into account.

The views of LEA officers and advisers

Before our fieldwork with the fifteen heads in twelve LEAs we interviewed an officer and an adviser in each LEA, about headship. The interviews were designed to elicit; (a) expectations of headteachers, and (b) the nature of their contact with their heads, and the basis of their knowledge of them. In particular, we asked about the characteristics of good and bad heads in their authorities. From their descriptions, we built up a picture of desirable headship traits as perceived by these officers and advisers.

Delegation was associated with good headship practice. Respondents said of particularly good headteachers they worked with:

He delegates a lot of admin.

Good at delegating ... working parties galore.

> It's well run 'cos there's large degree of delegation. The headteacher is advised by groups of committees.

Conversely, bad heads delegate insufficiently:

> He fails to delegate.
>
> He should delegate finance.
>
> He must consult more ... *thorough* delegation ... so the head can become free of routine responsibilites.

They also pointed to the dangers of over-delegation:

> The weak head delegates everything, lets the school run itself.
>
> (Of an allegedly badly run school): Over delegation ... King John.

There was no one overall style associated with 'good' headship practice. One chief adviser said that, of the two he saw as his best heads, 'one delegates a lot ... the other is more hierarchical'. Another said of those he saw as his worst two heads, 'one is authoriarian, the other over delegates'. Or, again, 'one has very centralised decision-making—an autocrat ... The other has an extremely complex participatory decision-making structure'. So, rather than equating quality of headship with autocratic, participatory, or democratic structures, what was seen as important was that the structure should be made explicit. A chief adviser described those he saw as his two worst heads as characterised by 'inconsistency of decision making; lack of definition of roles'. Another respondent said of similar heads 'no long term goals or consultation mechanism on these'. Best run schools had 'clear decision-making processes'.

Consultation was associated with good headship:

> He always discusses everything with his staff, and will stop it if they are not willing to go along with it.
>
> Heads should try to arrive at all decisions by consensus.
>
> Democratic, prepared to listen, uses staff meetings to arrive at a consensus ...
>
> There's a feeling of togetherness.
>
> Frequent meetings. They discuss the problems openly. They listen to what people are saying. Attempt to get a consensus. Try to involve everybody.

Conversely, a head running a bad school was described as:

> Secretive. Quick decisions are made by the senior management team without consulting staff ... a lack of consistency ... pretty autocratic.

Most respondents referred to the association of less well-run schools with weak working relationships with or between members of senior staff.

There's a lack of direction from the senior management team . . .

The senior management team is totally disorganised. It shows everywhere.

There's probably too much reliance on the deputies providing the answers.

He doesn't have a strong enough senior staff; Doesn't draw them out and inspire them.

The good head was identified by most as one who, whatever his or her style, was able to carry staff with him or her, in spite of diminishing staff morale in a contracting situation and the ever present diversity of staff views.

Heads have got to carry with them people who are sticking. It's all about man management.
Good management is the capacity of the head to get on the right side of staff and make them feel they have a part in the total management of the school.
Heads have got to be able to manage teams of thinking individuals. They've got to make sure different groups aren't going in different directions.
Heads need training in interpersonal skills, to learn not to alienate people, to build on their strengths and weaknesses.
The staff trust her, regard her judgements as sound. She takes the view, give us whatever staff, we'll get on with it.

In contrast, less successful heads were described in terms of managerial inadequacies.

A staff member was saying to the Area Education Officer what a terrible manager he is. The AEO said she should not comment personally. She said, 'Don't worry, he says it about himself.'
There's a divisiveness about the staff. Dissatisfaction . . . the head can either be extremely autocratic or show fumbling ineptitude.

Several described 'good' heads as having selected their staff carefully and well:

This (well-run) school relies on charisma and the astuteness of the headteacher in selecting and developing staff.
The success of the (well-run) school depends on the personality of the head and the staff he had appointed. He has been in post long enough to appoint staff who are sympathetic to his aims.
He was ruthless in the evaluation of staff . . . Those who were unsuitable, he drove out. He would send teachers cuttings from the TES; then, if that didn't work, he sent for the application forms on school notepaper, with the teacher's signature . . . Staff were handpicked.

Conversely, weaker heads were described as appointing staff of only average quality.

Others pick the less able in their own image. They get them to follow and then don't lead.

(Good heads) recruit around them a management team of quality. On the other hand with less good headteachers, without the personal quality—one gets insecurity. The people around them will be those who do not threaten them.

Of 'good' heads it was said:

One does it in a paternalistic way, one through meetings.

The staff respect the views of the head. She gains the respect of the staff because of her views and actions.

Curriculum aims must be agreed by staff, and staff committed to them.

. . . The head, senior management team and staff have clear goals, which are understood by all, so there's a unity of purpose.

A sense of purpose and the possession of long-term aims were also seen as attributes of well-run schools. Schools which were referred to as badly run were said not to have clear aims and objectives. Of schools described as badly run, it was said:

There's a lack of clarity about aims, a general wooliness, staff not knowing where they are and no means for working out aims . . . there's a lack of consistency, unexplained changes . . .

The head is unclear about his school's aims or the aims are not in the interest of the children.

Turning to heads' work with pupils, respondents spoke of badly run schools having disaffected pupils, and *vice versa*. Several respondents spoke highly of heads who knew most of their pupils:

He knows all nine hundred children in the school.

I'd be firmly at the extreme of saying it's the head's job to know the children and be known by them. One of the good heads (cited) deliberately teaches around the school

Respondents spoke of good heads achieving the maximum potential of all pupils, and maximising their aspirations: and contrasted this with pupil disruption and frustration which resulted from bad heads being in post.

Good administration was seen as important, and well-run schools led by heads with a synoptic view:

Well run and administered. She uses flow charts and structures everything.

Good administration—in one (school). It's down from the head, the other (school) it comes up from the staff, for example, if it's decided to change the curriculum, this actually gets organised on the timetable.

Other heads were criticised for their high involvement with trivia.

. . . heads caught up in day to day difficulties. Heads of faculty meetings won't go beyond capitation—if that.

> There's a danger of officers and heads being too narrow about administration. Heads shouldn't babble too much about administration, the trivia of running a school, and miss what's at issue.

In come cases 'good' schools were associated with the head's active role in encouraging parental involvement and winning parental support:

> Parents think school is like it was thirty years ago. The head must help them understand the changes, explain them to parents. In some things it's sensible for parents to come in *en masse*, be welcomed to the school, the informal availability of staff. But they need to make the school genuinely available to parents by encouraging them to come in.

> Heads have to see them (parents) all. Some don't react to them as they ought. Some parents are pretty obstreporous. An authoritarian head will react differently. Any parent who comes or writes has to be dealt with courteously and properly.

Heads were described by some in terms of their ability to respond to the particular needs of the parents in the community served by their school. In one Authority, two less effective heads were seen as differing in their ability to handle parental expectations:

> His school serves a downtown area...He's a good PR man...so probably parents don't react too badly. In the other, also a downtown one, there's a feeling from parents of wanting to shoot the headmaster. He'd never have survived elsewhere. But because of a battering from parents he's being careful not to put a foot wrong...The first has survived by manipulating parents. He wouldn't survive in a more sophisticated area either.

> The pupils' and parents' perception is that it works, because it's providing the discipline the children need. It's serving an ill-favoured area where parents wouldn't normally choose the school for their children.

Several respondents saw the head's ability to foster good relations with the community as an essential feature of the school's effectiveness:

> The head is firm, sympathetic, very friendly, has a wide range of interests outside of education and is strong on developing good relations with the community.

> He follows the principle of embracing as many people in as many ways as he can. He's brought in people from the local community and has a successful voluntary organisation based there.

> In these two schools the head and staff seek and capitalise on the opportunity for getting the school out into the community.

There was agreement among the officers and advisers that a head needed to be a good public relations person for his or her school:

> He is also a public relations man for his establishment, a function which is often undervalued. The image of the school and of the headteacher is often

concordant...And lastly, he is the ambassador of the education service in the community, dealing with employers...it is a big job.

The community is wanting someone who looks, sounds, and behaves like a head, who presents to the community at large the credibility of the organisation...a lot of them are becoming public relations experts, salesmen.

As a result of this belief, poor heads were often described as those who, among other things, were failing in their public relations.

As well as discussing the characteristics they associated with heads whom they saw as running their schools well or badly, respondents commented on a number of other aspects of heads' work. All emphasised the increased demands on heads' interpersonal skills, particularly in the context of falling rolls and redeployment.

They have also got to deal with staff morale. That means a real change to previous management styles.

The effects on staff are serious. They look at the number of parents making the school first choice. If they get more applications they feel they are doing well. It means the head's counselling role will become important, something for which they aren't trained.

Relations with teachers' associations

With the exception of one Authority, officers and advisers did not see relations between heads and teacher associations as creating problems, although there was seen to be some variability in how effectively heads dealt with the unions in schools.

We'd expect a head to manage not to be beaten by them, handle them reasonably by consultation. We try to support the headteacher, though if he steps out of line, we don't.

One officer referred to the fact that some heads were more tested by teacher unions than others.

... a head who has inherited a difficult situation. In the school one union dominates, it's virtually a mafia. The previous head had bought them off.

A chief education officer thought that heads had an easier time in his LEA, because of its climate of non-militance and his own attempts to ensure cordial relations.

I've worked hard on making sure that the unions and county are in step. If a head gets difficulties with the unions in schools, it's probably his own fault. (Here), if teachers are dissatisfied they don't express it via the union but via the head.

In contrast, heads in one of the London boroughs wer/
and advisers as being under a lot of pressure, parti
which dominated the Authority politically. They d
tion, which was in contrast with the relative con
counties:

> The NUT (here) is another source of pressure on hea.
> a highly political vocal group. The unions have recently .
> LEA level meetings with individual heads to put the union ┌
> across, rather than doing it via the local branch. They want to bypass ι.
> and go straight to elected members, to put pressure on heads.

In the same Authority, the advisers described their heads as dealing with the
increasing demands on them from unions 'by withholding information as
discreetly as possible'.

Curriculum matters

We found some variation between LEAs in the relative roles of the LEA and
the head *vis à vis* the curriculum. In one Authority, heads were described
as seeing the curriculum as the responsibility of the chief education officer.
In another, it was seen as the head's responsibility. The chief inspector told
us:

> We've asked our heads to look very hard at curriculum—in part and as a
> whole. This is a big shift, the head's role in curriculum.
>
> The Secretary of State requiring schools to have statements of aims and objec-
> tives adds weight. We're looking for heads well qualified in curriculum.

Some respondents pointed to the increasing role of governors in curriculum
matters:

> Governors want a part in curriculum decisions, which makes the head's job
> difficult. He has to say, 'I have overall responsibility for the curriculum'.
>
> Heads were and still are unwilling to involve them (governors) in what heads
> consider a professional matter.

Nevertheless, it may be as one chief education officer put it, that 'leaky roofs
still predominate'. In particular LEAs, we found an increasing LEA
intervention in such areas as peace studies and sex stereotyping in the
curriculum.

Our respondents also commented on heads' educational philosophy.
Advisers, in particular, saw the head as the leading professional.

s a curriculum leader, curriculum inspirer . . . the head has to be a profes-
nal, keeping himself up to date, looking after the professional development
f staff, providing overall direction for the curriculum.

As a prerequisite to this, they stressed that the head has to know what he
or she wants.

(The head) has to really know the area: people, community, pupils, views and
expectations of the governing body and the LEA.

When I go into X, (a well-run school) I think 'what am I going to need, have
I got this or that'; whereas in many schools you go in and take it from there.
(A head must have) an educational philosophy and a clear view about the role
of the institution.

The majority mentioned parental support and involvement as characteristics
of the schools they identified as well-run, though one mentioned a school
that was not successful but had strong parental support. The general
assumption was that heads would delegate many of the more personal problems relating to parents, but set the tone for parental contacts.

Two officers referred to the situation of parents nowadays and the additional demands this makes on the heads:

There are a lot of frightened, unsure adults around here. The head ought to
be able to put them at ease.

The greatest change is in the increase in pressures on the head from the clients,
that is, pupils and parents, as a result of rising parental expectations and increased competition for jobs. This generation of parents is the first who've
received secondary education themselves. They therefore have some standard
to judge what their own children are receiving, and see their children's education as an investment.

Most respondents had specific ideas about the strategies heads might adopt
in relations with their governing bodies. Some Authorities had devised rules
for structuring the headteacher's report to the governing body:

We insist that curriculum is always item two on governing body meetings.

Some heads will say they have nothing to report at this point, others will tell
governors what they are doing. In the officers' view it is for the heads to tell
governors how they have allocated the money.

In this Authority, you always had to put exam results at the end of your report
to governors, and comment on them.

In one Authority the governors are party to the scrutiny of curriculum review
statements required of schools by the Authority, as well as having the right
to be informed of the outcome of inspections and visits. An adviser pointed
out the implications of more strident demands made on heads by governors

in his Authority:

> They are giving heads a bumpy ride...I sometimes attend governing body meetings. The calibre of governors has improved, they have a more professional approach than in the past...What actually happens in terms of micropolitics is different from the articles of government. The clever head gets the governing body on his side.

In another Authority, the officer was critical of one head's handling of his governing body.

> They trust him but slightly fear his overbearing manner. His approach is at a child-like level, all black and white. He won't consult and can land himself in difficult situations.

The officer in another Authority gave his view of heads' relations with their governors.

> If you take on your governors, the school is the loser. We've four or five schools where the governors have got the bit between their teeth. They're highly articulate, middle class governors. They want to run the school...Taylor would say it's good, but they're not talking about it, they're just ganging up on him...The head who avoids a perpetual row with his governors is necessary. You don't go for conflict or clash. The skills are maturity and judgement, not putting your head on the block.

Overall, the emphasis was on heads judging how to handle the governing body, not being its puppet but equally, not trying to dominate and impose. It was considered important that heads should know the views and expectations of the governing bodies so that they could judge accurately how to present the necessary information. In some cases, the governors were seen to expect a high level of involvement which the head would need to accommodate in his own strategies. In others, the governors were described as content to let the head proceed, as long as adequate information was made available.

Women headteachers

Finally, we also questioned interviewees about women headteachers. We asked about this because we wanted some views to inform our selection of four heads: the response did not suggest that it was crucial for us to have a woman amongst the four.

Four points were made about women heads. First, most respondents said that women heads did not face any distinctive problems. Second, respondents generally had a high opinion of women heads: one cited a woman as one of the best heads in the LEA; another said that some of the best heads were women; another said that women heads were exceedingly good; another that women were the better heads. No respondents reported women heads to perform *worse* than men heads.

Third, respondents referred to differences between men and women heads. Advantage with aggressive parents was cited by two. Some also expressed traditional sex stereotyping: women headteachers 'tend to react a little more emotionally', are 'more sympathetic, especially to youngsters' and they have a better style of management because they 'haven't got a big voice'. Women heads were reported as being better with underperforming women, but some were likely to face difficulties in dealing with older men or boys' welfare.

Fourth, a small number of respondents raised the question of the difficulties women face in their career. They said that it is harder for women to get appointed; that they have to be better to be appointed; and that less came forward due to child/parent commitments. One officer saw their professional development as a problem: in his view, women deputies did not want the ultimate job of headship. In another Authority, a woman adviser described the major hurdle as getting a head of department post—they hardly ever went to women, she said.

Ethos and personality

In describing the role of the head in creating school ethos, many respondents referred to the personal characteristics of the head. One head, for example, decorated the corridors himself, knew all 900 children, and had 'personal charisma'. Heads were described as having 'a funny style', being 'reserved, not outgoing', and having 'a personal style'.

A chief education officer told us that 'a head has got to have the personality to lead . . . needs a clear mind and authority in his personal bearing'. Another said that 'a balanced head would play golf'. As we found in our study of the selection of headteachers (Morgan, Hall and Mackay, 1983), on the one hand there was a general acceptance of the notion of an appropriate personality or person for headship;

It depends on the personality of the head, the way staff respond.

The personality of the head is all important. If that's lacking, the school suffers.

The success of the school depends on the personality of the head.

On the other hand, they expressed the notion that different people might be acceptable, or perform well—by leading in a different way or in a different situation.

> They can have quite different personalities.
>
> Style is school-specific.
>
> There's no rules for managerial style—it depends on personality.
>
> There are many different styles. It's tied in to personality. It's no good transferring styles ... They do it in different ways, and that comes down to personality ... When I analyse and see why one is successful and another not, I have to say, it's personality.

School ethos was seen by respondents as important, assumed to be understood, yet at the same time eluding definition. They described the ethos of schools run by 'good' and 'bad' heads as follows:

> The feel of the school...is manifest in the staffroom.
>
> The first impact is the commitment of staff and pupils—the spirit of anything being possible—which springs from the head's attitudes and determination.
>
> I judge a good school by good order, self discipline from the pupils, a caring atmosphere, attractive visually—wall displays.
>
> You notice a slightly cold atmosphere. You don't feel everyone is at one.
>
> The atmosphere is bad...You can tell it when you go in. Some schools have relaxed, confident kids strolling down corridors between lessons—no running, not dawdling. Kids seem happy to be there. It's purposeful.
>
> The atmosphere is relaxed.
>
> The atmosphere is convivial but not particularly demanding...A jolly place, nice to be there.
>
> Has a caring ethos; pupils are encouraged to be mature...looks lived in and enjoyed by pupils.
>
> A happy atmosphere amongst pupils and staff.
>
> A slightly depressed atmosphere. A fair amount of vandalism and graffiti.

Relations with the LEA

Expectations of how heads should work with their LEAs varied. All of the officers and advisers valued close working relationships with heads—although there were variations in judgements of the practical form that relationship should take. One chief education officer referring to a local head, said:

> The LEA find (him) remote. He refuses to go to heads' meetings. If the head is remote to the LEA he's likely to be remote across the board.

This was in an Authority where strong emphasis was placed by officers and advisers on the head's ability to make and sustain contacts with the community.

Most saw regular phone contacts with the heads as desirable.

> It is a partnership... the (good) head might ring up and ask for advice. Some see that as a weakness.
>
> You're looking for someone who will ring up, talk it through; not the arrogant bloke who thinks it's a sign of weakness to ring up an officer.

Advisers in two London boroughs said that they encouraged a hot line between themselves and heads, facilitated by the small size of the LEA which made it more likely that heads would reach for the phone before a crisis. One officer commented unfavourably on heads who use the phone too readily.

> A bad head would be one who is perpetually ringing up asking, 'what am I to do?' They should get it done, not just pass it on, sort it out themselves.

In general the officers and advisers expressed the need to balance their expectations of heads as line managers carrying out the Authority's policies; and as leaders of their own schools, with the autonomy that implies. The emphasis was that heads should see themselves as part of line management rather than just responsible to their schools, although the degree of expected adherence to LEA policies varied.

> I am against legislating in great detail for all that our heads should do. But I am also against total autonomy for heads.
>
> One of the most difficult things facing heads is that they are teachers with a particular loyalty to their own school. They need to maximise their own resources. At the same time they are on the receiving end of exhortations and requirements which they cannot alter. They are managers themselves. Officers have to remind heads that they are the Authority too. In management terms, what the Authority wants is not a slavish adherent but someone who will recognise and accept when certain things are necessary.

The officers in two Authorities put more emphasis on heads being sympathetic to the Authority's policies:

> If the headteacher does not share the aims of the Authority, it is very difficult. It has to be a sensible relationship... unless headteachers understand the Authority's position they can't act sensibly.
>
> The vast majority of heads see our explanation as simple, feel they have shared in decisions. The bad head kicks up a fuss and starts nobbling members.

Some advisers echoed some of the conflicts for heads described by the officers:

It's very difficult for our heads. They might be on the programme planning committee, one of the instruments of cooperation of the Authority, and involved in decisions which conflict with the management of the school.

One added that he had known well-run schools at loggerheads with the Authority.

Heads are pretty ignorant of LEA procedures. They are unwilling to recognise the extra school dimension to school. That's why we are running courses to rectify this—to help heads realise the limits as well as the extent of their authority.

In a Labour controlled Authority, the officer and adviser separately described heads as being on the receiving end of directives from the centre.

We have clear management from the centre. Don't get me wrong, that I'm advocating democracy for headteachers and autocracy here. I am just making it clear to headteachers that they have no choice.

The activity of the council is important—the abolition of corporal punishment and school uniform, political education, careers education, peace education, equal opportunities, multi-ethnic.

In contrast, the adviser in a Conservative-controlled Authority pointed out that, in spite of the LEA's streaming policy, 'we still have some heads who are strongly mixed ability'. In another Conservative Authority, the officer said.

In the LEA's view a good head will put up a strong fight for his school if threatened with reorganisation or closure, even if LEA policy is decided.

Keeping informed

Finally, we were interested in what and how LEA officers and advisers knew about headteachers' work. We asked respondents if they had any school or headteacher performance data. None had anything systematic beyond such records as parental complaints appeals and so on. In general, officers and advisers described themselves as working on the basis of assumptions or impressions about particular heads, based on contact in schools or on courses.

Our headship data relates to their performance on previous courses. We've kept a record on how they did at an inter-personal level, but nothing on how they are in school.

I get feedback from colleagues. I have to be very careful that I bring images up to date.

We have no systematic system in writing.

> The adviser will know the head well, in a subjective sense. But we accumulate a fund of information.

When a head is in serious trouble, more records are kept.

> There's no reason why we shouldn't if we felt that someone was performing badly.
> We have no data on headteachers performance until we're really worried... we don't keep judgemental records about headteacher ... assessment of performance is coming.

There was one exception to this picture; in one London borough the role of its heads had been monitored through curriculum monitoring. The chief education officer told us that the following had been agreed with headteachers:

1 Curriculum review: five-yearly submissions from each headteacher to the LEA on curriculum and organisation.
2 In-depth inspection of each school every 10 years.
3 School-based teacher appraisal; each headteacher submits report on teachers' performance, according to procedures agreed within the school; and always involving discussion with staff.
4 Weekly inspectors' visits to schools.

In his view, in doing this the Authority was monitoring headteachers. He described his headteacher performance data as the feedback he received in terms of expressed concern about performance. He gave us a recent example: the fact that he had taken his inspector's reports to a governing body and said that the reports pointed to serious problems in senior management in four schools—one of them a secondary school. This led to the removal and transfer of staff, and the head of the secondary school being 'taken seriously to task'. She had not responded as expected, and so the LEA had required her to report monthly to her governors on the progress to meet the shortcomings. The chief education officer described himself as having 'used curriculum review as a door to headteacher appraisal'.

On school performance, the only 'hard' data we found LEAs to use were exam results, although use of these appeared as mainly impressionistic. Only one LEA took input factors into account in a systematic way.

Our interviewees' knowledge of heads had bases which fell into eight categories:

1 Committees/working parties/meetings—some residential.
2 Courses.
3 Visits to schools.

4 'Crisis' e.g. complaints/ suspensions/ staffing appeals/ educational welfare office/ educational psychologist etc.
5 Other writing or phone, e.g. regarding staffing or development.
6 Governors' meetings; and heads' reports to these.
7 Members and governors.
8 Social (i.e. personal) contact.

Some stressed the large number of school visits they or their colleagues made; others met heads at social events; and a few referred to a complex nexus of information systems—involving members, heads, advisers, PTAs, and governors. Exam results and written and telephone contact were also cited, as well as heads' governors' reports.

Summary

We did not find that LEAs had any comprehensive records of their headteachers' performance, nor system for appraising this. Rather, individual officers and advisers relied on their judgement, which was based on a composite picture, built up from a variety of sources over a period of time.

They stressed that no one model of headship was necessarily the best—be it participatory or autocratic; but that, whatever the model, it should be made explicit. They emphasised the need to work with staff to generate a unity of purpose, which was related to selection of staff, as well as their motivation—which, in turn, was seen as an increasing problem due to contraction. Over-involvement of some heads in administrative matters and a failure to deal with parents and others outside the school were identified as weaknesses in some heads. Except in some of the London boroughs, dealing with unions (and non-teaching staff) was not seen as problematic; but the requirements regarding governors were described as changing. The general emphasis on ethos and personality, however, indicated the elusiveness in their eyes of the characteristics associated with good or bad headship practice.

·VI·

Conclusion

Conclusion

In this final section we aim first to draw together four distinctive approaches to the job of headteacher and its common elements; second, to consider secondary school headship from the perspective of present policy. We began by setting our description and analysis of the work of four headteachers in the context of our observations of the working days of fifteen heads. Like Wolcott (1973) we saw out task as providing descriptive data about the job of the secondary school headteacher. Our single day observations of fifteen heads showed their daily work to be fragmented, people-intensive and to encompass a range of tasks. Teaching emerged as the longest sustained activity for many headteachers and formal scheduled meetings constituted a low proportion of the job. The majority of the heads' activities were interpersonal, predominantly with individuals and groups within the school, although they gave vastly different emphases to the importance of building and maintaining interpersonal relations and motivating staff. They differed substantially in their levels of involvement in the tasks to be carried out as a result of their contrasting interpretations of the head's role. In general, they spent more time on teaching activities than on 'leading professional' matters of curriculum and other educational policy; more time on 'operations' and 'human management' than on 'educational policy'; and about ten per cent of their time daily in the school on 'external management' matters. Routine administration dominated the time spent within the 'operations management' category. Pupil issues claimed just over half of their 'human management' time.

The general features of the job (its fragmentation, people-intensive character and varied range of tasks) were reflected in our in depth study of four headteachers. The striking characteristic of secondary headship is that the baseline of a formal description is missing, making it all the more important to know how it is actually done. In the course of the year the four heads all faced demands from staff, pupils, parents, and the LEA; the choices they made in responding to them and the constraints on proposed action varied considerably.

In observing four secondary headteachers we found that little had changed in the scope and character of heads' performance of the job since Lyons'

(1974) description of its fragmentary quality. As then, the tasks of three of the heads we studied ranged over all the work of the school, although with differing levels of input. The preference of the fourth for considerable delegation made possible intense involvement in teaching and advising older pupils. While the managerial role of each of the heads was characterised by fragmentation, only Mr Shaw took a predominantly proactive and strategic stance and appeared less at the mercy of events. In common with Wolcott (1973) we found a tendency among heads to respond to every problem as important, involving them in a multiplicity of 'little decisions'.

Our subsequent chapters focused on different aspects of the work of the four heads, in particular their relations with staff, pupils, parents and the LEA; and their performance of routine administrative tasks, buildings supervision and maintenance, the presentation of the school to the outside world and their professional work beyond the school. We showed in Chapter 4 how each head's style of working with staff was significantly tied to the kind of relationship they had with senior staff; and the extent to which they had consciously instituted systems into the school management structure for ensuring tasks were carried out. The emphasis of two heads was on creating and limiting opportunities for certain kinds of action, mainly through a vigilant watchfulness over what teachers were doing. In contrast, Mr Shaw and Mr Dowe were as much concerned about the ways in which teaching staff thought about their work. In general, three of the heads were uncomfortable about instituting formal monitoring systems of teacher performance, perhaps reflecting some of their own feelings as former teachers rather than as heads. Hargreaves described teachers' attitudes to observing and being observed:

> The most startling feature of teachers in their relations with adults, including colleagues, is their sensitivity to observation when teaching. Like sexual activity, teaching is seen as an intimate act which is most effectively and properly conducted when shrouded in privacy ... There is no doubt that this reflects the professional's concern with autonomy. (1980, p.141)

Only Mr King, who had limited teaching experience and a non-collegial approach to his teaching staff, took pleasure in dropping in unannounced on teachers at work in the classroom.

In times of industrial action, each of the heads differed in their views of the teachers and their cause; and in the ways they chose to respond to a multiplicity of conflicting demands from the unions, the LEA, parents, governors and pupils. They had considerable freedom to choose individual responses, which were generally in keeping with their approach to managing staff relations in more harmonious times. Our interviews with heads prior to the onset of industrial action on the part of teachers showed that the rules governing heads' responses to issues relating to collective bargaining were not defined. During the dispute that began in April 1984, we saw their uncertainty about how to act in unfamiliar circumstances, their reliance on each other for advice and example, and the influence of their own professional association and other allegiances on their response. Interviews with the larger sample of heads revealed a composite stance with potentially conflicting elements: a resistance to regular meetings with union representatives for fear of giving them too much status; a preference for being reactive rather than proactive towards union matters; and a primary concern that the interests of the pupils come first.

Richardson (1973) pointed to a growing stress in heads, relating to uncertainty about the boundaries and subsequent difficulties over the exercise of authority by those in leadership positions. Some fifteen years later, clarification of roles and responsibilities still remains elusive. In our profile summaries of each head, we show the extent to which boundaries marking off areas of responsibility within the school have or have not been clearly identified and communicated by the head.

In their work with pupils (Chapter 6) each head enacted a figurehead role in the school, responding differently to the possibilities it offered for teaching, counselling, and maintaining control. Among other features of their work within the school was the high proportion of time spent by three of the four heads on routine administrative tasks and their different systems for ensuring the completion of these. One mainly delegated this area of work; one chose to handle as many aspects as possible himself; two retained a high level of involvement whilst delegating substantial areas. Two were closely involved on a daily and often practical basis in the maintenance of buildings; one took a close interest without becoming practically involved; and the fourth delegated it almost entirely.

In responding to the situations and tasks associated with their leadership role, each head further acted to influence the style and behaviour of teaching staff in different ways. Mr King sought to achieve this through his presence and office. This accounted for his high visibility, allowing him to present a model of appropriate behaviour and ensuring constant supervision. He distinguished himself from his teaching staff by presenting himself as better than they were at the same tasks he expected them to accomplish. Mr Dowe also presented himself as a model for behaviour he desired from staff, but almost exclusively in the role of teacher and as a colleague rather than as a superior. Mr Shaw made his values and priorities clear in every working context, both as a colleague and a manager, though with greater emphasis on managerial aspects. Mr Mercer took upon himself an almost exclusive concern for ensuring desired outcomes to the school's immediate and longer-term needs. He was less apparently concerned to demonstrate through his own actions and behaviour the kind of stance he hoped teaching staff would adopt.

In their work outside the school, we looked at four areas: their work with parents, with the LEA, in the community and in the educational world beyond the school. They differed in whether they saw parents as partners or clients and in the extent and ways in which they sought to involve parents in school activity. Their relations with the LEA were affected by the extent to which they saw the LEA as having a legitimate involvement in the organisation of their schools; and as taking action which was in the interest of their school as well as the Authority.

In common with the headteachers in Kogan's (1984) study, governing bodies were seen by the heads as agencies belonging to the school rather than the LEA. Mr Mercer and Mr King both demonstrated a preference for centralised decision-making, but their relations with their governing bodies differed. Mr King was secure in his knowledge that they supported the objectives and the values of the school and accepted his leadership style as legitimate. Mr Mercer was less confident in his governor's support for his centralised style of leadership or their agreement about the school's aims and objectives. He was more likely to try and control the information made available to them. Both Mr Shaw and Mr Dowe put a greater emphasis in their leadership style on consultation and sharing decision-making. However, while Mr Shaw's relations with his governing body demonstrated a recognition of the expectation that they would 'call the school to account' and express views on policy, Mr Dowe's relations were more passive, in response to the governing body's own passivity.

The approach of the heads to the media was similar: suspicion of media motives based on past experiences prompted a proactive rather than reactive stance to pre-empt media hostility. The community served by each school was seen and responded to by three of the heads as another potential ally in promoting the interests of the school. Each of these three, though not Mr Dowe, devoted some time to cultivating personal links with members of their school's community.

The freedom allowed in the job to interpret its demands differently was most apparent in each head's involvement in the educational world beyond the school. This was particularly extensive in one case and limited in another. One of the heads was unusual in not seeking out frequently the views and support of colleague heads in the Authority, which provided a frame of reference for the other heads' assessment of what they were doing.

LEAs' views of headteachers in their Authority derived more from informal *ad hoc* sources of information than from face-to-face contact or hard documentary data. There was no evidence of attempts to systematise information on the performance of individual headteachers and criteria for judging heads as 'good' or 'bad' varied widely. Personal characteristics were cited more frequently than knowledge or skills, though the precise nature of each head's characteristics always remained elusive in their accounts.

Having summarised the heads' responses across different aspects of the job, we now present a cameo of each of the four heads observed. First we draw together the main features of Mr King's approach to the job.

Mr King was a lively, active head, highly visible though not always communicating easily with colleagues, as a result of the often critical stance he adopted. He started work well before the official start of the school day; and had a large number of interactions, especially with pupils, throughout the working day. In dealing with people he was loud and direct. His relations with staff were uneven; with a few he enjoyed friendly relations; with many—and this was highlighted during the teachers' industrial action—his relations were characterised by antagonism and conflict. He depended on vested authority rather than interpersonal skills, to achieve what he wanted from staff. There was a marked contrast in this respect between his interpersonal style within and outside the school. Decision-making was centralised and he was personally involved in the detailed aspects of administration—writing cheques and counting cash, for example. He was prominent in all matters concerning the physical fabric of the school, its condition and appearance. To this end, he cultivated and enjoyed friendly relations with cleaners, cooks and caretakers and even carried out minor repairs to the school buildings and plant himself. His omnipresence compelled him into involvement in matters demanding immediate attention.

He was in frequent contact with the LEA, often 'clearing' things before he proceeded with them. He got on well with senior officers in the Authority, who had a high opinion of him as a head. He worked closely with pupils on pastoral matters and expected staff to take his behaviour as a model, rather than his specifying rules for action. He usually attended an assembly; and was out of his room and around the school for the full duration of both breaks and the lunchtime; after school he personally supervised pupils boarding the buses. Much of this contact with pupils involved enforcing discipline, often by meting out physical punishment himself. He got on well with—and devoted much of his effort in this area to—older boys who were in trouble at school; he empathised with their position. He did not dwell at length or systematically on curriculum matters. He had close working relations with his governors, who strongly supported him in the school. He worked hard promoting his image and that of the school—in the media and in the community. He invited notables along to social events at the school and sat on a number of committees in the community. He had lived in this community since his own childhood. He attached considerable importance to the role and rights of parents, and particularly enjoyed his work with the PTA.

Mr Mercer most resembled those heads described in Lyons (1974) as being rarely 'able to plan their day in other than nominal terms, inevitably leaving a large part of it free in anticipation of the many minor crises that will occur' (p. 90). He combined high visibility through presence in assemblies and frequent tours of the school, with a degree of inaccessibility and non-availability, using his secretary as a gatekeeper. His approach to decision-making was more autocratic than participatory. His attempts to involve staff were tempered by his scepticism regarding their motivation, over which he saw himself as having little influence. Guidelines for desired behaviour were *ad hoc* rather than formalised or routinised. The organisation of the school over four sites involved him in many activities aimed at securing smooth school administration as well as the increased complexity of determining and implementing longer-term goals. He saw himself as mainly effective in influencing the school's appearance and its day to day operations (chiefly outside of the classroom). His preference was for an informal style of leadership, with few regular meetings though frequent *ad hoc* meetings. His approach was tactical rather than strategic, to take account of what he saw as the potentially negative consequences of the micro-politics of staff relations. He gave a high priority to interpersonal relations with non-teaching staff and to continued vigilance over the state of the buildings. While he often expressed his intention to manage time effectively and respond to a whole range of the school's activity, his days were spent more in assisting staff with routine tasks and responding to 'happenings' rather than planned events. The boundary between policy and administrative decisions was clear with a greater concentration of time on the latter. Mr Mercer encouraged in parents a confidence in the school's traditional approach to curriculum and pastoral matters, resulting in fairly limited contacts with them, occasionally as individuals and rarely as a group. His approach to the community served by the school was businesslike. While remaining apart from it, he cultivated a network of contacts whose help could be enlisted to the school's advantage.

Mr Dowe's headship style emphasised the academic. He had a strong interest in curriculum, more in and around his own subject area than on a whole school basis. He taught nearly a half timetable of sixth-form classes, and dealt largely with pupils from this end of the school. He did not attend assembly and saw relatively little of other pupils. His main contribution to the school ethos was his academic emphasis, a result of his perception of the need for improvement in 'A' level results. He preferred a collegial rather than hierarchical approach to staff relations. The extent of his availability to staff, to whom he was always considerate and respectful, was curtailed by his extensive teaching and examining commitments, as well as his practice of going home to lunch. Beyond the school, he was actively involved in other work with several exam boards. He sought to demonstrate through his own professional competence as a teacher the ways in which he wanted staff to see their own teaching roles. Thus he played a large part in defining the school's instructional goals. Otherwise, he delegated running the school extensively. As a result he was required to spend relatively little time in dealing with matters requiring immediate attention; his teaching commitments dominated the space made available.

He encouraged participatory forms of decision-making, emphasising good interpersonal relations in the school, though not always clarifying on a systematic, 'whole school', basis the factors contributing to the achievement of school goals. On financial matters, Mr Dowe dealt with policy rather than administration. He respected the rights of parents as consumers, although on several occasions experienced the problems which are always potential with highly articulate parents, in defining the school's instructional objectives. He was not active in the local community, nor did he have much contact with his governors. He saw little of, and spoke rarely with, colleague heads in the Authority; and often failed to attend county heads' meetings, though was active in his regional heads association. In a similar vein, he did not rate highly as educationalists officers of the Authority; on staffing matters, in particular, he came into considerable conflict with them. He was more concerned with the individual interest of his school than the broader policy concerns of the Authority; his relations with the LEA were sometimes antagonistic.

The main features of Mr Shaw's approach to his work as a head were his systematic involvement in the whole range of the school's activity, in spite of extensive commitments to activities outside of the school; his strategic view of school matters, ensuring continuing attention to longer-term planning; and his proactive stance towards innovation and change. He put great emphasis on being regularly visible and available to all the groups working in and with the school. In particular he approached systematically the task of building and maintaining interpersonal relations with staff, pupils and parents; as well as creating mechanisms for providing staff with the knowledge and skills to do their job effectively. He did this by involving staff consistently in the school's decision-making processes, making extensive use of his close working partnership with his senior management team to secure the staff's support. Having developed his preferred formula for running the school at its inception fourteen years previously, he remained wedded to these well-tried strategies which had, in his view, proved their worth.

He sought to combine an approach which encouraged staff to plan their goals (internalised rather than prescribed) with a view of the system as a whole, to be responded to as an entity, not just concentrated on in parts. In spite of its occasional, unanticipated (but not unfamiliar) fragmentation, his working day appeared organised, punctuated by regular events, with no gaps and considerable momentum. The control he was able to exert over the pace of his work, through the systems he had instituted to manage its demands, made it possible for him to include regular appraisals of longer-term issues, for which solutions were less well known, as well as to deal with matters requiring his immediate attention. He was active in the community served by the school although not a member of it.

Having shown in profile four distinctive approaches to the job of the head, we consider now the relevance of our analysis for policy development. The profiles show only one of the four heads as having made any substantial revision in the way comprehensive school heads arrange their working days since Lyons's work (1974). Unlike other managers, few of the headteachers that

Jenkins (1983) or we studied had regular scheduled meetings or timetabled, extended blocks of time to study specific policy issues. In other words, they had created few opportunities to think out and develop strategies and instruments to meet the complexity of demands on them for the development of school educational policy and classroom practice. Much of the time of many of the heads was taken up by teaching and other pupil-related matters; in other words, in activities performed directly for the customers or consumers. In most cases the time taken for this can be seen as at the expense of attention to overall planning and executive tasks.

Practice-orientated management theory (e.g. Katz, 1974; Mintzberg, 1973) distinguishes between the tasks and responsibilities of top, senior and middle management, reflecting the balance between overall planning and executive tasks and direct contact with the customers or clients. An implication of this distinction for headteachers would be that they would not, for example, expect to have a high level of pupil contact. Rather, as a characteristic of 'top management' in schools, they would demonstrate little involvement in the more generic professional activities—for example, teaching—which have previously occupied them on their career path to headship.

We have shown that this is not a model which many headteachers practice. We have commented on the lack of prescription of the job of the head and the way in which this leaves individual heads considerable licence in their interpretation of it. Continuing with our example, we found a major attachment by heads to a personal teaching timetable. They argue that this is useful to enable them to know what life is like for their colleagues at the chalkface; and that it is necessary if they are to retain the respect of classroom teachers. Some choose to teach because they enjoy it or find it a therapy or welcome retreat from other pressures. Clearly, with this choice as any other which they make, there will be opportunity costs, in that other activities may not be carried out while they are teaching.

In common with Jenkins (1983), we found similarities in the way in which heads do the job and differences from their counterparts in other occupational settings. We have also shown, in our detailed descriptions as well as our account of our single-day observation of fifteen heads, differences in how they view and perform the job. The four heads could be characterised by a particularly dominant feature of their style. Mr Dowe's emphasis, reflected in the proportion of time given to it, was on his involvement in teaching activities; his approach thus typifies that of the 'teacher educator'. A high number of scheduled meetings was a prominent characteristic of Mr Shaw's approach to the job, for whom attention to professional matters and to efficient procedures in the control of all organisational activity went hand in hand. In this respect he demonstrated the characteristics of what Hughes (1972) has called the 'leading professional' and 'chief executive' models of headship. Mr King's working day was characterised by a high number of contacts compared with the other three heads. His approach can be described as that of the 'pastoral missioner' because of its Arnoldian overtones in terms of the constant use of personal interactions to affect values and events. In our single day observations of the larger number of heads we found examples of these three models. The fourth head, Mr Mercer, combined features of the 'pastoral missioner' and 'leading professional' models.

The four heads studied in depth are therefore to be seen not as four exceptions in the spectrum of headship interpretation but as representatives of four recurring interpretations. What we cannot say, of course, is exactly what proportions they constitute in secondary headship interpretations as a whole; nor what the hallmarks are of other interpretations which may exist but which did not show up in our sample.

The problem facing policy makers, selectors and trainers is that variety remains the chief characteristic of how secondary headship is practised in England and Wales today. These varied performances need now to be set in the context of central government's increasing concern with the content of what schools do and the head's part in school success or effectiveness. Three recent publications carry explicitly or implicitly government expectations of secondary school headship. They are: 'Ten Good Schools' (DES HMI, 1977), 'Teaching Quality' (DES 1983); and 'Better Schools' (DES 1985). We consider each in turn.

'Ten Good Schools' argued the centrality of headship for school success and defined the elements of effective school leadership. While the problem of deciding what is to count as a measure of school success or effectiveness remains unresolved empirically it is interesting to link the criteria identified in 'Ten Good Schools' with our own observations of headteachers at work. We have summarised these links in Table 13.1.

'Teaching Quality', although primarily concerned with the initial training, supply and deployment of teachers, carried an important statement about the government's view of the core requirements for headship and its associated functions. It states:

> Headteachers and other senior staff with management responsibilities within schools are of crucial importance. Only if they are effective managers of their teaching staffs and the material resources available to them, as well as possessing the qualities of effective leadership, can schools offer pupils the quality of education they have a right to expect. (1983,para.83,p. 25).

Effective management is thus added to the criterion of 'Ten Good Schools' as another criterion of leadership for school success or effectiveness. The document also identifies performance appraisal and staff development as key managerial functions:

> But employers can manage their teacher force effectively only if they have accurate knowledge of each teacher's performance. The Government believe

Table 13.1 Four headteachers judged on the criteria of 'Ten Good Schools' (DES HMI, 1977)

Ten good schools criteria	Shaw	Dowe	Mercer	King
Communication of specific educational aims to staff, pupils, parents	Systematic and comprehensive approach to all three groups	Communicates to all three groups but generally more concerned with the upper end of the school and more able pupils	Informs staff of developments from outside the school. Communicates specific educational aims on an *ad hoc* basis	Informs all three groups of developments from outside the school. Not a source of specific educational aims
Human management displays sympathetic understanding of staff and pupils; is available	Places a high priority on interpersonal relations with both. Not always available	Interacts well on a collegial basis with staff and the more able, senior pupils. Not always available	Variable sympathy and understanding towards staff. Availability restricted	Unsympathetic to staff. Highly sympathetic to some pupils, especially older delinquent boys. Readily available
Personal qualities good humour; sense of proportion; dedication to task	Committed educationalist and skilful manager. Good humour and a sense of proportion consistently present	Committed educationalist concerned about others' feelings. Good humour and a sense of proportion consistently present	Committed to the school's rather than staff's interests. Good humour and sense of proportion frequently evident	Totally committed to the school. Good humour and a good sense and proportion selectively demonstrated
Devolution of power Conscious of the corruption of power; power-sharing a keynote of the school	Extensive power-sharing combined with a high level of personal involvement	Extensive delegation and devolution of power, general lack of concentration of power on himself	Limited power-sharing. Holds most of the power himself	Limited power-sharing. Holds most of the power himself

> that for this purpose formal assessment of teacher performance is necessary and should be based on classroom visiting by the teacher's head or head of department, and an appraisal of both pupils' work and of the teacher's contribution to the life of the school. (DES 1983, para. 92, p. 27).

There are currently no systematic school-based policies in these matters: we did not find headteachers undertaking teacher appraisal as an explicit policy, nor did they visit classrooms for that purpose. We did observe heads actively assisting individual teachers' aspirations for courses; but, altogether, what was observed did not constitute the implementation of a systematic policy for in-service training and staff development, involving subject updating, job rotation and other enrichment experiences. Of the four heads, we would judge only Mr Shaw to have demonstrated elements of a more comprehensive and systematic approach.

It is more difficult to judge the performance of the four heads in terms of what 'Better Schools' (DES, 1985) describes as the weaknesses and implicitly, strengths of secondary schools, since it is not easy to isolate the head's contributions to school effectiveness. Some of these weaknesses were: the absence of schemes of work; the concentration of teaching towards the middle band of ability; inappropriate teaching styles; lack of detailed assessment policies for pupils; mismatch between subject expertise and teacher allocation; lack of a systematic approach to career development; absence of policies for curriculum review; absence of regular and formal appraisal of all teachers; the need for more outreach work with parents; and inadequate attention to developing multi-cultural understanding.

Taking the first weakness, the absence of schemes of work: Mr Dowe, Mr Shaw and Mr Mercer discussed these with individual teachers on a number of occasions. Mr Shaw demonstrated a consistent concern with teaching across the whole ability range; Mr Dowe was more personally involved with the more able; Mr Mercer's focus changed at different points in the year; Mr King put most energy into promoting the interests of the low achievers.

Mr Shaw kept himself informed, mainly through consultation with others, about what teachers were doing in the classroom, the content and methods of their teaching. There were no systematic monitoring procedures, though heads of department were given time and scope to involve themselves closely in curriculum planning and optimising the use of staff. He welcomed the opportunity to try out the profiling system proposed by the LEA and actively encouraged staff to make maximum use of a multiplicity of non-staff resources. In contrast we rarely saw Mr Dowe discuss schemes of work with individual teachers and he had no formal way of monitoring what was happening in the classroom. Discussions with staff about career development were *ad hoc* rather than planned.

Mr Mercer dealt mainly with heads of department in considering schemes of work, discussing general principles rather than detailed proposals. His main concern was to promote the interests of the middle band of ability for whom he thought there was inadequate provision. He was satisfied that the provision for lower ability pupils was adequate and high ability pupils did not have a high profile in the school. Changes in the school's organisation as a result of projected falling rolls necessitated a more systematic approach (through interviews) to career development. He did not intervene with any regularity in departmental planning or the use of staff and non-staff resources. A recent HMI inspection had ensured that all staff had schemes of work available in Mr King's school and he monitored closely what was happening in the classroom, though on an impromptu basis. He actively promoted and supported a frequent, regular pupil assessment policy which was traditional in its approach. He was more concerned about the needs of low and underachieving pupils than those in the higher ability range. He was not concerned to develop a systematic approach to staff career development in the school.

Mr Shaw had instituted a system for curriculum review in the school; the other three heads approached the task on a more *ad hoc* basis. Profiling was most advanced in Mr Shaw's school, where teachers played an active part in agreeing the overall goals of the school. Mr Mercer in the same Authority was more cautious in his response to profiling. Mr King and Mr Dowe continued to use the traditional form of pupil reports in the absence of proposals for alternatives from the Authority. None of the heads had any system for the regular or formal appraisal of teachers.

They differed in the degree of proactivity of their work with parents; Mr Shaw and Mr King were most concerned about actively involving parents in the school's affairs; Mr Mercer and Mr Dowe only did so when necessary. In a mainly white school, Mr Shaw actively sought ways to enhance multi-cultural policies through the curriculum. We were not aware of Mr Dowe's specific promotion of a multi-cultural policy. Mr King and Mr Mercer both had multi-ethnic schools, and sought to secure multi-cultural understanding though in more traditional ways than advocated by recent ideas on multi-cultural education, such as the Swann Report (1985).

When reflected against the various policy declarations in the documents we have discussed above, our findings as a whole would suggest two broad conclusions. First, many of the activities now being expected of headteachers in these three government documents are not presently being carried out: in particular, classroom supervision, performance appraisal, departmental evaluation and systematic curriculum review. Consequently these recent policy expectations imply the need for substantial investment in training to equip heads for these tasks. Second the policy expectations which have been declared by the DES for schools imply the need for heads to re-interpret how they themselves carry out the job. All of the new policy requirements are demanding in time and imply detailed systematic policies under the head's constant supervision.

If all of the new policy expectations are to become a regular part of school management, a review of how heads spend their time will be necessary. Along with others in schools who are specifically paid for managerial responsibility, heads will have a great deal more of a specialist nature to do if the full implications of the expectations expressed in these documents are to be met; heads would face substantial and unavoidable challenges to their ways of working.

There are implications in an understanding of how headteachers do their work not only for policy makers, but for selectors and trainers too. As well as raising a range of issues when considered against current policy demands, our findings also raise the question of whether new policy is needed. Taken together these issues appear to us to fall into three, though not mutually exclusive, categories: (a) the implications of our findings for secondary headteacher selection: (b) the implications of our findings for headteacher training provision: and, (c) school-centred issues that arise from the differences between the public policy expectations of headship and its observed performance.

Our observations of heads at work confirm and extend some of the conclusions of our earlier work on headteacher selection (Morgan, Hall and Mackay, 1983). Observation has shown the job to be still more complex than we posited it to be. We have already demonstrated the failure of current selection methods to embody a systematic assessment of the abilities required in headship. From our earlier research we can add to this our observation of a degree of variance in headship interpretation of which headship selectors were unaware. Nothing deriving from our observation of headship alters our view of selection methods as a shot in the dark; in fact, they point to a still darker shade of darkness to be resolved. The complexity of the job and the degree of variance in interpretation have two important implications for headteacher selection methods. In a rigorous system, selectors need to assess overall competence across the whole range of job tasks and abilities; and to evaluate the appropriateness of the particular emphasis of interpretation which each candidate would bring to the job.

In respect of headship training, we see three main reasons why our findings imply complex and numerous issues of policy. First, there are the consequences of the complexity of headship in practice, that make it hard to believe that any deputy head, however competent and wide the experience in that post, could be ready for elevation to headship without prior formal training and management development. Whilst there are opportunities for deputies to receive training under Circular 3/83, the policy document for senior school staff management training, it is not obligatory for deputies to receive training before presenting themselves as candidates. In any case the current training provision places are overwhelmingly taken by heads. It could be argued therefore that the sequence is wrong; that a widespread training provision should be made first for deputies. Second, there are far-reaching training implications arising from the different interpretations we have observed across the tasks of headship. Heads describe themselves as having, and demonstrate, highly varying strengths and weaknesses. These both reflect and are reflected in the individual interpretation of the job. Any training and management development policy would need to be tailored to meet this variety of individual need: a bespoke rather than mass provision for heads' management development would seem to be required.

Third, there is the issue of who is to devise the policy to meet these detailed individual needs? As we have indicated, the LEAs at the present time have no techniques for evaluating the individual school or its head. Their methods are impressionistic rather than systematic, and the mismatch between the views of headship held in some LEA offices and the performance observed is not only unjust to the heads concerned but reveals an inadequate and shaky basis on which to found management development policies.

Finally, we turn to school-centred issues that arise from the differences between the DES expectations of headship and its performance as we observed this. First, there are what might be termed 'omissions' on the part of some or all heads: failure to carry out classroom supervision, performance appraisal, departmental evaluation, and detailed curriculum review, for example. Whereas at present these activities do not have the status of being mandatory, all of them—directly or by implication—would constitute obligatory responsibilities of headship if the detailed terms of salary restructuring proposals as set out in the Joint Working Party on Salary Structure paper, come to be accepted (see Figure 13.1).

Our description and discussion of how secondary school headship is performed has recorded how different individual role interpretations can be. This degree of variance raises the question of whether government in England and Wales should set out some guidelines for school management. Minimum guidelines of this nature do not exist in England and Wales, although in Scotland central government has defined the minimum required management tasks for schools—for heads, deputies, middle and junior managers, as well as for subject and pastoral leaders in the school (SED 1984). The Scottish Education Department lists the responsibilites of these staff, and expects and assumes that such tasks are carried out in all secondary schools.

In England and Wales, current government expectations of headship challenge heads to review the responsibilities of all management role holders in their schools. The thrust of government policy is, as we have suggested, to achieve more systematic curricula and staff effectiveness policies within schools. They are likely to require sustained planning by heads. The time demands to carry out these could be incompatible with some interpretations of headship which we observed. The main issue raised for heads by the policy demands from the government, therefore, is how to find the time for these important developments within the constraint of the day

Figure 13.1 Joint working party on salary structure 1984—Proposals by employers

---

Headteachers:
55 The duties and responsibilities of a head shall include:

1 Formulate and gain approval for the school's overall aims and objectives and policies for implementation.
2 Establish and modify as required the school's internal organisation, deploying finance and staff so as to implement policies and maintain staff motivation and initiative, all within the requirements of LEA policies and of staff conditions of service.
3 Clarify to individual staff members the contribution required of them through the provision of job descriptions, consulting individuals as required.
4 Establish and maintain appropriate professional and performance standards for staff of all kinds including the conduct of performance appraisals and reviews.
5 Secure assistance and support from those whose activities and support can contribute to the attainment of the school's objectives.
6 Liaise and cooperate with governors, LEA members and officers and other heads.
7 Participate in arrangements for assessment of his or her own performance and identification and meeting of training needs.

---

to day traffic of school life. Our observation of the different interpretations of secondary headship suggest that analysis and synthesis of the current variety would offer options to resolve this dilema; at the very least it implies the need for a review and explicit demarcation of the division of duties between heads themselves, their deputies, and their heads of years and departments.

Appendix

Methods of Research

We preceded our in-depth work with four heads by a broader study, which consisted mainly of interviews and also one-day observations of each of fifteen headteachers. The reasons for this first phase of our research were threefold: first, to learn something about headship that would give us direction for the rest of our work, and in particular to enable us to select heads for this. Second, it gave us fieldwork practice in observing heads at work, which was to prove useful, preliminary experience. Third, given a study which focused on four heads in-depth, we felt that we would want to test the generalisability of our findings to the broader sample.

Starting with an idea of the number of schools and LEAs we could fit in to the time available, we followed a sampling procedure which gave us a range of LEAs across a number of classifications: geographical area of the country, type of Authority, and classification on socio-economic grounds (as per DES cluster analysis). These are shown in the table below.

Table A1

LEA	Area of GB	Type of local authority (see Note 1)	DES cluster group (see Note 2)
A	SW	C	A
B	NE	C	B
C	Midlands	MB	E
D	S	C	A
E	L	LB	D
F	NE	C	B
G	NW	MB	C
H	L	LB	F
I	NE	MB	B
J	SW	C	A
K	W	C	See Note 3
L	SE	C	A

Notes

1 Type of local authority refers to county, metropolitan borough, or London borough council.
2 The cluster analysis groups LEAs into six relatively homogeneous groups, by comparing six socio-economic indicators (e.g., indicator one is children born outside the UK or belonging to non-white ethnic groups). The groups are described in summarised form as follows:
Group A All percentages in the 'percentage profile' below average
Group B All percentages close to the average.
Group C All percentages in the 'percentage profile' above average except for indicator 1.
Group D All percentages close to the average except above average for indicator 1.
Group E All percentages above average.
Group F All percentages above average, that for indicator 1 substantially so.
3. DES cluster analysis applies to England only; our research covered England and Wales.

Our main approach was to LEA chief education officers, to whom we wrote explaining our interests and requesting to interview an officer, adviser and member; and to spend about two and a half days in each of two schools interviewing staff and interviewing and observing the head.

At the same time, we negotiated our access with a range of professional and other associations and unions; we contacted the two headteacher associations, four teacher associations and one union for each of blue- and white-collar non-teaching staff in schools.

We interviewed the following number of individuals in this part of our work:

Table A2

Category of interviewee	Total no. Interviewed	No. of LEAs in which members of this category were interviewed
Officers	18	11
Advisers	12	12
Members	5	5
Teacher associations' officers	18	3
Non-teacher unions'	11	11
Total	64 interviews	12 LEAs

It was at these initial interviews that we negotiated our access to the schools in the LEA. We said that we wanted to study heads who had been in post at least four years; we felt that four years was long enough for a head to settle in to his or her headship. No nominated heads refused us access, although it is likely that (a) in their selection, officers or advisers would have taken account of heads who were likely, in their view, to be enthusiastic or uncooperative; and (b) heads may have turned us down to their officer or adviser, and another head then have been selected for us. Due to pressure of time and research priorities, we ended up with fifteen heads in nine LEAs.

The schools had a wide range of catchments, including urban inner city, rural, and affluent suburban; three of the schools had multi-ethnic catchments. All were mixed, and one was voluntary aided. Two heads were women, and three schools were split-site. The size and age range of each school, and the number of years each head had been in post, are shown in Table A3.

Table A3

LEA	School	no. on roll	Age range	No. of years held in post
A	1	1950	11-18	8
A	2	1420	11-18	14
B	3	540	11-16	4
B	4	920	11-16	8
C	5	1300	11-18	14
D	6	900	11-16	18
D	7	1350	12-18	13
E	8	720	11-18	9
F	9	1000	13-18	13
F	10	1600	11-18	13
G	11	1200	11-16	12
H	12	1940	11-18	4
H	12	1240	11-18	12
K	14	1440	11-18	4
K	15	1720	11-18	8

In each of these fifteen schools, we carried out an interview with the head about their perceptions of the job. We also spent a day interviewing a range of those with whom each head interacted, mainly teaching staff. We were interested in what they chose to say about the head, and encouraged them to say how their head worked. We interviewed the following in these fifteen schools:

Table A4

Deputy heads, senior master, senior mistress		42
Middle managers (heads of department/year/house)		22
Teacher association representatives:		
	NAS/UWT	13
	NUT	14
	AMMA	8
	PAT	1
	Total	36
Non-teaching staff		28
Governors		13
Parents		9
Pupils		16
Total number of interviews		166

Finally, we observed each headteacher for a whole day. With one exception, we had already spent time with the head by interviewing him or her and, to this extent, had made clear our interest and established some kind of relationship. We asked the head not to re-arrange anything on the day we were to observe because we were to be present. We arrived at the time the head started work and left when he or she did. During the day, we accompanied the head and recorded as much as possible about what the head did and said.

The second phase of our fieldwork was the in-depth study of four headteachers. The actual heads were chosen from those with whom we had worked with in the first phase of our work; they were selected for us by LEA officers, on the basis we have described for selecting the heads in the first phase of our research. These four were all heads of large 11-18 comprehensives, and they provided us with a variety of headship styles.

In addition to our Phase 1 interviews with each of these four heads, we spent an average of 174 hours with each of the four heads: an average of 15 whole days (a continuous period of 7-9 hours) and 18 part days (either a period under 7 hours, or the part of a day which exceeds 9 hours). In other words, we were in each school for a year for an average of about 1 day in 6, half of these being whole days and half part days. Only very rarely did we observe the heads working at home, at weekends, in the evening, or during school holidays; this omission appears particularly significant in the case of Mr Dowe.

Whilst with the four heads, we took abbreviated long-hand notes, recording as much as possible. We tried to be as unobtrusive as possible, physically and socially. When in the head's room we sat in a corner where we could see the setting well, but impinged on it as little as possible. We did not use tape recorders for a number of reasons.

Over the period of the research we became very close to the four heads. We were in the unusual position of being able to observe something approaching the totality of their work activities. Although it was not a central part of our project, inevitably we spoke with others, particularly teachers, about heads. When we were excluded from the head—which happened very rarely, as we discuss below—we sometimes took the opportunity to speak with other staff—mainly deputies and secretaries.

We always arranged with heads in advance when we would next be visiting them. None of the four discouraged us from going in—indeed, with some of them we often had to turn down invitations or requests to observe particular events.

We have mentioned that we took every opportunity to discuss with the heads. In doing this, we were aware that we were interrupting their normal routine, so we had to make judgements about how willing they were for this to happen. Often, in something of a lull, they were happy to talk with us for quite some time. During the day, all of the heads offered us a certain amount of explanation of what they were doing. They might comment on the typicality of what had just gone on or comment on particular aspects of their work. One often began the day by saying 'You may be interested...' and would then enlarge on a particular recent event to us. Another said, 'I'm talking out loud so you'll know what I'm thinking.'

On rare occasions we were asked to leave the head, for him to deal with a specific matter. There was never any acrimony over this, and usually the head told us something about the interaction afterwards; sometimes we could not help hearing it through the wall!

In each school we were excluded from accompanying the head as follows:

Table A5

Head	Occasions	Length of time	
		Hours	Mins
Mr Dowe	1		4
Mr Shaw	4		30
Mr King	13	1	28
Mr Mercer	4		50
Total	24	4	52

Table A5 excludes two significant matters: first, one LEA refused to allow us to attend several of its meetings; the chief education officer's meeting with heads, the ATCC, and a careers committee. Second, HMI asked that we leave or not attend on several occasions at two of the schools; this led to our absence from some meetings of the head with HMI, governors, and the LEA. Overall, though, it was very unusual for us to be asked to withdraw. We observed the disciplining of a head of department, the selection of deputy heads, career discussions with teachers and a whole host of other activities.

In summary, our method included semi-structured interviews—with a range of those the head deals with, both inside and outside the group. It centred, however, on our observation and recording of what heads actually said and did.

Finally, we should mention that we presented drafts of this work to all four heads, and discussed it at some length with three of them. In the light of this we made some minor changes to our text; but nothing, we feel, which changes the central themes which we have identified as constituting each head's interpretation of the job.

Bibliography

B. Allen (1968), *Headship in the 1970s*. Blackwells: Oxford.

G. Baron (1975), 'Some Aspects of the "Headmaster Tradition"', in V. Houghton, R. McHugh and C. Morgan (ed.) (1975).

C.H. Barry and F. Tye (1972), *Running a School*, Temple Smith: London.

G. Bernbaum (1976), *'The Role of the Head'*, in R.S. Peters (ed.) (1976).

A. Blumberg and W. Greenfield (1980), *The Effective Principal: Perspectives in School Leadership*. Allyn & Bacon: USA.

T. Bush (1981), 'Key Roles in School Management', Course E323 'Management and the School', Block 4, Part 3. Open University Press: Milton Keynes.

J. Callaghan (1976), 'Towards a National Debate', *Education*, 22 October.

DES (1982) 'A Classification of Local Education Authorities by Additional Educational Needs (Cluster Analysis)'. *Statistical Bulletin* 8/82, DES: London.

DES HMI (1977) *Ten Good Schools: A Secondary School Enquiry*. Her Majesty's Stationery Office: London.

D.D. Dill (1984) 'The Nature of Administrative Behaviour in Higher Education'. *Educational Administration Quarterly* 20, 3: 69-99.

R. Glatter (ed.) (1976), 'Control of the Curriculum'. *Studies in Education* 4, Institute of Education, University of London.

W.D. Greenfield (1982), 'Research on Public School Principals: A Review and Recommendations'. Paper presented at the National Conference on the Principalship covened by the National Institute of Education, October 1982.

D. Hargreaves (1980), 'The occupational culture of teachers', in P. Woods (1980).

V. Houghton, R. McHugh and C. Morgan (eds) (1975), *Management in Education*. Ward Lock: London.

M.G. Hughes (1972), 'The Role of the Secondary Head'. PhD thesis, University of Wales.

H.O. Jenkins (1983), 'Job Perceptions of Senior Managers in Schools and Manufacturing Industry'. PhD thesis, University of Birmingham.

R.L. Katz (1974), 'Skills of an Effective Administrator'. *Harvard Business Review*, 52:90-102.

M. Kogan *et al.* (1984), *School Governing Bodies*. Heinemann: London.

G. Lyons (1974), *The Administrative Tasks of Head and Senior Teachers in Large Secondary Schools*. University of Bristol.

G. Lyons (1976), *Heads' Tasks: A Handbook of Secondary School Administration*. NFER, Slough.

Martin and D.J. Willower (1981), 'The Managerial Behaviour of High School Principals'. *Educational Administration Quarterly*, 17:69-90.

L. McCleary and S. Thomson (1979), *The Senior High School Principalship*. NASSP: Reston, Virginia.

H. Mintzberg (1973), *The Nature of Managerial Work*. Harper & Row: New York.

C. Morgan, V. Hall and H. Mackay (1983), *The Selection of Secondary School Headteachers*. Open University Press: Milton Keynes.

J. Murphy, P. Hallinger and A. Mitman (1983), 'Problems with Research on Educational Leadership: Issues to be Addressed, *Educational Evaluation and Policy Analysis*. 5,3: 297-305.

R.S. Peters (ed.) (1976), *The Role of the Head*. Routledge & Kegan Paul: London.

C. Poster (1976), *School Decision-Making*, Heinemann: London.

E. Richardson (1973), *The Teacher, The School, and The Task of Management*. Heinemann: London.

SED HMI of Schools (1984), 'Learning and Teaching in Scottish Secondary Schools: School Management'. HMSO: Edinburgh.

Secretary of State for Education and Science and Secretary of State for Wales (1983); 'Teaching Quality'. Cmnd. 8836, HMSO: London.

Secretary of State for Education and Science and Secretary of State for Wales (1985) 'Better Schools'. Cmnd. 9469. London.

K. Walsh *et al.* (1984), *Falling School Rolls and the Management of the Teaching Profession*. NFER, Nelson.

Q. Willis (1980), 'The Work of School Principals'. *Journal of Educational Administration*, 18:27-49.

H. Wolcott (1973), *The Man in the Principal's Office*. Holt, Rinehart and Winston: New York.

P. Woods (ed) (1980), *Teacher Strategies*. Croom Helm: London.